Economic Development of South Korea

The Praeger Special Studies program, through a selective distribution network, makes available to the academic, government, and business communities significant and timely research in U.S. and international economic, social, and political issues.

Economic Development of South Korea

The Political Economy of Success

L. L. Wade
B. S. Kim

Praeger Publishers New York London

Library of Congress Cataloging in Publication Data

Wade, Larry L
Economic development of South Korea.

Includes index.
1. Korea–Economic conditions–1945–
2. Korea–Economic policy. I. Kim, Byŏng-sik, 1919– joint author. II. Title.
HC467.W28 1978 338.9519 78-2665

PRAEGER SPECIAL STUDIES
200 Park Avenue, New York, N.Y., 10017, U.S.A.

Published in the United States of America in 1978
by Praeger Publishers,
A Division of Holt, Rinehart and Winston, CBS, Inc.

89 038 987654321

Printed in the United States of America

To Terrence and Chung-Wook

Preface

The startling rapidity with which the Republic of Korea has been transformed from the desperately poor and undeveloped country it was in the 1950s to the highly literate, industrialized, and increasingly affluent modern society it is today is unique in world history, a fact only now being internationally recognized. For that reason, policy-makers, scholars, journalists and others concerned with improvements in the circumstances in which so many of the world's people live have every reason to examine the Korean case, to ponder its meaning and to determine what lessons, if any, might be learned and applied to other developing nations. At the very least, the Korean experience demonstrates that despair over the possibilities of development is altogether unwarranted.

Certainly if one were to account for the cynicism and pessimism of the age, an important source would be found in the pervasive and seemingly intractable problems of hunger, malnutrition, disease and material impoverishment associated with the economic underdevelopment found in so many of the world's countries. The First International Development Decade has passed, the Second nearly so and, although some countries have achieved impressive economic progress, development in most has fallen short of plans and the disruptions to trade balances occasioned by soaring prices of certain strategic commodities, especially food and energy, have generated increased concern for the possibilities of launching and sustaining growth in the less developed countries (LDCs). Indifference to underdevelopment is neither morally nor practically possible, and the continuing question is not whether but how their plight might be alleviated.

It is true, as discouraged observers have emphasized, that many countries are situated unfavorably by history and geography; some lack raw materials, suffered malign colonial experiences, have poor population to land ratios (all characteristics of the country discussed in this book). But the Korean experience suggests that mismanagement and not original position is more often the cause of *continuing* underdevelopment, combined on occasion with social and cultural attitudes -- and not necessarily those associated with traditional values -- held by authorities hostile toward the entrepreneurial and pragmatic spirit required for development. That fashionable explanations of persistent underdevelopment are not at all apt is indicated by an examination of the growth leaders among LDCs: e.g., Hong Kong, Singapore, Taiwan and South Korea. All of these are resource-poor and overcrowded, and South Korea and Taiwan suffered under exceedingly harsh and exploitive colonial regimes. All have combined an absence of self-pity with resolute decisions to expand and sustain development through public policies which encourage the mobilization of once latent cultural strengths and offer tangible inducements to individuals to act developmentally in their own interests.

In this book, the public policy correlates of the prodigious economic achievements of one of these -- the Republic of Korea -- are probed and explored for several reasons: because they deserve attention on their own merits; because they are potentially instructive to other Third World leaders with the wisdom to consider them; and because of their implications for a larger moral -- that even under the most depressing circumstances, intelligence, courage and concentrated toil and organization can generate vast improvements in social welfare. There is a political economy of success, and one which does not depend on the lash of totalitarianism or the wish-dreams of escapist utopians.

In Chapter 1, the historical and social context of the Korean situation and the early developmental decisions taken therein are described. In Chapter 2, the overall growth pattern is placed in comparative perspective, while the relative performances of Korea and other LDCs in the fields of savings and investment, capital efficiency, taxation, manufacturing, exports, education, population and defense are examined in Chapter 3. The recognition that modern Korea has been a world leader in *all* aspects of economic development surveyed suggests its potential adherence to a comprehensive, integrated plan in which resources have been mobilized and worked into the intermeshed sectors of the economy and society in a phased, orderly and productive manner consistent at all points with some grand conception of social welfare. That such an image requires some modification is suggested in Chapter 4, where certain formal and practical problems of planning a social welfare function are identified and where the atypical Korean planning experience is contrasted with general planning efforts in the LDCs. The workings of the contemporary Korean policy-making system bearing on development are discussed in Chapter 5, where the system's institutional framework, key decision-rules, and processes of policy coordination, promulgation, review and termination receive attention in an effort to give some texture and dynamism to the analysis and hints into the human process through which Korean developmental goals and aspirations have been concentrated and advanced. In Chapter 6, the essay is summarized, the Fourth Five-Year Plan (1977-81) is discussed, and a hypothetical model of Korean development is introduced as a guide to further research.

It is important to note that it is no longer necessary to be fully comprehensive in analyzing the Korean case for a broad readership since, happily, Korean studies have grown significantly in recent years. Consequently, it is not the purpose of this study to describe fully the specific decisions, events and evolutions that have stimulated and accompanied Korea development, and redundancy in view of other recent studies has been avoided. It is the cross-national and comparative dimension of Korean development and the Korean policy-making system, especially its bureaucratic and governmental components, which are of primary interest in the following pages.

Acknowledgments

The authors are pleased to express their gratitude to the several institutions which extended financial and other support for the venture leading to the publication of this book. Specifically, both are indebted to the Joint Committee on Korean Studies of the Social Science Research Council/American Council of Learned Societies and to Kyung Hee University, while L. L. Wade wishes to thank the U.S. National Science Foundation, the Korean-American Educational Commission, Seoul National University, and the University of California, Davis.

Just as importantly, American and Korean scholars, too numerous to be identified fully here, gave invaluable assistance at many times during the preparation of this study. However, we particularly wish to acknowledge with profound appreciation the unstinting and indispensable aid of Professor Bark Dong-Suh, immediate past Dean of the Graduate School of Public Administration, Seoul National University, whose ideas and practical assistance were crucial to the entire enterprise. For critical and helpful readings of early drafts of the manuscript, we are grateful to Professor Rhee Hak-Yong of Yonsei University, Professor Robert L. Curry of California State University at Sacramento, and Professor Alexander J. Groth of the University of California, Davis.

We also wish to thank the many senior and working-level officials in the Korean public service, especially those of the Economic Planning Board, whose patience at times we must have surely tried, but who without exception responded so helpfully to our requests for interviews and data over the period from late 1975 to early 1977.

Of course, none of the above institutions or individuals is in any way responsible for the contents of this volume; that burden is the authors' alone.

L. L. W.
B. S. K.
Seoul, 1977

Contents

PREFACE vi

ACKNOWLEDGMENTS x

LIST OF TABLES xiii

Chapter 1: Korean Development in Historical Context 1

Chapter 2: Recent Korean Development in World Context 38

Chapter 3: Development Effort and Success: Korea and the Developing World 91

Chapter 4: National Planning: Obstacles, Strategies and Achievements 146

Chapter 5: Decision Rules and Economic Policy in Korea 204

Chapter 6: Conclusion 246

Index 259

List of Tables

Table		Page
1.1	Social Indicators in Korea	28
1.2	Private Consumption Expenditures (1970 Constant Market Prices)	29
2.1	International GNP Per Capita	47
2.2	Developing Countries: Distribution According to Degree of Industrialization and 1970-73 Growth in Manufacturing	49
2.3	Planned and Actual Growth of GDP and Manufacturing Output for Selected Developing Countries	59
2.4	Growth Score of Manufacturing Output for Selected Developing Countries	61
2.5	Rice Yields in Developing South and East Asian Countries	65
2.6	Estimated Additional Cost of Grain Imports for Selected Developing Countries in 1973-1974.	67
2.7	Additional Oil Imports in 1974 Resulting From Price Rises as Percentage of GNP (1971) for Selected Developing Countries	68
2.8	Index Numbers of Agricultural Production in Korea	70
2.9	Cross-Classification of Countries by Income Level and Pre-Tax Equality	80
3.1	Developing Countries: Net Inflow of Resources, 1965-1967	102-3

3.2 Foreign Direct Investment in Korea, 1967-73 105
3.3 Foreign Grants and Loans to Korea, 1967-73 107
3.4 Incremental Capital-Output Ratios in Selected LDCs 111-2
3.5 Rankings of Selected LDCs by Actual Tax/GNP Ratio (1960-65) and Rates of Growth in Per Capita GNP (1960-72) 117
3.6 Export Concentration in Selected LDCs (1969) 123
3.7 Per Capita Income (1972) and Median Years of Education of Young Adults (25-34 age group) for Selected Countries (Circa 1970) 128
3.8 Median Years of Education by Age, Sex and Rural/Urban Residence in Korea, 1970 129
3.9 College Level Fields of Study of Korean Students, 1971 130
4.1 Second Five-Year Plan (1967-71) Projections and Results (Billions of Won and Per Cent) 187
4.2 Manufacturing Production in Korea 193
4.3 Third Five-Year Plan (1972-76) Projections and Results (Billions of Won and Per Cent) 194
6.1 Principal Targets, Fourth Five-Year Plan (1976-81) 249

Chapter 1

Korean Development in Historical Context

The prodigious material feats of the contemporary Korean political economy discussed in following chapters have emerged from an unpromising and tragic one-hundred years historical experience. Since the late nineteenth century, Korea has been beset by successive calamitous events which have brought destruction and profound distress to all portions of society. Geopolitically situated where the convergent interests of states all larger and more powerful than itself are focused, it has been a battleground, an invasion route, a tributary, a colony, a divided nation, a country which has seen violence, bloodshed and physical, cultural and political devastation on an horrendous and rarely equalled scale. For the strong, Korea has been prized less for itself than for what it has been thought to provide: access to the Pacific, Japan, China, Central Asia, Russian Siberia; a buffer against other great regional or world powers; but also as a colony to exploit economically. China, the Soviet Union, Japan, European powers and the United States have all at different times judged Korean events as affecting their vital or expanding interests, judgments which have often imposed appalling costs upon the Korean people.[1]

Korea is a land with an ancient, advanced and remarkably homogeneous culture. Its written history is older than Japan's -- extending back to the early Christian era -- if somewhat less old than China's. Its cultural patterns bear a strong resemblance to those of pre-Communist China, although its distinctive language and strong national identifications have created a cultural system which is in many important ways unique. The Korean people are thought to have immigrated into their 650 miles long, 150 miles wide peninsula nation from Central Asia long before the Christian Era, and intermixed with smaller ethnic groups from China and southeast Asia. They came eventually to form three kingdoms out of a number of tribal states -- Koguryo, Silla and Paekche -- which in the seventh century were forcibly united by the Silla kingdom as a result of its alliance with Tang China in a war against Koguryo. For the next 300 years, Korean culture grew in sophistication, refinement and wealth, often influenced by Chinese developments. Korea succumbed, in the thirteenth century, as did China, to the Mongol invasions and remained under Mongol domination for the next 200 years. The aborted Mongol effort to invade Japan was joined reluctantly by Korea, solidifying an already ancient enmity between Korea and Japan which, for many other reasons as well, persists to the present day. In the latter part of the fourteenth century, the general Yi Taejo seized control of Korea, installed his government in Seoul and established the Yi dynasty, under formal Chinese tutelage and less formal Japanese influence, relationships which endured until the Japanese victory over China in the late nineteenth century gave Japan singular dominance, leading to the annexation of Korea in 1910. In 1592, the Japanese invaded Korea and were eventually defeated in a still celebrated naval battle but at devastating costs from which Korean culture has perhaps not even now fully recovered.

Western traders and military spearheads (Russian, French, American), although more interested in China and Japan, began to enter Korean waters in the 1850s and 1860s, and were met with suspicion, hostility and violent rejection. Ironically, however, it was an Asian power, Japan, which began to demand from Korea concessions similar to those the Western powers had recently wrested from Japan.[2] Following the overthrow of the shogunate and the empowering of the Emperor, a Japanese mission was dispatched to Seoul in 1872 demanding normal trade relations, an overture which was rejected by the xenophobic and arbitrary Korean regent, the Taiwoenkun. In 1875, a Japanese ship was shelled in Korean waters, provoking a Japanese assault, capture of the Korean fortifications and an ultimatum demanding a treaty -- concluded the following year as the treaty of Kanghwa -- opening the ports of Pusan, Chemulpo, and Wonsan to trade, extending extraterritoriality to the Japanese, and establishing diplomatic missions. The treaty formally recognized Korean independence, contrary to Chinese presumptions, and later became a point of dispute between China and Japan. Through the intercession of the Chinese,[3] who were concerned to balance Japanese power in Korea, the United States was extended most favored nation trading terms and diplomatic recognition in 1882. Similar treaties were signed with Britain and Germany in 1883, Italy and Russia in 1884 and France in 1886. The Western treaties, unlike the Japanese, recognized Chinese suzerainty over Korea, confirming Japan and China in their different understandings of their spheres of influence in Korea, subjecting Seoul to intense cross-pressures from each, and creating internal and often internecine conflicts organized around the stresses so introduced.

The Taiwoenkun, retiring as regent in 1873, remained influential among anti-foreign factions; the Queen's family, the Mins, came to represent the accommodationists' interests. As part of an internal conspiracy to displace the Queen, an attack was launched against the Japanese Legation, killing several Japanese, forcing the Japanese minister to flee and inducing Japan to impose terms of settlement in the Chemulpo Treaty of 1882, which, among other things, permitted the permanent stationing of Japanese troops in Seoul to protect the Legation. These events contributed to a vicious political dialectic in which China also sent troops to Korea, coerced a treaty extending preferential trading terms, and installed a resident overseer in Seoul whose function was to assist in converting Korea from a Chinese tributary to a protectorate. Internal instability continued as Chinese/Japanese aspirations in Korea clashed and was manifested in a successful 1884 plot by the accommodationists, supported by the Japanese; power was seized, the Mins bypassed, and several conservative leaders assassinated. Japanese and Chinese troops were dispatched to the palace -- the Japanese to assist in the coup, the Chinese on behalf of the family of the Queen. This dangerous confrontation was, however, defused following some deadly exchanges of fire, negotiations were held and the Tientsin Convention of 1885 was signed, requiring both China and Japan to withdraw their troops from the peninsula but delaying the eventual war for only nine years.

The Sino-Japanese rivalry continued during the 1885-1894 period not only because neither power was prepared to forego its Korean concessions. The Korean polity itself was unable to forge a united front vis-a-vis its larger neighbors. Deep domestic factionalism -- a phenomenon which has continued to bedevil the Korean polity to the present day -- resulted in diverse appeals by various interests for Japanese and Chinese assistance, thus exacerbating interventionist tendencies already quite evident in China and Japan. There were additional ominous developments in world politics as well, which focused other great power rivalries on Korea. Russia was expanding eastward and alarming China as well as Great Britain, which was concerned with its own imperial prerogatives in Asia, in the process. China inaugurated moves designed to impose direct control of Korea from China and protect its border with Russia; Britain temporarily occupied the island of Port Hamilton off Korea to forestall a secret Korean/Russian agreement giving Russia use of warm water Port Lazareff. In 1886, China plotted clumsily to remove the Korean royal family to China and install the compliant Taiwoenkun in Seoul. The plot failed but succeeded in alarming the Japanese and disturbing the Koreans to the point where, in a search for broader international recognition and protection, a diplomatic mission was for the first time sent abroad to the United States over the objections of China. Economic rivalry in Korea between China and Japan mounted during the same period, anti-foreign and anti-government agitation in Korea expanded and the provisions of the Tientsin Convention were invoked by which both Japanese and Chinese troops were again introduced into Korea in June, 1894. This time there was no respite. The next month the Japanese began to impose their own solution to the Korean problem: the palace was seized and the puppet Taiwoenkun placed in "authority" and compelled to declare war on China. On August 1, war was declared by both sides. The Sino-Japanese war was concluded some eight months later in April, 1885 with the Treaty of Shimonoseki following the humiliation of the Chinese army in the field. Japan was confirmed as a significant, perhaps world, power, gained new possessions, the Liaotung Peninsula (given up for a time at European insistence, taken again in the Russo-Japanese War), Formosa, the Pescadores, and extracted from China an agreement, after centuries of its quite different relationship with China, that Korea was an "independent" country.

The Chinese defeat was one of the great watersheds of human history. Standing exposed as a paper tiger before Western and Japanese imperial and colonial ambitions, the oft-told story of the race to carve up ancient China began. For Korea, the Sino-Japanese War brought an end to its centuries old subordination to China but at the same time ushered in the most oppressive and bloodiest period in its history and led eventually to the dismemberment of the polity itself. The Hermit Kingdom was no more. It was also to be a period of deep, broad and intense change in social, economic and political spheres.

Often but not always misgoverned, frequently but not always oppressed by outsiders, traditional Korean culture had survived the centuries unchanged in many ways.[4] Confucian principles controlled interpersonal relations. The population was agrarian, often poor and impoverished, tilled the land with simple hand-made tools, lived in small self-sufficient villages. Public order was secured, even-handed justice often done if also often transgressed, intellectual feats of the highest order achieved (most remarkably, the simple hangul alphabet invented in the fifteenth century).

The end of the Sino-Japanese war gave the Japanese preeminence in Korea. "Advisers" were dispatched from Tokyo and, under their direction, a period of "reform" began. As with all colonial powers, pious intentions were publicly expressed which obscured the underlying exploitive reality. As in so many other colonial situations, the subjected population proved to be obdurate material upon which to work.[5] In October, 1895, Queen Min was killed in an uprising instigated beyond doubt by the Japanese Minister in Seoul, exacerbating the disorder in the country and inducing the Russians, whose own imperial aspirations were peaking, to send guards to "protect" their Korean Legation into which the successor king had fled. The Russians proceeded to expel the Japanese advisors (whose reforms were abolished), and extract economic concessions in North Korea. The jockeying for paramountcy in Korea between Japan and Russia continued apace and was formalized in the Rosen/Nishi Convention of 1898, in which both states pledged, altogether hypocritically, to protect Korean "independence", to consult on the sending of advisers, and to allow Japan economic penetration of the sort already achieved by Russia. (An earlier Japanese proposal to divide Korea along the thirty-eighth parallel into spheres of influence had been rejected by a Russia confident of soon taking the entire prize.) The competition continued, it becoming increasingly obvious that Russia's intentions were to secure hegemony over both Manchuria and Korea. As a counterweight, Great Britain and Japan signed a five-year mutual security agreement in 1902, in which, for the first time, a major Western power acknowledged Japan's peculiar interests in Korea. The inevitability of war between Japan and Russia, given Russia's continued efforts at expansion, was thus confirmed. A final Japanese initiative to Russia to share power in Korea failed. The severing of diplomatic relations followed and in early 1904 Japan attacked the Russian positions at Port Arthur. The Russo-Japanese War had begun from which, in the bloodiest international campaign since Waterloo, Japan emerged victorious in 1905. If the Japanese success against China ten years earlier had surprised the world, that against Russia startled it. Japan's status as a world power was unequivocally established. The first victory of an Asian power over a Western one had occurred, altering permanently, as now known, the position of Western imperialism in Asia. By the Treaty of Portsmouth, Japan acquired the Russian possessions in southern Manchuria and explicit recognition of its "rights" to virtually total domination of Korea.

As the specialist reader is aware, there remain many lacunae in the study of Korean history on matters bearing on Korean modernization. Scientific Korean historiography is only now emerging as a mature field in Korea. Historical research was discouraged during the Japanese colonial period except among Japanese historians who, in justifying the annexation, developed the so-called stagnation thesis which held that Korea by the late nineteenth and early twentieth centuries was still organized on a primitive, pre-feudal basis in which the seeds of modernization did not exist. This view has been challenged in recent years, most importantly perhaps by the Japanese historian Takashi Hatada, who perceived important instances of growth and progress in material welfare, participation and culture at many points in Korean history.[6] Hatada's interpretation may be contrasted with the views of historians during the colonial period, mostly Japanese, in which the allegedly benevolent and efficient Japanese administration is contrasted with the assertedly unrelieved mismanagement, myopia, abuse of power and official corruption of Yi Korean governments, which had resulted in a debased, impoverished, demoralized and inert body politic.[7] Such a thesis served to justify the "modernization" of Korea under Japanese direction.

Whatever was true of the period prior to the Japanese absorption of Korea, it is clearly the case that improvements in transportation, the emergence of industrialization, and the rationalization of agriculture were quickened during the decades of Japanese rule, facts acquiesced in even by the most ardent Korean nationalists.[8] The main beneficiaries of these economic improvements, however, were the Japanese, who came to occupy the leading roles in Korean business, finance, education, the professions, public service and, of course, politics. The Japanization of Korea meant that at the end of the colonial regime in 1945, few Koreans had been trained in the outlooks and skills required for self-directed economic progress and self-government.

Japanese Policy in Korea, 1905-1945

Since Japanese behavior in Korea cannot be understood adequately except in the context of the broader Japanese policy of Asian expansion (centering on China), the full story of Korean colonization cannot be told here.[9] For Korea itself, the conclusion of the Russo-Japanese War struck the death blow to even nominal national independence. Internal anti-Japanese and pro-independence agitation continued, however, and provided the pretext for annexation in 1910. Economic penetration increased concurrently. The monetary system was placed under the direction of the Daiichi Bank, the Japanese government assumed control of rail transport and communications, loans were made by Japan to underwrite the Bank of Korea and other financial associations, the Oriental Development Company was established to induce agricultural reform, tax collections increased, the Japanese legal system was imposed, traditional education was abolished and the Japanese model installed, a census was conducted (population: 12,934,282), ownership rights to the old communal properties were assigned, roads were built, sanitation improved. The costs to Koreans of these forced changes were immense. The land survey resulted in a government takeover of all lands previously controlled by the royal household, the municipalities and the Buddhist temples, which were then leased or sold to Japanese settlers. Ten years after annexation, one-third of the most productive land was in the hands of Japanese and over 300,000 (eventually nearly one million) Japanese had entered Korea in pursuit of economic advantage. An army of displaced Korean farmers was forced under the most arduous circumstances to wander aimlessly or to resettle, many of them in Manchuria and Siberia, where, subsequently, the politically active among them became attached to revolutionary communist politics: for this reason, Korean communism must be judged to have been initiated in Japan.

The disintegration of traditional Korean society, under the weight of the transformation imposed by military government, generated increased opposition, manifested most famously in the *Manse* (10,000 years, or Long Live Korea) movement of March and April, 1919. Some 500,000 out of a total population of roughly thirteen million Koreans, an extraordinarily high proportion of the population, participated actively in these initially Ghandi-like, non-violent demonstrations on behalf of national independence. Hatada records that during the *Manse* period 166 Japanese officials and police were killed, together with 29 civilians, while 1,962 Koreans were killed, 19,525 arrested, and 10,441 prosecuted. The movement was utterly suppressed and ended in failure: apart from the problems posed by a low level of continuing internal agitation and the persistent work of a small number of exiled leaders, the Japanese ascendency was complete. The Japanese did, however, in the glare of international publicity, alter their policy by which dominance was to be secured. The Governor General was replaced, the rule requiring a military governor was abolished formally (if not in practice), teachers were no longer to wear uniforms and carry swords, the military police were replaced by civilian (but largely Japanese) police, some expression of Korean cultural sentiment was allowed, and a very few submissive

Koreans were allowed to take part in politics.

The replacement of military by cultural rule coincided with a growing need in Japan for agricultural products and, in consequence, a fifteen year plan (1920-35) was launched to increase food production for export to Japan. Although the plan fell short of targets, production and exports grew substantially. In 1918, rice production totaled 13.7 million soks; in 1933, 16.3 million. Exports of rice to Japan in 1918 totaled 2.2 million soks; in 1933, 8.7 million. The consequences for the rice-dependent Korean population were staggering. In 1918, 11.5 million soks of rice were available for internal consumption compared to 7.6 million soks in 1933. The realignment of Korean agriculture, from a diversified, self-sufficient system to a one-crop, export-oriented one, confirmed Korea in the classical colonial pattern. Undeniably, Korean agriculture improved technically -- new seeds and planting schedules, a measure of mechanization, improved irrigation and flood control, larger-scale operations were introduced -- but these developments did not accrue to most Korean farmers. Indeed, tenancy increased, farm ownership decreased and, for many, standards-of-living fell.

Concommitantly, mining activity was stimulated (the yen value of mining output increased five times from 1925 to 1936) and in 1920 new rules governing economic activity were promulgated which placed Korea in the Japanese tariff and customs system and provided for the free movement of private Japanese capital into Korea. With few exceptions, investments were made initially in small-scale, labor intensive, agriculturally-related activities but, with the construction of hydroelectric dams in the north, larger investments in the fertilizer and chemical industries became feasible. Perhaps ironically, the international depression from 1929 on spurred Japanese capital movements to Korea, where cheap energy and low wages made large profits still possible. The growth of industry (yen value) rose two and one-half times between 1925 and 1936 and, as a proportion of total output, from 17.7 per cent to 31.3 per cent. Agriculture, reflecting the growing importance of industry, fell from 72.7 per cent to 51.8 per cent of total output during the same period.[10]

In all sectors, the emerging pattern was towards a dual economy in which the benefits of modernization went almost entirely to Japanese interests. The same was true of the cultural system, in spite of the imperial rescript of 1919 which proclaimed a policy of "universal brotherhood and non-discrimination between Japanese and Koreans." In 1939, the proportion of Koreans represented in university studies was .0093 per thousand population compared to 1.06 per thousand among the Japanese. Korean teachers, forbidden altogether before 1919, were permitted after that date, but very few were appointed to principalships and were paid far less than Japanese teachers. By 1924, there were only 69 Korean teachers in the 38 schools maintained by the Governor-General compared to 811 Japanese; 99 Korean teachers in 71 schools maintained by provincial governments compared to 474 Japanese; 2 Korean teachers in the 835 schools supported by school associations compared to 2,048 Japanese. Only in the District Educational Bodies were there really significant numbers of Korean teachers: 4,588 in the so-called Common Schools which were confined exclusively to elementary offerings.[11]

There is no gainsaying the fact that enrollments of Korean children in some types of schools increased sharply under the Japanese. Prior to the take-over, and excluding one university and four preparatory schools in Seoul (where work was organized along the Chinese model involving the study of the Confucian classics as a route to government careers), Korean education was primarily conducted in the *sohtang* schools where the sole subject of instruction was the reading and writing of Chinese characters. At the end of 1910, some 141,604 children attended such schools, a number which had increased to 275,920 by 1920. Korean children in common schools rose from 32,384 to 107,282 and from 446 to 3,513 in higher common schools during the same period. Beyond that, however, Korean representation in liberal, professional and other university curricula was pathetically low.[12]

In the 1930s, Japanese educational policy sought to extend education in the countryside in practical skills in an effort to enhance the quality of community leadership. However, by restricting admission to high schools and colleges, the development of an able, educated and genuinely national Korean leadership was prevented. The consequence of such policies is indicated by the growth and distribution of Korean teachers in the educational system: by 1941 the number of Korean teachers in primary schools had increased to 11,673; in secondary schools to 1,347; in normal schools and colleges to 289; and in the university field, to exactly 1 Korean professor. As late as 1941, there were only 304 Korean students at university; 3,639 at college; and 3,414 at normal schools. Korean students in primary schools increased from 407,292 in 1925 to 716,730 in 1935 and to 1,576,352 in 1941.[13]

As primary enrollments expanded, the aims of the educational system were altered toward the utter suppression of Korean culture. In 1938, Korean language lessons were replaced by Japanese, except in the first three primary grades; loyalty to the Japanese Emperor was inculcated; teachers and students were required to visit Shinto shrines; Koreans were pressured to adopt Japanese names and to speak only

Japanese at home. The evidence is persuasive that leading developmental roles were to be reserved exclusively for Japanese.

With Liberation in 1945, therefore, Korea was left with a minuscule number of trained and experienced citizens, professionals, businessmen, administrators and political leaders. Just before Liberation, perhaps 90 per cent of the population was illiterate (the obverse is now approximately the case); there was one physician for every 8,300 people (30 per cent of whom were in Seoul);[14] there were virtually no Koreans experienced in administering national policies (e.g., in the non-sensitive Department of Agriculture and Forestry in 1941 there was only one Korean higher official and he was a grade six -- a general pattern duplicated in all other ministries); no Korean served on the Supreme Court, while only four were numbered among the 35 judges on the Courts of Appeal, and only 10 per cent of all local judges were Korean.[15]

It was the Manchurian "incident" in 1931 and the establishment by the Japanese of the puppet Man-Chou-Kuo state that sparked a new and final phase of the Japanese in Korea. Industrial development and agricultural policy became organized candidly around the needs of the Japanese military. Farmers were assigned quotas for the delivery of rice and other grains; mining of gold, iron oar, coal, copper, tungsten and other minerals was accelerated; metal refining and chemical and light metallic industries were expanded. The number of Koreans employed in the industrial sector grew to some 750,000. Laborers drafted for war-related employments exceeded 2.0 million and another 723,000 were transported to Japan and the South Sea islands.[16]

Liberation to the Present

In the sixteen years between the end of colonial rule following the defeat of Japan in 1945 and the rise to power of the elites who were to transform South Korean society following the military coup d'etat in April of 1961, the South Korean people struggled to develop and survive in the face of a severed polity, an incompetent American military government (1945-48);[17] the increasingly inept Syngman Rhee government (1948-60);[18] a devastating war (1950-53); the April Revolution, which brought an end to the Rhee rule (1960); the short-lived and often chaotic Chang Myon regime (1960-61);[19] and the military revolution itself (1961).[20] With the compressed political turmoil, massive social dislocations and horrifying destruction of life and property that occurred in this period, consistent economic policy and sustained progress were impossible. Nonetheless several decisions taken during this period may be cited which, in their ultimate consequences, seem to have contributed to the developmental explosion of the 1960s and 1970s described in Chapters 2 and 3.

Liberation from Japan was accompanied by the division of Korea by the United States and the Soviet Union into two political entities (dissolving a highly integrated nation that had existed for some thirteen hundred years) between whom sharp antagonisms quickly mounted. The collapse of trade between the north and south and with Japan brought utter economic chaos to the south. Rice production, which had depended on fertilizer produced in the north, fell, while what rice was produced failed to reach the urban populations and was consumed in the countryside. Mass starvation was prevented only by large quantities of wheat from the United States. What industry had been located in the south was unable to function for lack of raw materials and then energy (after electrical power from the north was cut off in 1948). Brown records that, in 1946, South Korean manufacturing plants had been reduced by more than half of the pre-1945 number and that those still in operation were producing at only 20 per cent of capacity.[21] The concentration of heavy industry in the north (86 per cent, including chemicals, metals, cement and electricity) left South Korea (with 74 per cent of light industry, including textiles, food processing, machinery and lumbering) with an unbalanced and unintegrated manufacturing sector.[22]

The political division at the thirty-eighth parallel also severed what had been a rather highly developed transportation system (under Japanese rule, railroad length had by 1945 extended to a total of 5,671 kilometers and was perhaps the least underdeveloped sector in the entire economy).[23] Partition left South Korea with only 41 per cent of the railroads (2,642 kilometers); 42 per cent of locomotives (448); 51 per cent of freight cars (8,424); and 61 per cent of passenger cars (1,280).[24] With the departure of the Japanese transportation managers in 1945, control was assumed by the U.S. Military Government. A succession of reorganizations finally restored normal operations in late 1947 and, by 1950, under Korean management, new peaks of efficient operation had been achieved. These accomplishments were more than obviated by the Korean war, however, when some 41 per cent of total facilities and equipment were destroyed.[25]

The Republic of Korea (henceforth South Korea or simply Korea) was founded in 1948. The first two years of the First Republic under Syngman Rhee (1948-50) was a period of substantial progress in other areas as well, e.g., coal production was increased by 40 per cent; electrical power by 33 per cent; industrial production by 50 per cent. The Korean war, however, wiped out these gains in a few short months as the North Korean armies advanced south in June, 1950, overran three-fourths of the country and then either retreated or were captured and destroyed when the Pusan perimeter held and the Inchon landing of September, 1950, one of the most daring stratagems in military history, succeeded. The level of destruction was extremely high even by the standards of modern warfare. Brown cites figures showing that more than one of every twenty South Korean civilians, or 991,000 people, were casualties – 667,000 were killed or missing, 230,000 were wounded, 84,000 forcibly removed to North Korea.[27] The South Korean military suffered in excess of *40 per cent* casualties, or some 320,000 killed or wounded.[28] While some estimates differ from these,[29] the relative magnitudes are very large by any accounting: the overall military casualty ratio (both sides) was approximately 1:2.7 compared to a ratio of 1:2.18 in the First World War; the ratio of South Korean civilian casualties was 1:19, close to the proportion of civilian losses suffered by the Soviet Union in the Second World War of 1:19.3.[30]

Physical destruction was huge. Brown reports that physical losses were equal to the entire 1953 national product.[31] Some 661,000 buildings and facilities were destroyed,[32] 40 per cent of which were dwelling and 20 per cent transportation goods and other infrastructures. Inflation during the war reached such extremes that the currency became valueless. As the military front stabilized in 1951, reconstruction efforts began and it is perhaps from that date that the growth of the modern economy is best studied. The prospects for development were dismal at best: urban areas and the countryside in three-fourths of the country were in ruins, a large proportion of the most vigorous members of society had been decimated, the confidence necessary to begin anew was altogether lacking, an attitude that remained pervasive well into the 1960s.[34]

Two policy lines were adopted in the period just prior to the war, however, that were to have enduring and important effects on subsequent economic development: one concerned agriculture, the other education. The first was consciously contrived, the second much less so.

In June, 1949, a land reform program was inaugurated to redistribute some 23 per cent of the total arable land in South Korea (lands previously owned by Japanese, plus Korean farms over 7.5 acres). The effect was to reduce the average size of individual farms to less than 2.2. acres and to virtually eliminate large farms altogether -- by 1959 only 0.3 per cent of all farms exceeded 7 acres in size, while 42 per cent were 1.2 acre or less.[35] The result was to create even more petty farmers in a country of petty farmers and to make it difficult to achieve the economies of scale which larger farms might have encouraged. Even so, Korean agriculture has shown steady increases in productivity and, by international standards, is highly efficient in some areas, especially rice. Most importantly, however, land reform worked to the immediate benefit of some 62 per cent of farm families and removed potential agrarian unrest from the political agenda. Subsequent industrialization was able to proceed in the context of a politically pacified countryside.

Developments in education were truly of revolutionary proportions in the post-Liberation period. Educational aspirations, always keen in Korean culture, had been thwarted by Japanese policy; Liberation brought an explosion in numbers of students at all levels and in the growth of new elementary and high schools and colleges. Neither the

American military government nor the administration of the First Republic sought very effectively to direct this growth in socially optimal directions. The Japanese model was abruptly rejected, the American system uncritically installed, and educational entrepreneurs, often moved more by monetary than pedagogical motives, created new schools with, usually, inadequate staffs, equipment and standards. Imbalances were created which still persist, e.g., 70 per cent of all university students are in Seoul, as are 37 out of 74 colleges and universities;[37] student-teacher ratios are still far too high -- 1:69.7 in 1945 compared to 1:62.6 in 1964 in elementary schools;[38] employment opportunities were not commensurate with levels of training and education. Adjustments were made -- pre-admission examinations for higher education, enrollment limitations, new opportunities in developmentally-related programs -- which, although rather ineffective in earlier years, have shown considerable effect more recently.[39] The sweep of these movements is indicated by school enrollments in 1945, when there were 1.37 million elementary students, 85,000 high school students and 7,800 third level students, compared to 1964, when elementary students numbered over 4.7 million, high school students over 1 million, and college students 142,629.[40] Virtually universal elementary education had been achieved by 1964 in a population that in 1945 had been overwhelmingly illiterate.

Education grew haphazardly, like Topsy, and doubtlessly inefficiently as well. Balanced growth in all sectors, including education, may be conceptually preferable to wide oscillations and disequilibrated movements in development,[41] but as a practical matter the inelegant expansion in educational activity was an expression of a deep impulse in Korean culture which, after centuries of artificial repression had found its release. Judged by its consequences, it has been an indispensable factor in the economic progress of more recent years.

South Korean political history from the Liberation to 1961 could scarcely be more complex, and it is beyond present purposes to unravel that history here.[42] In brief, it concerned efforts to create liberal representative democracy by acts of will, as if democratic institutions on the Western model were themselves unrelated to peculiar and, by historical accounting, rather temporary circumstances, including such diverse influences as Greek philosophy, Roman law, the pluralism of power between church and state, feudal rights, and, in later periods, relative affluence, literacy, urbanization and industrialization.[43] No such conditions existed in Korea when Syngman Rhee became president in 1948. His great popularity, based on his long service in the independence movement and his immensely respected erudition in both Western and Oriental scholarship, accounted for the 92 per cent of the vote in the National Assembly by which he became president. The First Republic allocated power primarily to the Assembly while the political culture continued to rest upon the persistent authoritarianism of the past. Rhee's tenure was one in which traditional practices accumulated over newly posited ones. The process by which autocratic tendencies replaced representative government was accelerated by the outbreak of the Korean war and the chronic incapacity of the politically active population to form a stable and responsible competitive party system. The result, in Henderson's evocative phrase, was the "politics of the vortex."[44] Homogeneous to a degree unparalleled among nation-states in race, language, culture, class, economy, national identifications and, in the face of a hostile regime in the north, political ideology, no social and economic differentiation existed which otherwise might have provided a stable basis for political party groupings. The lack of a social basis for political party differences and the historic and continued centralization of power at the capital in Seoul prevented the formation of a responsible and socially-connected party system, generated a drift of all ambition toward the center, and gave rise to the incessant building, coalescing, collapsing and regrouping of "political parties" rarely distinctive or even clear in social outlook or policy orientations.

If modernization had been the first priority of the increasingly autocratic Rhee, the concentration of authority in the context of the times might have been consistent with such a goal. In the view of some, however, Rhee's "caesaristic" tendency emphasized personal power, extreme nationalism and anticommunism, while neglecting the more mundane but essential tasks of institution-building, including the building of a competent developmentally-oriented bureaucracy.[45] Cabinet instability, insecurity of tenure and excessive centralization of administrative decision-making made concerted attention to development impossible, especially given the thin stratum of administrative talent available in any case. By way of illustration, ministers served an average of eleven months during Rhee's twelve years in office; Rhee himself at one time approved all allocations of foreign exchange above $500; virtually no administrators were experienced in national planning and programming.[46] Most importantly, Rhee, for all his high intelligence, was unable to articulate a sense of national mission and direction, that is, an integrating and mobilizing ideology essential to nation-building. Cynicism and hopelessness, unavoidable to some degree in the existential circumstances, were reinforced by an increasingly corrupt and arbitrary regime.

Rhee's Liberal Party government came to an end with the student-led uprising of April 19, 1960 in which, in Seoul alone, some 130 persons were shot dead and 1,000 wounded. Continuing demonstrations, and army security forces who refused to contain them, led to Rhee's resignation on April 26 and exile to Hawaii. It is well to remember, however, that political party and oppositional activity continued even during the high tide of Rhee's atavism and that Korean totalitarianism, if not authoritarianism, remains a northern and not southern phenomenon.

The abbreviated Second Republic was inaugurated in August of 1960 and was overthrown in May, 1961 by the military coup led by then Major General now President Park Chung Hee. Its brief history was characterized by considerable idealism, a commitment to civil liberties, broadened participation and, at the same time, an irresponsibly captious press, governmental vacillation, instability, continued lack of party discipline and, arguably, ideological polarization on issues concerning the type of economic order to be pursued, attitudes toward the roles of the state's coercive instruments (police and army), the means of achieving national unification, and dependency on the United States.[47]

The military government under the direction of its young officers imposed stability on a politically disordered country. Unlike the previous governing elites, they brought with them the military virtues of discipline and dedication, considerable administrative experience gained in managing the large national security sector, a strong nationalistic ideology and, as it turned out, a capacity to recognize, accept and implement expert advice on developmental questions. On the other hand, a voluntary consensus on a political formula that would constrain as well as liberate political activity has not yet been fully formed in Korea, although the social differentiation produced by economic development in recent years, combined with a growing awareness that the stakes involved in maintaining stability are now broadly distributed, may lead eventually to the shared understandings and self-restraints which are a prerequisite to ordered democracy. The Third Republic was established in the elections of 1963 by which, in October, Park Chung Hee was narrowly elected president and, in November, when the Democratic Republican Party (Park's party) won 110 of the 175 seats in the National Assembly.

It is from 1963 that the great surge in economic growth began, although it is well to observe that economic performance under the post-Korean war Rhee regime was by no means a total failure. Growth in GNP during 1954-55 was about 5.5 per cent; in 1956, 0.4 per cent; during 1957-58, about 6.5 per cent, and in 1959, 3.9 per cent. In 1960, the year of Rhee's deposition, growth was only 1.9 per cent, but in 1961, in spite of the Chang government's difficulties and the military coup, growth was 4.8 per cent, which was greater than the 3.1 per cent achieved in 1962 during the first full year of military rule.[48] The index of industrial production (1960=100) rose from 43 in 1954 to 91.8 in 1959 and, under the Financial Stabilization Plan of 1957, the chronic post-war inflation was ended and price stability achieved.[49] These achievements, however, obscure some important facts. Population growth was such as to prevent significant increases in per capita income; much growth reflected temporary American relief and reconstruction assistance; much economic activity was still more welfare than growth-oriented; and there was no effective long-term development strategy and a still retarded institutional basis for producing one.

It is true that efforts at economic planning began as early as the Korean war itself.[50] The first plan (1954-58), proposed by Robert R. Nathan for the UN Korean Reconstruction Agency, had the objective of achieving economic self-sufficiency by 1958 through increases in the primary sectors of agriculture, fishing and mining and by import-substitution policies. Although production in these areas did increase to some degree, the plan failed, first, because the Korean government chose not to implement it and, second, because it was in any case fundamentally flawed in conception: as is now clear, the Korean comparative advantage consists in manufacturing, not primary commodities. In the last months of the Rhee administration, the government's own Economic Development Council put forward a seven-year plan to be pursued in two phases, 1960-62 and 1963-66, which was aborted by the 1960 revolution. The Chang government initiated a five-year plan in early 1961 which again was stymied by the political events of May and the subsequent rejection of the plan by the military regime.

The First Five-Year Plan, 1962-66, reflecting some prior planning, was promulgated by the Park government and, with various interim modifications, was the first economic plan carried through to (a very qualified) conclusion. The First, Second (1966-71), Third (1972-76) and Fourth (1977-81) Five-Year Plans are discussed in later chapters; here it is sufficient to note that the planning period from 1962 to the present proceeded without political interruption and ineptitude of the sort which had plagued earlier efforts; that the plans became recognized internationally as responsible and attainable in their objectives; that they were associated with, if not the total cause for, the great economic progress which occurred simultaneously; and that the apparent success of the plans produced rising confidence in, and enhanced legitimacy for, the government. The Korean polity continues to face serious questions of legitimacy and authority -- as the current history of the Western liberal democracies reveals, crises of legitimacy are not peculiar to less developed systems but are continuing problems for all governments -- but has greater psychological and material resources available now than at any time in its history for the peaceful resolution of such crises, effective performance being the first requisite of political persistence in the modern world.[51]

Since 1963, the Korean government has stabilized under the administration of President Park, who was re-elected in 1967 and, following constitutional amendments, again in 1971 and 1972.[52] Sporadic student agitation, some press commentary, occasionally politicized religious activists and a few deposed or resigned politicians continue to spearhead oppositional tendencies. Political control was imposed by martial law in 1964 and 1972, by the garrison decree of 1965, by closing of campuses in 1964, 1965, 1969, 1971, 1972, 1973, and 1974 and by the several emergency decrees, most recently in 1975, which placed limits on demands for constitutional changes. The process of nation-building in Korea continues and the value dissensus between the government and some -- by no means all -- of the intellectuals who regard themselves as the repository of the nation's conscience remains a source of conflict which, if not moderated, might at some point inflict deep lacerations on the society and upset the prospects for further improvements in national welfare. A resolution of these tensions would require the development of a political code characterized by a supportable balance between order and dissent or, more precisely, agreement on values and conflicts on interests.

If the universe of diverse, stable, practical and overlapping interests grows[53] in Korea; if governmental and non-governmental authority patterns should more and more converge;[54] if effective governmental performance and economic development continue,[55] the way may be open to the formation of that essential social consensus and moderate antagonism on questions of rights, welfare and participation which practical advocates of democracy have always found most attractive.[56]

In subsequent chapters, economic and social development are taken as generally synonymous for operational purposes. One is aware that other analysts make a sharp distinction between those two terms, arguing that, whatever economic development may entail, it does not necessarily carry with it improvement (or development) in social welfare and that, consequently, development should properly be measured by other indicators. There is considerable good sense in this argument. However, there is evidence that, while the correlation is imperfect and special cases aside, economic growth has meant general improvement in general welfare in most systems in which it has occurred and certainly in Korea. In Nordhaus and Tobin's important paper, the general conclusion is reached that, "although G.N.P. and other national income aggregates are imperfect measures of welfare, the broad picture of secular progress which they convey remains after corrections of their most obvious deficiencies."[57] It is also a fact that efforts to develop alternative theoretically-based welfare, progress, improvement or development indicators have not, thus far, been particularly successful,[58] although certainly much non-economic data which convey useful information on the quality of life in some countries are available.[59] Whatever the case elsewhere, growth in Korea has made possible the obvious spread of many amenities, services and opportunities to larger proportions of the population than ever before. The spread is a palpable fact impressed upon the senses of all travelers in Korea, and in addition to the development indicators discussed in chapters 2 and 3, is reflected in any number of statistical series: housing construction, radios and television sets in use, caloric consumption, paved roads, electrical power generation, private cars, air travel, telephone subscribers, compensation of employees as per cent of national income, numbers of physicians and hospital beds, shifts in private consumption expenditures. It would be unnecessarily tedious to discuss each of these (or other possible series) in detail, but inspection of Tables 1-1 and 1-2 should serve to confirm the general and in some cases very striking trends and are consistent with the data on income distribution discussed in Chapter 2.

In Table 1-2, it will be observed that personal household expenditures show a trend from 1960 to 1974 toward greater consumption of more luxuries and amenities (tobacco, beverages, household furnishings, personal and health care, recreation and entertainment) and less on necessities (household operation, rent and water charges). The relative reduction on food expenditures indicates that basic food needs are now being met in average households, a vast improvement in a once chronic social problem.

Compared to fifteen or twenty years ago, the Korean situation of today has improved immeasurably, although major economic, political and administrative problems remain. The achievements are the striking thing, however. In Badgley's study of Asian development projected into 1980, South Korea ranked (with Taiwan and Thailand) as the "most viable" of the thirteen countries surveyed. Badgley's viability index involved national power (resources of popula-

Table 1-1

Social Indicators in Korea

	1960	1973-74
Physicians per 10,000	3.1	5.2
No. Hospital Beds	9,951	19,828
Caloric consumption (per day per person)	2,280 (1963-65)	2,600
Residential construction (1,000 sq. meters)	650	16,572
Electrical energy (million KW)	1,699	16,832
Paved roads (Km)	727	6,762
Passenger cars	12,776	76,462
Buses	4,195	19,583
Civil Aviation		
Domestic	71,081	990,826
International arrivals	13,314	572,403
International departures	14,660	616,145
Telephone subscribers		
Business	37,330 (1959)	441,564
Residence	24,647 (1959)	435,138
Public	575 (1959)	12,847
Radios in use	333,000	4,000,000
Television sets in use	25,000 (1961)	1,186,806
Compensation of Employees	21% (1955-59 average)	38.5% (1973-74 average)
National Welfare Pension System	–	40% of average salary at age 60 for workers in plants with 30 or more workers (1977)?

SOURCES: *UN Statistical Yearbook for Asia and The Far East, 1971;* Bank of Korea, *Economic Statistics Yearbook,* various years; *Korea Annual, 1975.*

Table 1-2

Private Consumption Expenditures (1970 Constant Market Prices)

	1960	1970	1974	Change 1960-74
Food	57.2 %	50.3 %	44.9 %	-
Beverages	4.5	4.4	5.8	+
Tobacco	1.3	3.3	3.8	+
Clothing and other personal effects	10.6	10.6	13.4	+
Rent and water charges	5.3	4.0	3.7	-
Fuel and light	4.4	4.6	4.4	same
Furniture, furnishings and household equipment	1.5	2.7	3.9	+
Household operation	1.3	1.0	1.0	-
Personal care and health expenses	4.2	4.9	5.2	+
Transportation and communication	3.3	5.8	6.0	+
Recreation and entertainment	4.1	5.3	5.0	+
Miscellaneous services	2.3	3.1	2.9	+
	100%	100%	100%	

SOURCE: The Bank of Korea, *Economic Statistics Yearbook, 1975.*

tion, manpower, transportation and communication, energy and productivity, materials); national integration (of cultural, political, economic and military institutions); national morale (public confidence, optimism, state legitimacy); and perceived national capability (confidence of leaders in their nation's capacities vis-a-vis other nations).[60] Badgley defines viability as "... a condition in which a state maintains sovereignty, sustains political and economic processes that advance the conditions of civility and mutual trust among the population, and is able to pursue courses in domestic and foreign affairs that serve its interests."[61] For Korea to stand relatively high on such a measure is a Korea fundamentally transformed from its historic poverty, weakness and vulnerability.

It would be overly facile to ascribe the growth and spread of material improvements in Korea to the performance of the government alone, but it is surely the case that government policy and its administration have been crucial factors in creating the general atmosphere and social rules which have both compelled and encouraged the Korean people to act developmentally. The public sector institutions, rules and personalities that have been instrumental in these recent achievements must figure importantly in any full understanding of the success of the Korean political economy and are the subjects of later chapters.

Summary

The ancient tributary and recent colonial status of Korea ended with the establishment of the First Republic under President Syngmon Rhee in 1948. The nation's human resources had been left undeveloped by the Japanese and the integrated industry and infrastructure built during Japanese rule – always oriented toward Japanese interests in any case -- was severed by the partition of the nation at the 38th parallel when the United States and the Soviet Union were unable to agree on the basis for a new Korean polity following the Second World War. Disruption in trade with Japan and political inexperience contributed to the pervasive distress of the period. Nonetheless, substantial progress was made in the immediate post-Liberation years only to be largely destroyed during the Korean war of 1950-53. The Rhee government did succeed in stimulating investment, controlling inflation and generating respectable rates of growth. The moral authority of the Rhee government, made difficult by the persistent factionalism of party partisans and the absence of a broadly accepted political formula, was eroded also because of its relative inattention to social reconstruction, excessive centralization, arbitrariness and gathering corruption. The revolt against Rhee signalled the effective political mobilization of new groups (students, intellectuals, the press, the military) and resulted in the installation of the short-lived Second Republic, leaders of which were unable to consolidate their power or to compromise the aspirations of the newly mobilized interests. The military revolution of 1961 imposed stability on the country and, after initial vacillations, succeeded in establishing development as well as security as its first priorities and showed a capacity to mobilize and allocate resources in a manner consistent with those goals. The Third Republic, instituted with the elections of 1963, evolved policies which stimulated economic development to levels far beyond the earlier expectations of most informed economists and administrators both at home and abroad, an achievement which has increased the legitimacy of the regime among the population generally if not among some segments of intellectual opinion, raised confidence of both elites and masses and provided a foundation for future progress. The performance of governmental institutions, policies and personalities implicated in the raising and dispersing of material welfare are considered in subsequent chapters.

Notes

1. Korea's international relations prior to the Western penetration of Asia are described in Frederick M. Nelson, *Korea and The Old Orders of Eastern Asia* (Baton Rouge: Louisiana State University Press, 1940).

2. The Japanese colonial ascendency in Korea is related most fully in C. I. Eugene Kim and Han Kyo Kim, *Korea and The Politics of Imperialism, 1876-1910* (Berkeley: University of California Press, 1967). See also Arthur J. Brown, *The Mastery of The Far East* (London: G. Bell and Sons, 1919); Hilary Conroy, *The Japanese Seizure of Korea, 1868-1910* (Philadelphia: University of Pennsylvania Press, 1960); and Homer B. Hulbert, *The Passing of Korea* (Seoul: Yonsei University Press, 1969).

3. Late nineteenth century Chinese policy toward Korea is analyzed in Frederick Foo Chien, *The Opening of Korea: A Study of Chinese Diplomacy, 1876-1885* (Hamden, Conn.: Shoe String Press, 1967).

4. Traditional Korean (particularly political) culture is described, from rather different perspectives, in Gregory Henderson, *Korea: The Politics of The Vortex* (Cambridge: Harvard University Press, 1968), pp. 36-55; and Pyong-Choon Hahm, "Toward a New Theory of Korean Politics: A Reexamination of Traditional Factors," in Edward Reynolds Wright (ed.), *Korean Politics in Transition* (Seattle: University of Washington Press, 1975), pp. 321-355. A seminal work by James B. Palais, *Politics and Policy in Traditional Korea* (Cambridge: Harvard University Press, 1975) rejects the conventional emphasis on monolithic autocracy stressed by most writers, including Henderson, in favor of a systems (interactive) model in which interests, ideology and politics combined to produce stability as well as marginal adjustments. Also relevant are Pyong-Choon Hahm, *The Korean Political Tradition and The Law* (Seoul: Royal Asiatic Society, 1967), and Yi-Sup Hong, *Korea's Self-Identity* (Seoul: Yonsei University Press, 1973).

5. The story of the Japanese colonial period and the Korean reaction is available in Chong Sik Lee, *The Politics of Korean Nationalism* (Berkeley:

University of California Press, 1964); Andrew C. Hahm (ed.), *Korea Under Japanese Colonial Rule* (Kalamazoo: Western Michigan University Press, 1973); Harold H. W. Sunoo, *Korea: A Political History of Modern Times* (Columbia, Missouri: Korean-American Cultural Foundation, 1971); and Henderson, *Korea,* pp. 72-112.

6. *A History of Korea* (Santa Barbara, CA: American Bibliographical Center, 1969). Also see Palais, *Politics and Policy in Traditional Korea.* Recent scholarly papers on this subject are cited in Edward W. Wagner, "Report on a Conference: Traditional Korean Society," in *Social Science Research Council Items,* Vol. 29, No. 4 (December, 1975), p. 47.

7. This is the theme expressed, for example, in the pro-colonial book by Alleyne Ireland, *The New Korea* (New York: Dutton, 1926).

8. See, for example, Henry Chung, *The Case of Korea* (London: Revell, 1921).

9. The wider history is told absorbingly in Nathaniel Peffer, *The Far East : A Modern History* (Ann Arbor: University of Michigan Press, 1958).

10. These figures are not altogether reliable (measurement error in agriculture is apt to be large) but the general trends are clear. See Hatada, *A History of Korea,* p. 120. The economy under Japanese rule is covered best in Andrew J. Grajdanzev, *Modern Korea: Her Economic and Social Development Under The Japanese* (New York: Institute of Pacific Relations, 1944). For the period 1910 to 1920, a volume published by the Bank of Chosen, *Economic History of Chosen* (Seoul, 1920) is useful, if clearly biased.

11. Ireland, *The New Korea,* p. 202.

12. *The New Administration in Chosen.* Compiled by The Government-General in Chosen, July, 1921, Appendix, p. XXV.

13. *Korea: Its Land, People and Culture of All Ages,* (Seoul: Hakwon-sa, 1963), pp. 374-375, Tables 1 and 2. This encyclopedic reference is an invaluable source on many facets of Korean life.

14. A. Wigfall Green, *The Epic of Korea* (Washington, D. C.: Public Affairs Press, 1950), p. 45.

15. Grajdanzev, *Modern Korea,* pp. 243-251.

16. *Ibid.*

17. The 1945-48 period is well covered in George M. Mc Cune and Arthur

L. Grey, Jr., *Korea Today* (Cambridge: Harvard University Press, 1950), and E. Grant Meade, *American Military Government in Korea* (New York: King's Crown Press, 1951).

18. The emergence and ultimate fall of the Rhee government is described in all current histories of Korea: particularly helpful are Henderson, *Korea,* pp. 113-182; Hahn-Been Lee, *Korea: Time, Change and Administration* (Honolulu: East-West Center Press, 1968), pp. 75-108; Young-Ho Lee, "The Politics of Democratic Experiment," in Wright, *Korean Politics in Transition,* pp. 19-25; and Richard C. Allen, *Syngman Rhee: An Unauthorized Portrait* (Tokyo: Tuttle, 1960).

19. The failure to achieve stable liberal government following the overthrow of Rhee is the subject of the excellent study by Sung-Joo Han, *The Failure of Democracy in South Korea* (Berkeley: University of California Press, 1974).

20. See Se-Jin Kim, *The Politics of Military Revolution in Korea* (Chapel Hill: University of North Carolina Press, 1971).

21. Gilbert T. Brown, *Korean Pricing Policies and Economic Development in the 1960s* (Baltimore: Johns Hopkins University Press, 1973), p. 31.

22. Mc Cune, *Korea Today,* p. 57.

23. *Korea: Its Land, People and Culture of All Ages,* p. 277. The relatively well-developed transportation system is commented on by Grajdanzev, *Modern Korea,* pp. 185-191, who notes that Korea, with a population one-third of Japan, had one-quarter the length of Japanese railroads.

24. *Ibid.*

25. *Ibid.*

26. David C. Cole and Princeton N. Lyman, *Korean Development: The Interplay of Politics and Economics* (Cambridge: Harvard University Press, 1971), p. 21.

27. Brown, *Korean Pricing Policies,* p. 35.

28. *Ibid.*

29. There are discrepancies in the casualty figures given by different authorities, not surprising in view of the prevailing chaos. See Cole and Lyman, *Korean Development* (p. 22) and *Korea: Its Land, People and Culture of All Ages* (p. 208) for somewhat varied estimates.

30. *Korea: Its Land, People and Culture of All Ages,* p. 209.

31. Brown, *Korean Pricing Policies,* p. 35.

32. *Korea: Its Land, People and Culture of All Ages,* p. 209.

33. Brown, *Korean Pricing Policies,* p. 35.

34. Princeton Lyman, "Economic Development in South Korea: A Retrospective View," in Wright, *Korean Politics in Transition,* p. 243.

35. *Korea: Its Land, People and Culture of All Ages,* p. 257.

36. Brown, *Korean Pricing Policies,* p. 39.

37. Byung-Hun Oh, "Students and Politics," in Wright, *Korean Politics in Transition,* p. 131.

38. *Ibid.,* p. 118.

39. *Ibid.,* p. 115.

40. *Ibid.,* p. 116.

41. Albert O. Hirshman's *Journeys Toward Progress* (New York: The Twentieth Century Fund, 1963) makes a strong case for the occasional virtues of unbalanced development.

42. A succinct descriptive account of this most tumultuous period (1945-1961) is available in *Korea: Its Land People and Culture of All Ages,* pp. 128-133. More contextual analyses are available in Cole and Lyman, *Korean Development,* Part I; Han, *The Failure of Democracy in South Korea, passim;* Henderson, *Korea,* Parts II-IV: Kim, *The Politics of Military Revolution in Korea, passim;* and Kyung Cho Chung, *Korea: The Third Republic* (New York: Macmillan, 1971).

43. An inventory of theories of democracy is available in M. Rejai, *Democracy* (New York: Atherton, 1967), none of which suggest that conditions in post-Liberation Korea were consistent with liberal constitutional democracy.

44. Henderson, *Korea.* But see Bruce G. Cumings, "Is Korea a Mass Society?" in James B. Palais (ed.), *Occasional Papers on Korea,* No. 1 (The Joint Committee on Korean Studies of the ACLS/SSRC, April, 1974), pp. 65-81.

45. See John K. C. Oh, *Democracy on Trial* (Ithaca: Cornell University Press, 1968).

46. Kim, *The Politics of Military Revolution in Korea,* pp. 21, 24.

47. Han, *The Failure of Democracy in South Korea,* p. 5 and *passim.*

48. The Bank of Korea, *Economic Statistics Yearbook,* 1975, p. 5.

49. Hahn-Been Lee, *Korea,* pp. 82, 84.

50. Excellent discussions of the evolution of economic planning from the Korean War to the Second Five-Year Plan may be found in Hahn-Been Lee, *Korea,* pp. 74-174 and Cole and Lyman, *Korean Development,* pp. 203-221. Earlier planning efforts are usefully described in W. D. Reeve, *The Republic of Korea: A Political and Economic Study* (New York: Oxford University Press, 1963) and Joe Won Lee, "Planning Efforts for Economic Development," in Joseph S. Chung (ed.), *Patterns of Economic Development: Korea* (Detroit: Korea Research and Publications, 1966).

51. David Easton, *A Systems Analysis of Political Life* (New York: Wiley, 1965).

52. The Korean Constitution and the nature of its recent amendments are discussed by Edward R. Wright, "The Constitution and Governmental Structures," in Wright, *Korean Politics in Transition,* pp. 46-49.

53. Samuel P. Huntington, *Political Order in Changing Societies* (New Haven: Yale University Press, 1968).

54. Harry Eckstein, *Division and Cohesion in Democracy* (Princeton: University Press, 1966).

55. Seymour Martin Lipset, *Political Man* (New York: Doubleday, 1960), pp. 45-96.

56. David Braybrook, *Three Tests for Democracy* (New York: Random House, 1968).

57. See National Bureau of Economic Research, *Economic Growth: Fiftieth Anniversary Colloquium, V* (New York: Columbia University Press, 1972). See also Hollis Chenery, *et al., Redistribution With Growth: Policies to Improve Income Distribution in Developing Countries in The Context of Economic Growth* (New York: Oxford University Press, 1974). Often growth may be associated with restricted distribution of benefits because little capital gets decentralized to the bulk of society. Land redistribution and wide educational opportunities in Korea have endowed many with

the resources necessary for sharing in growth. These effects can be far more important than strategies which rely on taxes, subsidies and price manipulation, as commonly practiced in developing countries (although far less so in Korea). See Philip Musgrove's review of the above study in *Political Science Quarterly,* Vol. 90 (Fall, 1975), pp. 610-11.

58. See the critique by Wilfred Beckerman, *International Comparisons of Real Incomes* (Paris: Development Centre of the Organization for Economic Co-operation and Development, 1966), pp. 7-10. The case for alternative ways of evaluating development is made in N. Baxter (ed.), *Measuring Development: The Role and Adequacy of Development Indicators* (London: Frank Cass, 1972) which, however, does not present any real answers to the evaluation problem. It has been pointed out in a review of the Baxter book by C. O'Loughlin that "The importance of interpreting the priorities and possible targets from the viewpoint of the communities to be developed also need to be considered; otherwise there is a danger that work on social indicators may become an intellectual exercise in do-gooding." *The Economic Journal,* Vol. 83 (June, 1973), p. 650. Another effort to measure the quality of life is J. Drewnoski and W. Scott, *The Level of Living Index* (Geneva: United Nations Research Institute for Social Development, Report No. 4, September, 1966) which is interesting if not compelling. Relevant also is Burkhard Strumpel (ed.), *Subjective Elements of Well-Being* (Paris: Organization for Economic Cooperation and Development, 1974), published as part of the OECD's social indicator development program.

59. For an interesting effort involving the United States, see Office of Management and Budget, *Social Indicators, 1973* (Washington, D. C.: U. S. Government Printing Office, 1973). For a somewhat similar approach in the United Kingdom, see *Social Trends,* No. 3 (London: Government Statistical Office, 1972).

60. John Badgley, *Asian Development: Problems and Prognosis* (New York: The Free Press, 1971), pp. 76-116.

61. *Ibid.,* p. 77.

Chapter 2

Recent Korean Development in World Context

The concept of economic development has different uses for different people. For some it is a criterion of performance; for others it is a party cry or pet phrase invoked to justify or condemn a policy or aspiration which is either detested or desired. Here economic development is used in the first sense, as a measure of the performance of an economy. The operational definition of economic development consists, at the very least, in significant and sustained increases in per capita income.

A second aspect might also entail an analysis of leisure -- if two individuals receive the same incomes but one works longer hours than the other, their incomes are actually different in a welfare context. The problems of measuring this dimension of development are profound if not insurmountable for obvious reasons: while industrial workers and civil servants may work more or less regular hours, the hours of labor of farmers, self-employed entrepreneurs and independent professionals are difficult to estimate for any particular country and almost impossible cross-nationally: does the small farmer in Korea work "more" for his income than his counterpart in China or India?

A third component of development would have to do with the extent to which increased community output is "reasonably" or "unreasonably" distributed among income groups; whether existing inequities, if maintained, are in some ways appropriate or, if inappropriate, are changed in more acceptable directions. The problem of measuring distribution is compounded by the fact that growth and equity may not be synchronized precisely. For example, sustained increases in per capita income may, in a particular country, be associated with heightened inequity in income distribution during the earlier periods of economic expansion and greater equity in later periods.[1]

A number of circumstances have contributed to the unusually equitable distribution of income in Korea compared to most other developing countries. These include the relentless leveling of Korean society under the Japanese, the destruction of wealth during the Korean war, the land reforms of 1947 and 1950, the rapid expansion in education following liberation and Korea's labor-intensive development strategy, not to mention specific redistributive policies of more recent vintage in pricing, taxation, subsidy approaches, and social welfare.[2] Relative equality of opportunity, imposed by both cruel fate and wise public policy, has meant that growth and equity have not been the antagonistic goals that they are in so many polities. For the LDCs which compare unfavorably with Korea in income distribution, history as much as policy may be the cause. In recent years, Korea has gained both increases in income and relative equity among income groups.[3] In other countries, the time spans involved in establishing an "appropriate" link between expansion and equity may be quite lengthy, as in the industrialized West, where one can say only with the experience of decades that increases in community output have produced greater rather than less equity.

A fourth factor in development might concern a country's foreign debt, if any, and its capacity to manage it. Foreign debt constitutes an obligation of the economy as a whole and, if excessive, can severely retard development. This has been a troublesome matter in Korea, where foreign debt outstanding rose from $3.3 billion in 1973 to $5.9 billion in 1975. Short-term debt in 1975 was $2.2 billion, which was twice that of net reserves, and payments of principal and interest on total foreign debt exceeded $1 billion. If large trade deficits should reoccur, borrowing will be required to finance merchandise purchases and debt service rather than capital investments, which will in turn undermine the country's debt management capability. The consequences for continued economic expansion would become profound should export earnings not continue at a high level. Although disquieting prospects exist, the pessimism that developed during the earlier phases of the 1973-74 world trade recession has dissipated, partly because of the larger than expected growth in exports in 1975 and 1976, and the recovery of the economies of Korea's chief trading partners, Japan and the United States. Barring unforeseen circumstances, Korea will over the next few years reduce its debt servicing burden to more easily manageable proportions.

The cross-national analysis of growth, leisure, distribution and foreign debt is a vexing matter. An adequate comparative analysis of income/leisure patterns would require some knowledge of the marginal productivity of labor in the comparison countries as well as cultural influences which is simply not available. Comparative studies on the allocation of costs and benefits associated with growth are in their infancy, and what findings have been reported are arguable in terms of meaning and significance. Foreign debt position and its relationship to growth depends on its composition, a country's export potential and management capability, international perceptions and such other contingencies as to make the import of cross-national comparisons difficult to judge if not altogether questionable.

The use of per capita income as a measure of development involves well-known problems as well. International economic data, while improving, are less reliable than one would prefer and some series for some countries are lacking altogether. Methodological problems also exist in using official exchange rates as the basis for international comparisons, particularly since such rates relate only to products in foreign trade and may have a remote connection to actual price levels in particular countries. Moreover, national income accounting does not provide data which would measure "welfare" as some observers would prefer to define it. National income accounting does not of course measure the welfare of societies in terms of whether the community is satisfying the "needs" of its members, even though it is to be observed that the expansion of output is a goal of virtually all polities. It is also true that cultures and hence tastes vary across nations and that national production or income data cannot therefore provide fully satisfactory measures of relative welfare. It is a mere truism to say that life is not necessarily more rewarding or fulfilling in a rich country than a poor one. What can be said, however, is that growth in output provides more *choices* for a society and that, as a general rule, an expansion of choices has been preferred in the modern era by most countries to the relatively restricted opportunities of traditional society. Actually, it is not clear that the range of national tastes is as disparate as sometimes supposed. The fascination with the fruits of modernity observed in so many apparently dissimilar societies suggests the opposite. Finally, as noted, alternative approaches to the measure and comparison of national welfare

are notoriously atheoretical or impressionistic, and hence of limited usefulness. In any case, national income accounting is an indispensable tool to policymakers and international comparisons based on national accounting provide models or suggestions as to how, in particular circumstances, national output might be expanded.

Korean Economic Growth in Comparative Perspective

The 1974 edition of the *World Bank Altas* lists 189 countries and territories and includes data on their population totals for mid-1972, population growth rates for the 1960-72 and 1965-72 periods, per capita GNP at market prices for 1972, and average annual growth rates in per capita GNP for the periods 1960-72 and 1965-72.[4] These political units are grouped into three main categories: the "industrial countries,"[5] with a combined population of 622 million people and 1972 per capita incomes of $3,670; the "centrally planned economies,"[6] including some 1.19 billion people and 1972 per capita incomes estimated at $580; and the "developing countries," with a total population of over 1.8 billion and 1972 per capita incomes of about $280. The developing countries so listed (although excluding such obviously less developed countries as the People's Republic of China, Cuba, North Korea and North Viet-Nam) are further sub-divided by the World Bank into four groups: the petroleum exporters[7] (275 million population and per capita incomes of $270 in 1972 -- risen dramatically since 1973) and "higher,"[8] "middle."[9] and "lower"[10] income countries. Altogether, the higher-income developing countries had a combined population of 356 million, per capita incomes of $740 in 1972 and include those developing countries with per capita incomes of more than $375 in 1972. The middle-income developing countries had a combined population of 272 million, 1972 per capita incomes of $260 and included those developing countries with per capita incomes between $200 and $375. The lower-income developing countries, with a total population of 942 million and per capita incomes of $110 in 1972 included those developing countries with per capita incomes in 1972 of less than $200.

The Republic of Korea, with a per capita income of $310 in 1972 (increased to $680 in 1976), ranked high among the middle-income developing countries, a fact made possible by the extremely high rates of growth and declining rates of population increase achieved over the last fifteen or twenty years. The Korean accomplishments may be put into international perspective. For the 1960-72 period, Korea maintained an average annual growth rate in per capita income of 6.8 per cent. Since population grew by an average of 2.2 per cent annually during those years, GNP increased at an average annual rate of 9 per cent. For the more recent 1965-72 period, average annual population growth fell to 1.9 per cent and per capita income expanded at an average annual rate of 8.5 per cent. GNP for that period thus grew at an average annual rate of some 10.4 per cent.

Growth in Per Capita Income

For the 1960-72 period, the average annual rate of increase in per capita income in Korea was exceeded only by Greece (7.2 per cent), Japan (9.4 per cent), Singapore (7.1 per cent), the Libyan Arab Republic (16.2 per cent) and Saudi Arabia (7.2 per cent) and equaled by the Republic of China (6.8 per cent) among the 124 nations of the world with populations of one million or more. Hong Kong's rate of per capita growth (6.1 per cent) was nearly as high. Growth in Libya and Saudi Arabia, of course, stemmed less from development as commonly understood than from their strategic positions as petroleum exporters. Thus, it is an intriguing and perhaps important fact that, with the exception of Greece, the Sino-cultures of Korea, Japan, the Republic of China, Hong Kong and Singapore have led the entire world in recent years in broadly-based rates of economic growth. (The People's Republic of China -- the Empire at the Center of the World which forms the cultural core of East Asia – had unremarkable increases of 2.6 per cent for both the 1960-72 and 1965-72 periods.)

Korea's economic achievements are underscored by an examination of several other comparisons. The average annual increase in per capita income for the 1960-72 period among the twenty-nine countries classified by the World Bank as higher income developing countries was 3.5 per cent. These include countries with 1972 per capita income between $357 and $2,610. If Israel, with a 1972 per capita income of $2,610 is not placed in this grouping, as seems reasonable, the upper range is set at $1,460, the income figure for Greece in 1972. The 3.5 per cent average annual growth rate in per capita income among these countries constitutes a rather respectable performance and would be higher if the poor performance of several countries (e.g., Uruguay, which had an average annual *decline* of 0.1 per cent and Lebanon, which had a slow annual average increase of 1.0 per cent during 1960-72) were omitted. However, the growth rate would still be far below that of Korea and the other Pacific-rim Sino-societies.

Among the twenty-three countries identified by the World Bank as middle-income developing countries (per capita incomes of between $200 and $375 in 1972), the annual average rate of increase in per capita income during 1960-72 was just less than 2.8 per cent. This is the group in which South Korea fell, with its 1972 per capita income of $310. The Korean achievement of 6.8 per cent average annual increase in per capita income is approached only by Swaziland (6.3 per cent), Papua New Guinea (5.6 per cent) and Botswana (5.5 per cent) among the middle-income developing countries. A number of the countries in this group were not developing economically at all during 1960-72. The Congo grew in per capita income at an average annual rate of 0.9 per cent; Ghana had a zero growth rate; Senegal a minus rate (-0.8 percent).

As for the nearly one billion people who live in the thirty-five countries included in the World Bank's category of lower-income developing countries, the 1960-72 period was not one of impressive economic achievement. For the group as a whole, increases in per capita income averaged less than 1.8 per cent annually. In five countries (Khmer Republic, Niger, Rwanda, Somalia, The People's Republic of Yemen), per capita incomes actually declined between 1960 and 1972. Nine countries grew either not at all or less than 1 per cent per annum. Only Togo (4.5 per cent) had a per capita growth rate of more than 4 per cent and only five other countries (Gambia, Kenya, Malawi, Pakistan and Zaire) had per capita growth rates of between 3 and 4 per cent. For many, perhaps most, of these countries, prospects for substantial economic growth are bleak and reference to some of them as "developing" has an ironic, not to say patronizing, connotation. It is well to remember, however, that only a few years ago, South Korea would have fallen within this group if anyone had then employed the classification scheme used in the World Bank's 1974 *Atlas.*

By almost any yardstick, the Korea of twenty years ago offered few ostensible possibilities for substantial economic development. The country had one of the highest population densities in the world, a meager natural resource endowment and per capita income in 1955 of perhaps $50. A per capita income of $1,500 by 1981 now appears likely.[11] The Korean experience suggests, therefore, that even under the most unpromising circumstances economic growth can occur. Whether it will be emulated is another question. That the Korean achievement is impressive not only with respect to other developing countries but in terms of world-wide trends as well is shown by comparing the average annual growth in per capita income in Korea during 1960-72 (6.8 per cent) with rates achieved in the industrialized world (3.97 per cent) and the centrally planned economies (3.5 per cent). The ratio of the rate of growth in per capita income in the industrialized countries to that in Korea over 1960-72 was .58; it was .51 in the centrally planned economies; .35 in the developing countries as a whole; .51 in the higher-income developing countries; .41 in the middle-income developing countries; .26 in the lower-income-developing countries; and .41 for all countries of over one million population, excluding the petroleum exporting countries.

The Korean performance would be even more impressive if the shorter 1965-72 period were examined. During those years, average growth in Korean per capita income was 8.5 per cent. This was the third highest rate in the world, next only to Singapore (10.3 per cent) and Japan (9.7 per cent). Singapore's development, while remarkable, occurred in a population of 2.2 million; Korea's in a population of 32.4 million. These data are summarized in Table 2-1.

Table 2-1

International GNP Per Capita

	Average Growth Rates 1960-72 (%)	% of Korean Growth	Amount US $1972	Annual Population Growth, 1965-72 (%)
Industrialized Countries (N=22)	3.97	58	3,670	1.0
Centrally Planned Economies (N=13)	3.50	51	580	1.4
Developing Countries (N=87)	2.40	35	280	2.5
High Income (N=29)	3.50	51	740	2.3
Middle Income (N=23)	2.76	41	260	2.7
Lower Income (N=35)	1.77	26	110	2.5
All Countries (N=122)	2.82	41		2.2
KOREA	6.8		310	1.9

NOTE: The median annual growth rate in per capita income for 1960-72 for all countries was 2.9%, which approximates the average rate. See end notes 5-10 for countries in each category. Computed from data reported in *World Bank Atlas, 1974.*

Most developing countries aspire to industrialization as the central means for improving standards of living even though industrialization does not bear an invariable relationship to per capita income. This is most obviously true for the petroleum exporting states. Even the members of the Organization of Petroleum Exporting Countries (OPEC) have justified their administered prices, however, partially on the grounds that their oil resources must be fully exploited and industrialization extended against the inevitable day when their strategic resource shall have been depleted. Other countries have achieved relatively high standards of living through the rationalization of agriculture (as in New Zealand), through the provision of banking and commercial services (as in Hong Kong where, however, manufacturing has grown apace), or through exports of primary products other than oil. Nevertheless, all twenty countries with per capita incomes of $2,000 or more in 1972 were industrial countries in the sense that at least 20 per cent of total output was accounted for by manufacturing. Only a handful of developing countries have manufacturing sectors larger than this: Korea, Iran, Singapore, Hong Kong, Brazil, Peru, Argentina, Mexico, Chile, Egypt, Uruguay and Taiwan.[12] (See Table2-2.)

Among these more industrialized developing countries, Korea, Iran, Singapore, Hong Kong and Brazil, achieved the highest rates of growth in extending their manufacturing sectors over 1970-73 (10 per cent per year or more). Among these, the Korean manufacturing sector was the fastest growing of the fast-growing industrialized LDCs. In 1972 per capita terms it was also the poorest (Korea, $310; Iran, $490; Singapore, $1,300; Hong Kong, $980; Brazil, $530; Taiwan, $490). Korea was also the poorest of all industrialized LDCs with the exception of

Table 2-2 Developing countries: distribution according to degree of industrialization a/ and 1970-1973 growth in manufacturing b/

Industrialized			Intermediate			Agrarian		
High growth	Medium growth	Low growth	High growth	Medium growth	Low growth	High growth	Medium growth	Low growth
Republic of Korea	Peru	Chile	Mauritius	Algeria	Nicaragua	Dahomey	Indonesia	Ethiopia
Iran	Argentina	Egypt	Dominican Republic	Colombia	Bolivia	Gambia	Liberia	Uganda
Singapore	Mexico	Uruguay	Rwanda	Ecuador	Paraguay	Upper Volta	Jordan	Somalia
Hong Kong			Malaysia	Honduras	Pakistan	Tunisia	Zambia	Burundi
Brazil			Syrian Arab Republic	Venezuela	India	Nigeria	Gabon	Sri Lanka
			Kenya	Philippines	Jamaica		Burma	Laos
				Thailand	Guyana		Saudi Arabia	Khmer Republic
				Panama			United Republic of Tanzania	
				Malawi			Haiti	
				Morocco			Iraq	
				Guatemala			Angola	
				El Salvador			Ivory Coast	
				Costa Rica				
				Afghanistan				

a/ Measured by the share of manufacturing in total output: up to 10 per cent, agrarian; 11-20 per cent, intermediate; over 20 per cent, industrialized.

b/ Low growth, less than 6 per cent a year; medium growth, 6-9 per cent a year; high growth, 10 per cent a year and over. In each column, countries are listed in descending order of average rate of increase in manufacturing production, 1970-1973 (1970-1972 in some cases).

SOURCE: *United Nations World Economic Survey, 1974* (Published in 1975).

Egypt ($240). If current growth trends remain unchanged, however, the per capita income ranking of Korea relative to other industrialized LDCs will change substantially over the next decade.

For example, an annual 8.5 per cent growth rate would more than double 1972 per capita income in ten years -- from $310 to $763 in constant dollars. This is not impossible, indeed it is slightly less than current planning targets. Even if Korea's growth rate were reduced to one-half of current trends, per capita income would increase by 146 per cent in twenty years. Such an increase would move Korea into that grouping of nations with 1972 per capita incomes of between $700 and $800, a group comprised in 1972 of Rumania ($810); Yugoslavia ($810); Jamaica ($810); Chile ($800); Portugal ($780); Uruguay ($700); Mexico ($750); and Lebanon ($700). In 1972, Korea was ranked sixty-eighth in per capita income among the states of the world. Extrapolating from current trends – a risky business at best -- Korea will move ahead over the next ten to fifteen years of many other nations in per capita income; for example, of Chile, Uruguay, Lebanon, Peru, Nicaragua, Guatemala, Colombia, El Salvador, Honduras, Paraguay and others. Compared with the desperate circumstances of 1955 or 1960, this would be a phenomenal achievement in view of the unparalleled population density, scarcity of natural resources, and national security burdens which have pressed heavily on the Korean developmental process.

The great surge of economic development in Korea and the other Sino-cultures on the Pacific rim of China has occurred, then, under objectively unpromising conditions. Singapore and Hong Kong might, because of their unusual position in international trade and finance and as "city" rather than nation-states, be regarded as possible exceptions to any general theory of economic development, even though the manufacturing sector is large in both places. Also, Hong Kong (with a population of over 4 million) is larger than thirty-five and Singapore (population: 2.2 million) is larger than twelve countries with populations of over 1 million.

As recently as 1962, per capita income in Korea was only $76 and its population density one of the highest in the world. Then as now there was little new land available for cultivation -- by the late 1930s virtually all arable bottom and hillside land was being tilled. Out-migration as a response to population pressures was to some extent possible earlier in this century but is no longer an option. The 200,000 Koreans who had moved to Manchuria by 1910 increased under the Japanese take-over to some 1.3 million. Between 1921 and 1938 some 750,000 Koreans had immigrated to Japan, a number which increased to 2.1 million as a consequence both of the draft and voluntary movement of Koreans into the Empire's war services and industries. The possibilities of major out-migration ended in 1945 with the defeat of Japan and, indeed, that year precipitated a major migration back to the Korean homeland, as perhaps 1.2 million expatriots from Manchuria and Japan returned. Another 1.8 million refugees moved into South Korea prior to the sealing of the 38th parallel under the Russian occupation. (Because some 550,000 Japanese left Korea in 1945, these population movements were offset to some extent.) During the Korean War between 500,000 to 1.5 million utterly destitute refugees came into South Korea, placing enormous additional strains on an already devastated economy and society. Nearly an equal number -- perhaps 1.3 million people, most of them civilians – were casualties of the war, 350,000 of whom were killed. In these circumstances, industrialization was a vital requirement for development.

Determinants of Economic Growth

No fully satisfactory theory of economic growth exists any more than a satisfactory theory of history exists. Indeed, if one were to have a theory of economic growth one would possess a large part of a theory of history. Many explanations of why economic growth has not proceeded in many societies are similarly less than compelling. The notion that geography and natural resources are determinant is not persuasive if only because economic growth has occurred in countries -- Japan is only the most obvious case -- with severely limited natural resources and remotely located from foreign sources of supply. Many European states developed with natural resource endowments of fertile land and mineral deposits far less than those possessed in many areas of Latin America, Africa and Asia. Korea also faced (and faces) profound natural resource constraints yet managed to launch an economic advance that has made it an industrialized developing country.

The view that colonialism obviates development by having submerged talent and opportunities, destroyed previously productive cultures, and distorted the position of the colony in international trade, all in the interest of the metropolitan country, is an oftstated Marxist and radical-leftist claim which, however vaguely stated, has an initial persuasiveness. A colonial history, however, has not always been associated with the incapacity to sustain economic growth in the post-colonial period.[13] Indeed, Singapore, Hong Kong, Taiwan and Korea, which have in recent years led the world in broadly-based economic development, are all former colonies, the first two of the British, the second two of the Japanese. The colonial experience of Korea, as a matter of fact, may have been unprecedented in its degree of exploitation and the imported Japanese ruling class was among the largest imposed on any colonial country. When the Japanese departed in 1945, the status of the Korean population was as underdeveloped in terms of skills, education, land, leaders and future prospects as any newly emancipated colonial people anywhere.

Another frequently cited limitation on development concerns the lack of capital and the alleged incapacity of a poor society to set aside any portion of its current output for saving and investment because of immediate survival needs. Yet, it would seem that many countries do in fact have sources of potential capital that will emerge when political stability has been secured and when public policies are realigned from the short-run welfare maximizing strategies which are so often pursued to those which make saving an attractive proposition even to populations in which there is extensive privation. Political turbulence, inflation, unproductive subsidies, investments in low priority land or construction will encourage hoarding, exporting of capital or current consumption. The political capacity to take the frankly painful decisions necessary to induce capital formation, both domestically and from abroad, is not a quality that is easily demonstrated much less measured. The Korean case, however, is one in which consumption-oriented policies were transformed into investment policies, with positive long-term consequences for both growth and welfare. If political competence is lacking, no amount of capital from external sources is apt to induce growth. The effective generation and exploitation of capital thus depends on ability, optimism, and a realistic outlook which, by eschewing the scape-goating of others for one's own failures, makes possible the disciplined development and concentration of organizations and policies which can stimulate growth. The Korean economic transformation was accompanied by a realistic understanding that only the Koreans themselves could create the conditions for growth. The ideological projections invoked by political elites in many developing countries as explanations of economic failure merely divert energy away from the tasks of institution building, rational analysis and self-criticism which are essential to growth. It is doubtful if any of these dispositions can be imported.

It is quite likely that the cultural values which are congenial to growth are not consistently distributed across the developing world; moreover, there is no reason why they should be, development having no value apart from the particular aspirations of a people. In Korea, on the other hand, a strong case can be made that the culture has reinforced, indeed may be basically responsible for, economic growth by providing the predispositions and values necessary to achieve it. Another structural circumstance in Korea may also have been important: The virtual destruction of the Korean social stratification system under Japanese rule created a population in which most individuals were similarly if poorly situated; the equity of poverty bequeathed a virtually classless society to the modern period, with the result that the often stultifying reaction of traditional elites, which has inhibited development elsewhere, did not have to be overcome.

In the remainder of this chapter, the Korean development pattern in industry, agriculture and services is placed in international perspective. These comparisons, together with those in the following chapter, seek to reveal the extent to which Korea has been a world leader in broadly-based and sustained economic development. It is a story of success on many fronts and, as later analysis suggests, the triumph of common sense over ideology in economic decision-making.

Industrialization and Development

For most countries, the road to increased welfare is through industrialization, a hard fact that will not disappear by the increasing journalistic and academic protestations to the contrary. Any notion that social welfare is actually harmed by industrialization will, if institutionalized in public policy, condemn the "beneficiaries" of that policy to permanently lower standards of material welfare. It is perhaps largely the practical failure of industrialization in many LDCs, not its potential benefits, that has occasioned recent questioning of its desirability.[14]

Aspirations in most LDCs have been for rapid industrialization, leading to rising incomes, greater savings, additional growth and diversification and still higher and more stable incomes. Economic diversification and heightened efficiency would lead to expansions in exports, making possible imports of commodities both to improve the quality of life and as inputs into an increasingly productive economy. Accompanying industrialization would be enhanced employment opportunities, "better" income distribution and regional development, or so it was hoped, thought and urged in the early period following World War II. By 1975 it was clear that such patterns had not been experienced in most LDCs: in fact, only Korea, Taiwan and possibly one or two other cases fit this developmental model at all points. In most countries, industrialization has not proceeded as hoped. Even, where it has to some degree, the economic and social gains have been less than anticipated. It is important to take some account of the reasons for this.

First, industrialization does not by itself produce growth. When it does not, industrialization as such is not responsible. Industry may be the most dynamic economic sector but unless policy and behavior in other areas of social life are adjusted accordingly, growth will not occur. The social transformation sought in most LDCs depends on the interaction of complementary activities and undertakings. Industrialization must, therefore, play an appropriate role but is not a substitute for improvements in the social and political spheres. Viewed in this light, industrialization is not all of one piece. It must be fitted to the resource endowment, comparative advantages, scale, and cultural and political goals of a particular country. If industrialization in a given country has failed to insure growth, reduce inequities and provide employment, the responsibility is apt to lie with an inappropriately selected pattern of industrialization and with failures of policy in other areas. Efficient industrialization must rest upon an appropriate level of investment in overhead capital and judicious choices of the kinds of industry to be encouraged (e.g., labor intensive industries during earlier periods).

To be sure, it is not the case that efforts at industrialization in the less developed world have invariably failed. The World Bank noted in 1972 that, for the First Development Decade, "... the manufacturing industry has been the most rapidly growing major sector in the developing countries and its contribution to over-all growth has increased with its rising share of the gross national product."[15] The

UN's 1972 *Industrial Development Survey,* V.4 shows that for the developing world as a whole growth elasticity of manufacturing relative to GDP was about 1.4 per cent for the 1960s, a period when GDP increased for all LDC at about 5 per cent annually. Growth in manufacturing was therefore about 7 per cent annually, a rather encouraging figure, even though much of this average was accounted for by the high performance of a few countries.[16]

In Asia, annual growth in manufacturing during 1960-71 was 7.0 per cent among LDCs; in Latin America it was 5.7 per cent; and in Africa 3.9 per cent. The fact that manufacturing output for the same period also grew considerably in the developed market economies (6.0 per cent) and centrally-planned economies (8.6 per cent) does mean, however, that at current levels of performance, the world share of manufacturing output will not be readjusted between the LDCs and the rest of the world. The developing countries will, given present trends, continue, as over the last decade, to account for some 8 per cent of the world's manufacturing goods.[17]

This does not mean that each LDC has kept its own relative position in contributing to this 8 per cent. In Asia alone, significant changes have occurred, with Korea showing the greatest increases in its share of manufacturing output. In 1960, Korea accounted for 3.5 per cent of the manufacturing output in Asia. By 1970, this had risen to 8.6 per cent. For some countries, percentage contribution to Asian output had fallen (as in India, from 40.4 per cent to 36.7 per cent; Indonesia, from 11.3 per cent to 7.0 per cent; and the Philippines, from 6.1 per cent to 5 per cent). The increased Korean share of Asian output captured in the 1960s was also greater than any increase in regional shares made by any LDC in Africa and Latin

America. In 1960, Korea produced 1.4 per cent of the developing world's industrial goods; in 1970, it produced 3.4 per cent. Korea's share of total world manufacturing doubled between 1960 and 1970, from 0.1 per cent to 0.2 per cent, relative increases achieved nowhere else.

As would be expected, Korea's rapidly increasing share of LDC and world manufactured output was accompanied by a significant shift in the composition of its gross domestic product (GDP). Manufacturing output was 14 per cent of GDP in 1960 and 21 per cent in 1970, a transformation in the structure of the economy greater than in any other LDC. Manufacturing output per capita in Korea grew from $15 in 1960 to $56 in 1970, a percentage increase of 273 per cent, or 27 per cent annually. This level was still far below that of the developed world for 1970 (U.S., $1,054; U.K., $643, for example) but was sufficient to move Korea ahead of many countries which had exceeded Korea in per capita manufacturing output in 1960 (e.g., Philippines, Tunisia, Southern Rhodesia, Algeria, Egypt, Morocco, Iran).[18] It is apparent that, while LDC manufacturing output may not have increased as a share of world production, absolute production has increased along a broad front and in some cases, such as Korea's, has done so in proportionate terms as well.

The often-cited "failure" of the industrialization strategy in the Third World may also stem from the rather general failure of national plans to achieve targeted levels of performance. The relationship of national plans to actual policy decisions is frequently attenuated.[19] Whether this is because national plans are in many cases mere political artifacts having limited impact on the actual policy process, or because, while taken seriously, they are based on an inappropriate development strategy, or because the vicissitudes of fate intrude, is a matter for investigation. All are probably true. The fact is that the relationship between projected and achieved rates of growth is not high. One study of the planned growth rates for GDP and manufacturing in eighteen comparison LDCs showed that, from the middle 1960s through the beginning of the 1970s, only two countries, Korea and Taiwan, exceeded their planned growth rates in GDP and only five -- Korea, Taiwan, Ceylon, Jordan and Argentina – met or exceeded planned growth in manufacturing output. (See Table 2-3.)

Table 2-3

Planned and Actual Annual Growth of GDP and Manufacturing Output for Selected Developing Countries
Average Annual Rate (Per Cent)

	Planned growth			Annual growth		
	Period	GDP	Manufacturing Output	Period	GDP	Manufacturing Output
Africa						
Tanzania, United Rep. of	1960-1970	6.7	14.9	1960-1968	4.1	11.7
Tunisia	1957-1971	5.3	8.0	1960-1968	3.7	6.0
Uganda	1966-1971	6.3	10.1	1960-1968	4.4	7.2
Asia						
Ceylon	1951-1968	6.0	11.7	1960-1969	4.3	13.5
China (Taiwan)	1964-1968	7.1	11.4	1960-1969	10.0	17.1
India	1967-1974	5.3	8.5	1960-1969	3.1	4.9
Iraq	1964-1969	8.5	11.3	1960-1968	6.3	4.4
Jordan	1963-1970	7.2	7.0	1960-1968	5.8	10.5
KOREA	1965-1971	6.8	10.8	1960-1969	8.5	16.4
Pakistan	1965-1970	6.5	10.1	1960-1969	5.5	7.8
Philippines	1960-1967	6.0	10.0	1960-1969	5.1	4.5
Latin America						
Argentina	1960-1967	4.0	4.3	1960-1970	3.6	4.7
Bolivia	1958-1971	8.9	7.7	1960-1970	5.4	7.2
Chile	1961-1970	5.5	6.3	1960-1970	4.3	5.8
Ecuador	1965-1969	6.5	10.3	1960-1970	5.0	6.5
Honduras	1965-1974	7.0	13.0	1960-1970	5.2	9.0
Paraguay	1966-1970	6.0	8.8	1960-1970	4.6	4.7
Venezuela	1964-1968	7.1	10.8	1960-1970	4.6	6.6

SOURCE: UNIDO, *Summaries of the Industrial Development Plans of Thirty Countries,* Vol. 1 (Vienna, 1970).

This is not to say that plans typically bear no relationship to achievements. Calculation of the coefficients of correlation for planned and actual growth for the countries in Table 2-3 show that r = .50 for GDP and .46 for manufacturing output. Thus, while expectations were not perfectly achieved they did not completely fail by any means. In the case of Korea, planned annual growth in GDP was 6.8 per cent for the 1965-71 period, while actual growth for 1960-69 was 8.5 per cent; in manufacturing output, for the same periods, plans called for annual growth of 10.8 per cent while actual growth was 16.4 per cent, a "surplus" of achievements over plans approached only by Taiwan.

It is important to isolate some of the factors which seem to be related to growth in industrialization. The UNIDO's *Industrial Development Survey* identified some twenty-six LDCs for which comparisons could be made with respect to six variables associated with growth in manufacturing.[20]

The variables selected (growth rate of GDP, growth rate of per capita GDP, growth rate of agricultural output, growth rate of exports, relevant age groups in secondary schools, growth rate of gross domestic capital formation) were highly related (r = .8) to growth in manufacturing. Correlations between manufacturing output and any single variable were rather low, suggesting that policy measures which focus on isolated growth-related elements will have limited results. Hence, policies to stimulate rapid growth in manufacturing should properly focus on these (and other) growth elements more or less simultaneously. The UNIDO study's "growth scores" for manufacturing and GDP for each of the twenty-six LDCs based on the correlations of these variables during the 1960s are shown in Table 2-4.

Table 2-4

Growth Score of Manufacturing Output for Selected Developing Countries, 1960-1968

	Score for growth of manufacturing output	Combined growth factor score
Africa		
Ghana	45	62
Morocco	16	98
Southern Rhodesia	13	74
Tunisia	31	92
Asia		
Ceylon	84	133
China (Taiwan)	100	268
Indonesia	0	64
Iraq	21	148
Jordan	60	185
KOREA	93	265
Philippines	23	129
Latin America		
Argentina	20	96
Bolivia	40	147
Chile	36	166
Colombia	28	103
Costa Rica	44	133
Dominican Rep.	6	59
El Salvador	60	132
Guatemala	44	118
Honduras	55	131
Jamaica	33	156
Nicaragua	33	152
Panama	65	210
Peru	46	140
Uruguay	1	57
Venezuela	38	121

SOURCE: UNIDO, *Industrial Development Survey, Vol. IV* (New York, 1972), p. 17. (For computation procedure, see *Ibid.,* p. 13.)

Korea, with growth scores of 93 in manufacturing output and 265 for combined growth had (excepting Taiwan, whose scores were in the same range) scores far above any of the other LDCs examined. As the discussion turns in later sections to a more detailed analysis of these and other elements associated with growth in industrialization, the dimensions of the very broadly-based Korean performance will be apparent.

The Korean industrial expansion has affected many industrial groups but production of transportation equipment, electrical machinery, textiles and chemicals and petroleum products has been particularly dynamic. The overall index of industrial growth (1970 = 100) rose from 22.7 in 1960 to 225.0 in 1974, an increase of 878 per cent. For the more recent 1965-74 period, the index grew from 36.8 to 225, or 321 per cent. The components of the index expanded very rapidly in two cases and more slowly in the third: manufacturing grew from 33.9 in 1965 to 237.5 in 1974, or 600 per cent, while electrical power production went from 35.4 to 183.7, or 419 per cent. The index in mining -- reflecting Korea's poor natural resource endowment -- grew only 37 per cent, from 91.0 to 125.1 The place of manufacturing in the composition of GNP has predictably grown. By 1974, manufacturing constituted 28.3 per cent of GNP, up from 17.9 per cent in 1965. The importance of agriculture declined during the same period from 38.4 per cent of GNP to 25.5 per cent. Service activities related to manufacturing expanded: wholesale and retail trade was 14.9 per cent of GNP in 1965 and 18.8 per cent in 1974, while banking, insurance and real estate expanded from 1.6 to 2.4 per cent of GNP. Education during 1965-75 grew from 2.0 to 2.7 and construction from 3.4 to 4.3 per cent of GNP. Interestingly enough, public administration and defense, which are under tremendous expansionary pressures in many LDCs -- inefficient government employment being one way of coping with unemployment -- declined in Korea from 5.0 to 4.1 per cent of GNP.[21] Rapid industrial expansion was the key to substantial improvement in living standards.

Faced, as it was in the period following the war of 1950-53, with a poor resource endowment, high population density and very limited capital in both private and governmental (social overhead) spheres, Korea did not have the luxury of choosing from a menu of developmental strategies. The only path to the sustained enhancement of output was to import from abroad large amounts of capital and raw materials and to add value in export-oriented industries. The financing of imports required foreign exchange, which could be earned from the expansion of exports and from inducements to foreign lenders, both private and official, to invest in Korea. Korea has been successful on both fronts. Large amounts of technology-embodied external capital has been attracted (largely from Japan and the United States) and manufactured exports have increased tremendously. Skilled and semi-skilled, relatively low-wage labor has been moblized in the process as well. The decision process which led to the export-expansion drive, the attraction of external financing, investments in social overhead (especially education), the organization of the labor force as well as other policies (in domestic savings, investment efficiency, taxation and pricing, agriculture and population) is examined in later chapters of this volume. The performance of the Korean economy in the agricultural and service sectors is discussed in broad and comparative terms in the next sections of this chapter.

Agricultural Productivity

In most LDCs, the agricultural sector is of crucial importance: lagging growth rates will retard growth in the entire economy merely because of the size of agriculture in most developing economies, while growth in agriculture generates increased demand for the products of manufacturing and relaxes pressure on the balance of payments. The relative efficiency of Korean agriculture is high by international standards. The growth in output has also been steady in recent years but, because of persistent population pressures and limited land, continues to be a nagging problem.

The cultural resources of the Korean people have been mobilized effectively to minimize this population to land ratio problem, although they have not been adequate to make Korea entirely self-sufficient in agriculture. The productivity of Korean agriculture now approaches Japanese standards and, relative to other Asian countries, rice yields are dramatic. Yields per hectare are, for example, more than twice those in Pakistan, and nearly double those in Sri Lanka, Malaysia (West), and Indonesia. They excel even more yields in other major rice growing and consuming nations in Asia. (See Table 2-5.) The fact that yields were comparatively high in Korea even before the application of modern fertilizers and before mechanical equipment became increasingly available indicates that agricultural productivity is not entirely a matter of applying material capital to the agricultural sector. Fully as important has been the diligence and perseverance of the Korean farmer working under conditions no more objectively promising than in many other countries.

Table 2-5

Rice Yields in Developing South and East Asian Countries

	Yield	(Quintals per hectare)
	1974	Average 1971-1974
Bangladesh	18.3	17.4
Burma	18.8	16.6
India	16.2	16.6
Indonesia	27.7	24.9
Khmer Republic	8.5	10.4
Laos	8.9	10.6
Malaysia (West)	28.9	29.3
Nepal	18.3	19.4
Pakistan	23.3	19.1
Philippines	16.9	16.3
Republic of Viet Nam	23.1	23.8
Sri Lanka	26.0	23.1
Thailand	18.7	17.4
KOREA	50.2	47.5

SOURCE: United Nations, *World Economic Survey, 1974,* p. 55.

Of some forty developing countries examined in a United Nations study of development effort, Korea ranked seventh in the rate of growth of agricultural production during the 1960-65 period with an average annual increase of 5.1 per cent. In terms of per capita increases, however, Korea did less well over a longer period (1955-65), ranking twelfth in a group of thirty-one countries.[22] Between 1960 and 1970, agricultural production grew by 61 per cent in Korea which, while high, was far below increases in industrial production.[23] What a satisfactory rate of growth in agriculture would be is impossible to say. It appears that, for the developing world as a whole, a 6 per cent increase in gross domestic product implies a 4 per cent rate of growth in demand for agricultural products.[24] In Korea, recent experience reveals an urban elasticity of demand of roughly 0.45 for rice; 0.24 for all cereals; 1.29 for meat, eggs and milk; 0.98 for fruit; and 0.62 for vegetables (e.g., for each percentage rise in incomes, demand increases 0.45 per cent for rice, etc.).[25] Given the already intensive and relatively efficient use of agricultural land in Korea, continuing population pressure, and the high income elasticity of demand for food generated by recent large increases in per capita income, it is to be expected that agricultural production relative to demand will continue to place pressure on the balance of payments, although by 1976 Korea had approached rough self-suffiency in food production, and dealt surprisingly well with the food import crisis of 1973-74 through export expansion and good harvests in 1975-76.

Table 2-6

Estimated Additional Cost of Grain Imports for Selected Developing Countries in 1973 and 1974

	1973		1974	
	% of GNP 1971	% of Total Imports 1970-72	% of GNP 1971	% of Total Imports 1970-62
Bangladesh	7	8	8	–
Sri Lanka	7	–	9	27
India	0	11	1	28
Pakistan	1	13	4	36
Egypt	5	44	8	73
Philippines	1	7	2	13
KOREA	5	19	6	25
Brazil	1	6	0	3
Mexico	1	7	1	11
Chile	2	15	4	33

SOURCE: O.E.C.D., *Development Co-Operation: 1974 Review,* p. 69.

As seen from Table 2-6, rising food prices and internal constraints on domestic agricultural production meant that, in 1973, the cost of grain imports for Korea was 5 per cent of 1971 GNP and constituted 19 per cent of total 1970-72 imports. The situation by 1974 was even more pressing. Grain imports had risen to 6 per cent of 1972 GNP and comprised 25 per cent of total imports.

Table 2-7

Additional Oil Imports in 1974 Resulting From Price Rises as Percentage of GNP (1971) for Selected Developing Countries

KOREA	9.0
Afghanistan	8.5
Thailand	5.4
Jamaica	5.3
Liberia	5.1
Uruguay	4.9
Lebanon	4.6
Sri Lanka	4.8
Philippines	4.5
Sudan	3.8
Tawain	3.7
Nicaragua	3.5
Turkey	3.3
Kenya	3.1

SOURCE: O.E.C.D. *Development Co-Operation: 1974 Review,* p. 37.

This, the rising cost of food, combined with a skyrocketing petroleum importing bill, perhaps the greatest increase for any developing country, presented Korea with grave problems. (See Table 2-7.) To have surmounted these problems is testimony to the dynamism of the Korean economy.

In developing countries where substantial new lands can be put into cultivation, and/or where existing lands are producing far less than optimum yields, policy makers might pursue the following agricultural strategy: Obtain an estimate of the growth of per capita demand for food by estimating the income elasticity of demand for food relative to the expected rate of growth in per capita income and add to this the population growth rate to obtain a figure for the growth of aggregate food demand. That figure could be compared with the actual rate of growth in agricultural output and used to assess the gap between performance and "needs." This is a difficult problem for Korea. Substantial expansion of new agricultural land is not possible, although arduous efforts did bring 14 per cent more arable land into production between 1960 and 1970 and double cropping has been extended with good effects. Irrigated arable land expanded at about the same rate and now comprises some 85 per cent of all arable land. The general index for total food production, excluding fishing, rose from 72.0 in 1960 to 125.8 in 1974 (1964-66 = 100). The general index for the vital grain crops rose from 73.9 in 1960 to 101.0 in 1974; for the same period, livestock production rose from 80.1 to 180.0; and for forest products from 55.8 to 152.2, all very creditable performances. Yet, population growth resulted in an increase in per capita food production of only 18 per cent and, in the area of cereal production (mainly rice) the increase in per capita terms was only 3 per cent for the decade of the 1960s.

Growth in the early 70s was much higher, reflecting increased mechanization, paddy realignments, new seeds, greater fertilizer and better financing and marketing systems. The level of fish catches, meanwhile, has increased dramatically in recent years, from 377.200 metric tons in 1960, to 2,026,221 metric tons in 1974, producing more protein for the Korean diet and substantially outrunning population growth. (See Table 2-8.)

Table 2-8

Index Numbers of Agricultural Production in Korea

(1964-1966 = 100)

	1960	1970	1974
All items	72.0	115.9	125.8
Grains	73.9	103.3	101.0
Livestock	80.1	157.0	180.0
Forestry	55.8 (1961)	137.9	152.2
Fish catches (metric tons)	357.2	816.2	2,026.0

SOURCE: United Nations, *Statistical Yearbook for Asia and The Far East, 1971* and The Bank of Korea, *Economic Statistics Yearbook, 1975.*

Services

As late as 1970, a study by the Organization for Economic Co-operation and Development was forced to conclude that "... with regard to the general importance of service activities in less developed areas, the paucity of relevant studies, either empirical or theoretical, is little short of astonishing."[26] Since then, little has changed, although one important study by Blades, Johnston and Marczewski has been published, which seeks to bring together whatever comparative data are available on the service as opposed to the goods sectors of LDCs and to offer recommendations for improvements in data gathering and policy-making.[27] Economic activity is often grouped into the broad categories of Industry, Agriculture and Services (Primary, Secondary and Tertiary activities provide another classification), but no internationally acceptable methodology exists for the unambiguous classification or measurement of the disaggregated activities which make up the service sector.[28]

The Blades' study defines the service sector as comprised of activities which issue no physical output, namely:

1) Transport, Storage and Communications
2) Wholesale and Retail Trade
3) Banking, Insurance and Real Estate
4) Ownership of Dwellings
5) Public Administration and Defense
6) Other Services: Community, Business, Recreational and Personal Services (including health and education)

Obviously, these very heterogeneous activities differ greatly in wage-rates, skill levels, capitalization, and productivity; hence, a general analysis of the service sector will obscure large differences among the components of the sector. Cross-national analysis is inhibited not only by often non-comparable classification schemes but by the relatively limited disaggregation of data even when classification has been made with common definitions. Within these strictures, Blades, *et al.* found it possible to analyze in very general terms the service sectors of some one-hundred LDCs for which reasonably reliable data were available, and to undertake a more detailed analysis on the basis of more complete data of (only) twelve LDCs, one of which, happily for present purposes, was Korea.

For most LDCs, the service sector is larger (as a proportion of gross domestic product) than either the industrial or agricultural sectors. In Korea, the service sector accounted for some 40 per cent of GDP in 1970, placing it in the median range of the sixty-six countries analyzed in the Blades, *et al.* study. Moreover, some 29 per cent of private consumption expenditures in Korea were for services (55 per cent of 29 LDCs examined had higher proportions; 41 per cent lower). And 61 per cent of gross domestic fixed capital formation in Korea occurred in the service sector in 1969 (largely in transport, housing and other services) compared to 30.7 per cent in industry and 8.3 per cent in agriculture, placing Korea again in the median range among the 28 countries for which there were data.[29] Clearly, descriptions of economic development and any policy recommendations which omit or slight the service sector will be seriously deficient given the scope and composition of that sector in the absorption and generation of social resources. In addition, recent rates of growth in the service sector of many LDCs, while apparently averaging less than in industry, have been substantially above those in agriculture, a trend which may well extend into the future. The preoccupation with industry and agriculture in studies of LDCs is consistent with the central concerns of developmentally-minded regimes; however, there are at least three important reasons why greater attention might be focused on services: (1) "appropriate" decisions concerning the mobilization and allocation of resources require a comprehensive understanding of total production and its distribution; (2) the more intangible "quality of life" available to a population, as opposed to the goods available for consumption, is tied to the availability of services (particularly security, housing, health and education); and (3) many services are closely connected to the goods-producing sectors and increased productivity in the former (in, e.g., transport, communications, banking, public administration, health and education) may lead to greater productivity in the latter.

For the period 1956-70, Korea's GDP increased at an average annual rate of 7.7 per cent. By sector, growth rates for the same period were: agriculture, 1.5 per cent; industry, 14.7 per cent; and services, 7.4 per cent. The growth rate of the service sector therefore approximated the total growth rate, a typical if not invariable pattern among LDCs.[30] However, if the growth of the total Korean economy for that period is unity (1.0), elasticities of growth in some service areas were greater: in transportation, storage and communications it was 1.9; in wholesale and retail trade, 1.3; in banking and insurance, 1.2. Slower growing service activities were public administration and defense (0.3); ownership of dwellings (0.4) and other services (0.8). Among the eleven other LDCs for which comparative data were available, no clear growth pattern for the components of the service sector is apparent which would permit the Korean growth rates to be placed in perspective, although the central tendency for total services in all twelve countries was between the rather narrow elasticity band of 0.9 and 1.4.[31]

With respect to the proportion of the economically

active population engaged in service employment, Korea, with 27 per cent of employment in services, was again in the median range of fifty-eight LDCs examined in Blades' study; countries with much higher proportions tend to be small, both in population and area, highly urbanized and, in several cases, characterized by large tourist and/or entrepot sectors. Countries with much smaller proportions of service employment typically have very large agricultural populations and low urbanization. (Comparative data on the distribution of employment within the service sector is scanty and unrepresentative.) The growth of service employment in recent years among fourteen LDCs, where more reliable data were available, had in all cases outstripped growth in agriculture and in eight cases, Korea among them, had exceeded growth in industry.[32]

The productivity of labor in the service sector (taken as the ratio of value added to numbers employed) was also examined by Blades, *et al.* for forty-four countries.[33] Labor productivity in services may then be compared to labor productivity in the economy as a whole and in agriculture and industry. If productivity for the economy as a whole is taken as 1.0, it was found that in Korea productivity in services was somewhat greater (1.3), largely because of the contribution of transportation and communications (2.5) and commerce (1.7). Productivity in other services -- public administration, defense, health, education, personal services – was less than unity (0.8) but still above agriculture (0.7). The output/worker ratio for industry was 1.7. The Korean pattern was reasonably typical, at least in broad outline, of other LDCs: in all forty-four countries, output/worker ratios in services exceeded those in agriculture and were greater than unity in all but four countries. Only in Malta, Uruguay and Jordan were the ratios for industry less than unity.[34]

Moreover, a strong central tendency existed, with thirty-seven of the forty-four LDCs having output/worker ratios of between 1.0 and 2.0. Korea, with a ratio of 1.3 fell, as in other comparisons, near the median of the cases examined. There was a tendency for the countries with higher per capita incomes to have somewhat *lower* output/worker ratios. The reasons for this non-obvious relationship are not clear. If measurement error is not responsible, as seems likely (there being no basis for supposing the error would be chronic in its relation to levels of development), service workers in LDCs would seem to be more productive than their counterparts in other sectors of the same society. This is not implausible: some service workers are necessarily highly skilled and heavily capitalized (railroad workers, for example), even in very poor countries with retarded agricultural sectors and low-technology industry. As growth occurs in the goods sectors, the relative efficiency of the service sector might be expected to decline. At any rate, Korea falls in the median range of the forty-four countries not only in labor productivity in the service sector but in per capita GNP as well.

Until improvements in data and theorizing are made, little more can now be done to assess the Korean service sector in global context. It is apparent, however, that the striking divergence of Korean growth patterns from most other LDCs in the area of industrial expansion and agricultural productivity does not hold true for the service sector. Whatever international data are available indicate that Korea is rather typical of tendencies in the service sectors of LDCs. For sixty-six LDCs examined in Blades' study, the share of services in GDP extended from 20 to 72 per cent. For forty-seven of those countries, the range was from 35 to 54 per cent; and for thirty-five of them it was 40 to 54 per cent. Compared to distributions to be found in agriculture and industry among these countries, the service sector shows a pronounced central tendency.

The reason why Korea should deviate from the apparent LDC pattern in goods production but conform in services production is to be found largely in Korea's position in the international economy. Relatively few services are traded internationally on a significant scale and services are, by and large, produced and consumed domestically. While this is not always the case (as in countries peculiarly situated with respect to some transport, recreational and financial activities), it is true for Korea, where the export of services is quite small. Korea must, as all countries, provide some minimal level of services for itself. But because its services cannot be exported on a significant scale it must produce some minimum level of goods either for domestic consumption or for international exchange for other goods. This requirement puts an upper limit on the potential size of the service sector. Industrial growth is less restricted, and broader deviations are possible, as shown on the one side by the atypical growth path of the export-led Korean industrial expansion and the very limited size of the industrial sector in some other LDCs. If there is a lesson in this for other LDCs, it would seem to consist in a reconfirmation of the importance of becoming integrated into the international economy, usually through industrialization. In peculiar and rare circumstances, external integration and internal growth might proceed from the export of services or primary products. In some few larger societies (e.g., China), growth might be sustained largely as the basis of internal developments. However, the world growth leaders among LDCs in recent years have tended to conform to the Korean pattern.

Comparative Income Distribution

The full meaning of economic growth for the distribution of income is by no means a settled question. There is no invariable relationship between the two and without some attention to political and social factors, what relationships can be discerned remain clouded as to precise meaning. Consequently, the comparisons on distribution introduced in this section rest on data which wise readers will view with appropriate skepticism. The data are fragmentary and the fact that many countries are unable or unwilling to engage in the empirical studies which would yield more reliable information means that no early resolution of issues concerning the measurement and comparison of income distribution is in prospect. The question of distribution is, however, of such critical importance in development that some attention must be paid to the subject.

One may note at the outset that several conceptual problems are involved in the analysis of income distribution, including, first off, the appropriate unit of analysis itself. Should it be per capita income or family income? How should business income be treated? Is absolute or relative income of first importance? How significant are actual and prospective *changes* in income for social welfare, personal satisfaction and motivation, political stability?[35] What are the consequences of different distributions for consumption patterns, for saving and investment, the demand for imports, economic growth? How should non-monetary income be treated, especially in the LDCs where it is of great importance in subsistence agriculture? How is income from consumer durable goods (e.g., cars, washing machines, housing) and public goods (e.g., roads, public health and safety, national security) to be assessed and compared? In view of these and other problems, supportable empirical generalizations concerning income distribution and degrees of inequality are rare indeed.

What evidence is available suggests a modest cross-national association between level of development (measured by per capita income) and inequality: wealthier states are, but not invariably, characterized by a somewhat more equal distribution of income. (The coefficient of correlation between level of development and the proportion of national pre-tax income going to the poorest 40 percent of the population for the sixty-six countries shown in Table 2.9 is only 2.4.) Other factors also bear a slight, but rather less, relationship to distribution, including rates of population and economic growth, the size of the agricultural sector, literacy rates. Other presumably important factors in income distribution -- the concentration of wealth, efficiency of markets, social mobility rates, cultural dispositions and, vitally, types of economic, political and ideological systems -- have yet to be related systematically and convincingly in theories of income distribution.[36] The data available suggest that, in point of fact, there are liberal democratic, traditional authoritarian and modern totalitarian states (e.g., Britain, Taiwan and Bulgaria) which rank comparatively high in terms of equality of income distribution. By the same token, both rich and poor states can be found which rank high (e.g., Japan, Sri Lanka) and low (e.g., France, Kenya) on equality of distribution. Both capitalist (e.g., United States) and Marxist states (e.g., Hungary) can be found among countries with more equitable distributions. Industrialized developing systems may be either among the less equal (e.g., Mexico) or more equal (e.g., Korea) national systems in income distribution. Rates of growth appear to be only remotely if at all associated with distribution patterns. (These particular comparisons are based on the data given in Table 2-9. Redistributive governmental interventions through taxation might change the relationships somewhat, as might data collected at the same point in time.)

For present purposes, however, the data in Table 2.9 make possible some noteworthy observations concerning Korean income distribution. First, Korea is among the top third of the world's states in equality of distribution as measured by the income shares of the top income receivers compared with the lowest income receivers. (This is perhaps the simplest and most useful measure of distribution, although it is in some ways less statistically manageable than the Gini coefficient. The latter can have the deficiency of showing similar coefficients on the rather frequent occasions when the Lorenz curves of dissimilar distributions intersect.) Second, Korea is a somewhat deviant case as concerns the overall international relationship between per capita income and income inequality.

In the world's states with per capita incomes of $300 or less (the group in which Korea fell in 1970), the proportion of national income received by the poorest 40 per cent of the population averaged, according to one study, less than 12 per cent; for the states with $300-750 in per capita incomes, the poorest 40 per cent averaged between 12 and 17 per cent of national income; in the more affluent countries (above $750 per capita), the poorest 40 per cent averaged above 17 per cent of total income.[37] Korea, with a per capita income of $235 in 1970, had a pattern of distribution which resembled the wealthier societies. The lowest 40 per cent of income recipients in Korea received 18 per cent of national income. (The middle 40 per cent received 37 per cent; the top 20 per cent received 45 per cent.) Korea, along with Taiwan, are the only

Table 2-9

Table 2-9 Cross classification of Countries by Income Level and Pre-Tax Equality

HIGH INEQUALITY — Share of lowest 40% less than 12%

Country(yr.)	Per capita GNP US$	L'st 40%	Mid 40%	Top 20%
Kenya(1969)	136	10.0	22.0	68.0
Sierra Leone (1968)	159	9.6	22.4	68.0
Iraq(1956)	200	6.8	25.2	68.0
Philippines (1971)	239	11.8	34.6	53.8
Senegal(1960)	245	10.0	26.0	64.0
Ivory Coast (1970)	247	10.8	32.1	57.1
Rhodesia(1968)	252	8.2	22.8	69.0
Tunisia(1970)	255	11.4	33.6	55.0
Honduras(1968)	265	6.5	28.5	65.0
Ecuador(1970)	277	6.5	20.0	73.5
El Salvador (1969)	295	11.2	36.4	52.4
Turkey(1968)	282	9.3	29.9	60.8
Malaysia(1970)	330	11.6	32.4	56.0
Colombia(1970)	358	9.0	30.0	61.0
Brazil(1970)	390	10.0	28.4	61.5
Peru(1971)	480	6.5	33.5	60.0
Gabon(1958)	497	8.8	23.7	57.5
Jamaica(1958)	510	8.2	30.3	61.5
Costa Rica (1971)	521	11.5	30.0	63.5
Mexico(1969)	645	10.5	25.5	64.0
South Africa (1965)	669	6.2	35.8	58.0
Panama(1969)	692	9.4	31.2	59.4
Venezuela (1970)	1004	7.9	27.1	65.0
Finland(1962)	1598	11.1	39.6	49.3
France(1962)	1913	9.5	36.8	53.7

MODERATE INEQUALITY — Share of lowest 40% between 12% & 17%

Country(yr.)	Per capita GNP US$	L'st 40%	Mid 40%	Top 20%
Burma(1956)	82	16.5	38.7	44.8
Dahomey(1959)	87	15.5	34.5	50.0
Tanzania(1967)	89	13.0	26.0	61.0
India(1964)	99	18.0	32.0	52.0
Madagascar (1960)	120	13.5	25.5	61.0
Zambia(1959)	230	14.5	28.5	57.0
Dominican Rep. (1969)	323	12.2	30.3	57.5
Iran (1958)	332	12.5	33.0	54.5
Guyana(1956)	550	14.0	40.3	45.7
Lebanon(1960)	558	13.0	28.0	61.0
Uruguay(1968)	618	15.5	35.5	46.0
Chile(1968)	744	13.0	30.2	56.8
Argentina (1970)	1079	16.5	36.1	47.4
Puerto Rico (1968)	1100	13.7	35.7	50.6
Netherlands (1967)	1980	13.6	37.9	48.5
Norway(1968)	2010	16.6	42.9	40.5
Germany,Fed. Rep.(1964)	2144	15.4	31.7	52.9
Denmark(1968)	2563	13.6	38.8	47.6
New Zealand (1969)	2859	15.5	42.5	42.0
Sweden(1963)	2949	14.0	42.0	44.0

LOW INEQUALITY — Share of lowest 40%, 17% and above

Country(yr.)	Per capita GNP US$	L'st 40%	Mid 40%
Chad(1958)	78	18.0	39.0
Sri Lanka(1969)	95	17.0	37.0
Niger(1960)	97	18.0	40.0
Pakistan(1964)	100	17.5	37.5
Uganda(1970)	125	17.1	35.8
Thailand(1970)	180	17.0	37.5
Korea(1970)	235	18.0	37.0
Taiwan(1964)	241	20.4	39.5
Surinam(1952)	394	21.7	35.7
Greece(1957)	500	21.0	29.5
Yugoslavia (1968)	529	18.5	40.0
Bulgaria(1962)	530	25.8	40.0
Spain(1965)	750	17.6	36.7
Poland(1964)	850	23.4	40.6
Japan(1963)	950	20.7	39.3
United Kingdom (1968)	2015	18.8	42.2
Hungary(1969)	1140	24.0	42.5
Czechoslovakia (1964)	1150	27.6	41.4
Australia(1968)	2509	20.0	41.2
Canada(1965)	2920	20.0	39.8
United States (1970)	4850	19.7	41.5

Income up to US$300 Income US$300-$750 Income above US$750

Original Source: S. Jain and A. Tiemann, *Size Distribution of Income: A Compilation of Data,* Development Research Center Discussion Paper No. 4, World Bank, Washington, D.C., 1973.

Table Compiled by Irving Swerdlow, *The Public Administration of Economic Development* (New York: Praege pp. 170-71. Used by permission.

poorer LDCs in the "low inequality" category in Table 2.9 which have shown sustained and rapid growth in industrialization and per capita incomes in recent decades. On the basis of that information alone, greater inequality might have been expected for both countries, since there may be a tendency for inequality to increase in the early period of modernization as an expanding middle-class captures a larger share of national income from lower-income earners.[38]

That Korean inequality is less than might have been predicted calls for an explanation. Part of the answer surely lies in the nature of its cultural and social systems: Korea is not characterized by particularly rigid or impermeable ethnic, religious, regional or linguistic pluralism and class lines are weak. The leveling of Korean society by the Japanese, the post-war land and educational reforms, the destruction of the Korean War, the elimination of misdirected subsidies in the early and mid-1960s, and the labor-intensive strategy of development have had the cumulative impact of maintaining relative equality during a period of explosive growth.

Notwithstanding Korea's international standing on income distribution, income inequality remains a potential problem. With some 45 per cent of national income going to the top 20 per cent of the income earners, a strong case for redistribution can be made, and, as a matter of fact, enhanced welfare is one centerpiece of Korea's Fourth Five-Year Plan (1977-81). The Plan is discussed in Chapter 6. In any case, Korea now stands quite high among the LDCs in relative equality of income distribution, and the facile generalization that its rapid economic growth has increased inequality must be resisted firmly. One important consequence of this fact is that, other things remaining equal, future improvements in income distribution in Korea should be more manageable than in many other LDCs, if only because such improvements would require smaller departures from current distribution patterns.

Summary

As K.J. Holsti has noted,". . . our image of underdevelopment is based on considerable pictorial or written evidence of widespread poverty, despair, disease, lack of opportunity and cultural deprivation."[39] Such an image, if accurate, would surely justify interest in the means by which political reconstruction and economic development could be stimulated to reduce or remove such a negative social design. Actually, there is little convincing evidence that "despair" and "cultural deprivation" form part of the underdevelopment syndrome. The social indices of despair, which is after all a psychological condition, might be manifested in irrational violence, crime rates, suicides, alcholism and drug addiction, divorce, lethargy in work, ideological incoherence, and so forth. Alienation and despair so conceived bear little or no relationship to underdevelopment, such tendencies being more apparent in economically advanced liberal societies than in poor ones. The notion that cultural deprivation is a feature of underdeveloped societies does not deserve serious comment as concerns the ancient and sophisticated culture of Korea. No, underdevelopment concerns the scope of material deprivation and the relative absence of opportunity by which general welfare can be improved. Whether material improvements provide a "better life" is impossible to say. A society that, having ranked its traditional patterns above those implicit in economic development, will not develop in any case; it will get what it wants. For societies whose elites seek, contrary to the aspirations of their peoples, rapid economic growth, very much the same results will ensue; development cannot be sustained by elite energy alone but requires the broad acceptance and participation of many social strata and sectors. Whether any countries actually exist which are strongly biased against economic development is questionable. There is no question, on the other hand, that the first priority of most underdeveloped nation-states is the generation of greater material welfare and the broadened choices accompanying it. It has become fashionable to regard the prospects for growth skeptically, to attribute the "dependency" of Third World nations on the "neo-colonialism" imposed by the developed world, and to seek alternatives to conventional routes to development. The facts are that growth is possible, even in the most unpromising circumstances, that the dependency argument is disproved by the Korean case alone (not to mention others), and that there are no sustainable developmental alternatives to increased productivity.

In 1955, Korea was a resource-poor, over-populated, under-educated, recently harshly colonized, war-devastated country. As we have seen, per capita income increased 6.8 per cent annually between 1960 and 1972, 8.5 per cent between 1965 and 1972 and continued at the same high rate through 1976. The Korean growth rate was equaled only by a few other countries, all of them at higher levels of development (only Japan and Singapore for the 1965-72 period). Korea's rate of growth in manufacturing, crucial to growth, was higher in recent years than any of the fast-growing industrialized LDCs, higher than any of the less-industrialized LDCs, and higher than any of the industrialized developed countries. Korea's share of world and LDC manufacturing output has increased significantly and manufacturing in the Korean GNP had risen to over 25 per cent by 1975, signaling a marked structural transformation of the economy achieved over a 10-15 year period. Per capita manufacturing output rose 273 per cent in the 1960s, apparently the highest growth rate in the world, a performance that substantially exceeded planning projections. Factors which correlate highly with growth rates of GDP (growth rates in per capita GDP, agriculture, exports, capital formation and education) gave Korea, with Taiwan, the highest growth score of the LDCs surveyed, indicating the broadly based and integrated nature of Korean economic development.

In the agricultural sphere, the efficiency of the Korean performance is extremely high by international standards, although the very limited availability of new agricultural lands and the high ratio of population to arable land presents continuing problems. That near maximum advantage has been taken of available opportunities is shown by comparisons with other large rice growing and consuming nations in Asia. Korean yields per hectare compare favorably with the highly efficient Japanese and Taiwanese and exceeded average productivity in thirteen other Asian countries by 157 per cent in 1974. The fact that rice yields were high even before the extensive application of fertilizers and small-scale technology testifies to the diligence and intelligence of Korean farmers. The rate of growth in agriculture, both in absolute and per capita terms, has been steady but, because optimum possibilities are being approached, slower than in some other LDCs, although still above the median levels of performance. Increased population size and higher incomes (the latter producing a high elasticity of demand for food) will continue to place pressure on the balance of payments and, consequently, on growth. The rapidly expanding fishing industry and developments in other agricultural areas, such as livestock and hillside farming, have moderated these pressures somewhat, as will, eventually, the stabilization of the population. As a practical matter, the agricultural dilemma is probably best addressed by continued expansions in manufacturing and exports.

The scope and composition of the service sector of most LDCs has not received sufficient attention from political economists and little reliable data are available for the making of international comparisons. Because employment and investment policies require, for greatest positive effect, a comprehensive understanding of the major components of the economy, and because the service sector is intimately connected to "quality of life" issues, there is a strong case for focusing greater statistical and policy attention on the service sector. In most LDCs, the service sector is (by some definitions) larger than either the industrial or agricultural sectors. In Korea, the service sector accounts for some 40 per cent of GDP (Blades, *et al.* classification) and is in the median range of LDCs for which comparative data exist. Growth rates in the Korean service sector have approximated growth rates in the economy as a whole and have been greater than in agriculture and less than in industry, a not atypical pattern among LDCs. The proportion of the work force engaged in the service sector (27 per cent) again was in the median range of fifty-eight LDCs surveyed. The productivity of labor in the service sector in Korea is somewhat greater than in the economy as a whole, largely because of the heavy capitalization of the transportation and communications components, a rather usual association among LDCs. Korea thus appears to have a more or less typical structure in its service sector, a fact due perhaps to the low "tradeability" of services in international trade (which fixes an upper ceiling on the production of services) and to internal needs (which fixes a lower limit). The Korean growth cycle has thus been induced by industrialization, inhibitions to rapid growth in both agriculture and services being insurmountable.

Korea also ranks among the top third of the world's states (judging from the inadequate data base available) in the equity with which income is distributed. Growth has not been inconsistent with the maintenance of this ranking and, indeed, there are some reasons for believing that equity will increase in future years. More concern with equity is a feature of the current Five-Year Plan, as discussed in Chapter 6, and would appear to be more attainable than in LDCs with more profound distributive problems.

In the following chapter, the Korean performance in several fields related to industrialization and growth is placed in international perspective, namely, its performance in mobilizing domestic and foreign savings and investment, the efficiency of capital investment, the mobilization of tax revenue for the production and distribution of public goods and services, export achievements, population growth, and defense. Investment in human capital, that is, education, is also considered.

Notes

1. Economic Planning Board, *Economic Survey* (Seoul, 1967), pp. 137-9. For a discussion of the problems in cross-national equity analysis, see Irma Adelman and Cynthia Taft Morris, "Who Benefits from Economic Development?" in *Planning Income Distribution Private Foreign Investment* (Paris: Organization for Economic Coperation and Development, 1974).

2. Irma Adelman and S. Robinson, *Income Distribution Policies in Developing Countries: The Case of Korea* (Palo Alto: Stanford University Press, 1977).

3. Gilbert T. Brown, *Korean Pricing Policies and Economic Development in the 1960s* (Baltimore: The Johns Hopkins University Press, 1973), pp. 269-271.

4. *World Bank Atlas: Population, Per Capita Product and Growth Rates* (Washington, D.C., 1974).

5. Including, with average annual per capita growth rates for 1960-72, Australia (3.1%), Austria (4.3%), Belgium (4.2%), Canada (3.6%), Denmark (3.8%), Finland (4.4%), France (4.7%), West Germany (3.7%), Ireland (3.5%), Italy (4.4%), Japan (9.4%), Luxembourg (2.5%), Netherlands (4.1%), New Zealand (2.1%), Norway (4.0%), Portugal (5.4%), Puerto Rico (6.0%), South Africa (2.8%), Sweden (3.2%), Switzerland (2.9%), United Kingdom (2.3%), and the United States (3.0%).

6. Including, with average annual per capita growth rates for 1960-72, Albania (4.6%), Bulgaria (5.9%), China (2.6%), Cuba (-1.2%), Czechoslovakia (3.4%), East Germany (3.4%), Hungary (3.9), North Korea (4.8%), Mongolia (-0.4%), Poland (3.7%), Romania (7.7%), USSR (6.4%), North Viet-Nam (0.7%). The methodology used to arrive at GNP comparisons for the centrally planned economies (whose national accounting systems vary from the standard UN System of National Accounts) is discussed in the *World Bank Atlas,* 1974, pp. 21-22.

7. Including, with average annual per capita growth rates for 1960-72, Algeria (3.2%), Ecuador (2.3%), Gabon (7.0%), Indonesia (2.1%), Iran (6.3%), Iraq (2.7%), Kuwait (-2.1%), low because of an average annual population increase of 9.7%, Libya (16.2%), Nigeria (2.0%), Saudi Arabia (7.2%), and Venezuela (1.8%).

8. Including, with average annual per capita growth rates for 1960-72, Argentina (2.7%), Barbados (3.2%), Brazil (3.2%), Chile (2.1%), Republic of China (6.8%), Colombia (1.8%), Costa Rica (3.1%), Cyprus (5.9%), Dominican Republic (2.4%), Fiji (2.5%), Greece (7.2%), Guatemala (2.2%), Guyana (1.4%), Israel (5.7%), Jamaica (3.1%), Lebanon (1.0%), Malaysia

(3.1%), Malta (5.9%), Mexico (3.3%), Nicaragua (3.3%), Panama (4.5%), Peru (2.2%), Singapore (7.1%), Spain (5.8%), Trinidad and Tobago (2.8%), Tunisia (3.1%), Uruguay (-0.1%), Yugoslavia (4.8%), and Zambia (2.0%).

9. Including, with average annual per capita growth rates for 1960-72, Bolivia (2.1%), Botswana (5.5%), Cameroon (4.0%), Congo (0.9%), Egypt (1.5%), El Salvador (2.2%), Ghana (0.0%), Honduras (1.5%), Ivory Coast (4.2%), Jordan (1.7%), South Korea (6.8%), Liberia (2.6%), Mauritius (-0.2%, Morocco (1.4%), Papua New Guinea (5.6%), Paraguay (1.5%), Philippines (2.2%), Senegal (-0.8%), Swaziland (6.3%), Syrian Arab Rep. (3.4%), Thailand (4.6%), Turkey (3.9%), and South Viet-Nam (0.8%).

10. Including, with average per capita growth rates for 1960-72, Afghanistan (0.3%), Bangladesh (0.0%), Burma (0.8%), Burundi (1.1%), Khmer Rep. (-0.9%), Central African Rep. (2.2%), Chad (0.5%), Khnomey (0.9%), Ethiopia (2.6%), Gambia (3.5%), Guinea (0.0%), Haiti (0.3%), India (2.6%), Kenya (3.6%), Laos (2.1%), Lesotho (0.0%), Malagasy Rep. (0.4%), Malawi (3.6%), Mali (2.1%), Mauritania (5.2%), Nepal (0.7%), Niger (-0.4%), Pakistan (3.3%), Rwanda (-0.4%), Sierra Leone (2.6%), Somalia (-0.6%), Sri Lanka (2.0%), Sudan (--), Tanzania (2.9%), Togo (4.9%), Uganda (2.2%), Upper Volta (0.9%), People's Rep. of Yemen (-4.5%), Yemen Arab Republic (2.0%), and Zaire (3.3%).

11. The planning estimates of the Economic Planning Board call for a per capita income of $1,500 by 1981.

12. United Nations, *World Economic Survey, 1974* (New York, 1975). Taiwan, for absurd reasons, is no longer included in the UN statistical reports, which does not alter the fact that the Republic of China has been a world leader in economic development over the last two decades and in many ways constitutes a striking parallel to the Korean case.

13. As B. J. Cohen concludes in *The Question of Imperialism: The Political Economy of Dominance and Dependence* (New York: Basic Books, 1973), there is neither logical nor empirical validity to most such claims.

14. See Robert L. Ayres, "Development Policy and The Possibility of a 'Livable' Future for Latin America," *American Political Science Review*, LXIX (June 1975), pp. 507-525, for an argument that creating "livable" societies – emphasizing equity rather than growth – might substitute for a growth strategy which allegedly creates "hyper-urbanized, semi-industrialized, permanently underdeveloped, permanently inequitable countries" (p. 514-15). While Ayres' analysis and recommendation are, in our view, both misdirected and ill-advised, his strategy would require policies no more likely, in fact less likely, to be adopted than policies which would end current inhibitions to growth.

15. "Industry," Sector Working Paper (Washington, D.C.: World Bank, April, 1972).

16. UNIDO, *Industrial Development Survey, V. 5* (New York, 1973), pp. 2-3.

17. *Ibid.*, p. 2.

18. United Nations, *The Growth of World Industry,* V. I, 1969 edition, and United Nations, *Monthly Bulletin of Statistics,* various issues.

19. Naomi Caiden and Aaron Wildavsky, *Planning and Budgeting in Poor Countries* (New York: Wiley, 1974).

20. *Industrial Development Survey,* pp. 13-18.

21. The Bank of Korea, *Economic Statistics Yearbook* (Seoul, 1975).

22. UNCTAD, *The Measurement of Development Effort* (New York, 1970), pp. 15-16.

23. Brown, *Korean Pricing Policies,* p. 296.

24. *Official Records of The Economic and Social Council of The United Nations,* Forty-ninth Session, Supplement No. 7, n.d.

25. Brown, *Korean Pricing Policies,* p. 116.

26. David Turnham, *The Employment Problem in Less Developed Countries: A Review of The Evidence* (Paris: OECD Development Centre, 1970).

27. D.W. Blades, D.D. Johnston and W. Marczewski, *Service Activities in Developing Countries* (Paris: OECD Development Centre, 1974).

28. No digression into the methodological problems facing national accountants in this area is possible here. For a full discussion of the issues, see *Ibid,* "Technical Appendix."

29. Definitional and classification variations account for the discrepancy in investment figures given here and in the following chapter.

30. Blades, *Service Activities in Developing Countries,* p. 69.

31. *Ibid.,* p. 70.

32. *Ibid.,* p. 94.

33. This is necessarily a very gross measure given lack of better data. Not only can value added be affected by other factors, especially capitalization, it happens that value added (the *numerator* of the ratio used) in the service sector is in some cases estimated in terms of employment (the *denominator* of the ratio). In Korea, this is true only for the public administration and defense çomponent of the service sector. See *Ibid.*, p. 37.

34. *Ibid.*, pp. 104-105.

35. An English study found that unskilled workers were relatively content with their incomes because they believed that advancement into the skilled working class, either for themselves or their children, was possible. Discontent was greater among higher paid skilled workers because of pessimism that they or their children could enter the less permeable middle-classes. See Walter G. Runciman, *Relative Deprivation and Social Justice* (Berkeley: University of California Press, 1966).

36. See Irving Swerdlow, *The Public Administration of Economic Development* (New York: Praeger, 1975), pp. 172-73.

37. See S. Ahlvwalia Montek, "Income Inequality: Some Dimensions of the Problem," in *Finance and Development* (Washington, D. C.: International Monetary Fund, September, 1974), p. 4.

38. D. J. Turnham, "Income Distribution: Measurement and Problems," Society for International Development, 12th World Conference, Ottowa (May, 1971), pp. 3-4.

39. "Underdevelopment and the 'Gap' Theory of International Conflict," *American Political Science Review*, LXIX (September, 1975), p. 828.

Chapter 3

Development Effort and Success: Korea and the Developing World

In normal circumstances, few countries in the modern era can develop economically without strenuous efforts on the part of their governments and populations to realize their potential for a better life. The very different settings in which particular countries are placed by history means that the problems of development are to some extent different for each society. For that reason, cross-national comparisons of developmental success are intrinsically flawed. A country with strategic natural resource endowments, such as possessed by the petroleum rich states, has opportunities to develop which are by and large unrelated to the efficiency of its public institutions or the skills and diligence of its population. For some countries a program of population control is unnecessary while for others it is essential. For some, a tax system that is responsive to growth in output is desirable while for others, at other stages of development, it is of secondary importance. Increased savings ratios in most countries are important to future growth but may be less a function of a determined effort to defer current consumption than a natural result of successful growth itself.

With the above caveats in mind, it is still useful to examine indicators which might reasonably be regarded as measurements of developmental effort as a means of identifying countries that have launched more successful developmental programs and which may serve as models of development by alerting policymakers to those areas in which effective action is necessary to more adequate performance.

In one cross-national study of development effort and success, the following were selected as particularly important indices of development: (1) the growth of agriculture; (2) investment and saving (foreign savings were not isolated); (3) the efficiency of investment; (4) the mobilization of tax revenue; (5) export performance; and (6) the growth of population.[1] With the exception of agriculture, which was discussed in the previous chapter, these and three additional factors -- the mobilization of foreign savings, human resource development or education, and the application of the security forces to development activity -- are examined below as they relate to Korea and its position vis-a-vis the performance of other LDCs. As noted, the achievements of the Korean economy provide a leading example of successful growth and development. In accounting for this success, it is useful to examine the above indicators of effort, recognizing that "effort" is difficult to distinguish from "success" in any completely satisfactory way. Effort of course has many dimensions, not the least of which concerns the public policy pattern which is a precondition for success in the fields examined in this chapter. Following the present discussion, then, attention will be given to the nature of the Korean policy process.

Investment and Savings

It is now generally understood that no invariable

relationship exists between the rate of capital formation and economic growth, although it is true that, other things being equal, higher rates of investment will generate higher rates of growth.[2]

There are several reasons why, in actual circumstances, the investment/growth relationship may be weak: (1) some investment serves to replace rather than augment a nation's productive capacity; (2) some investment (e.g., some infrastructure investments) may have only very long run consequences for the rate of growth; and (3) demand may be inadequate to call forth full production from available capacity. In the case of Korea, strong external demand has stimulated investment and consequent supply. Investment in these circumstances is not controlled by limited domestic capital since expansion can be financed directly from profits – a typical pattern in LDCs. This structural circumstance (high demand for exports) means that high growth can occur from relatively modest increases in investment. In the absence of such demand, investments will not be made by private investors. Aside from agriculture, where the lowering of supply contraints will usually affect the rate of growth directly, a decision by government to act as an "automonous" saver and investor in other sectors will not necessarily lead to commensurate rates of growth, at least in the short run. This is not to suggest that direct government investments as part of a comprehensive development plan should not be made; there are important implications in these facts, however, for public policies relating to savings, investment and growth. Government investment is apt to be in major projects, e.g., hydroelectric dams, large-scale irrigation projects, highway construction, and their direct effects on the level of production may be less (in the short-run at least) than that part of total output which is more directly due to demand factors.

This suggests that if satisfactory growth can be sustained *without* increasing significantly the rate of savings, international comparisons of savings efforts among LDCs must be qualified appropriately. It should also be recognized that investment and growth stimulated by external demand lower the decision-making burden on national policy-makers since they need not be involved deeply in all investment decisions. Investments and investment decisions can be decentralized to firms (which may finance investments out of profits) and private investors. The role of the government in such cases may be to maintain orderly capital markets, adjust the money supply, offer special concessions, provide related social overhead and, indeed, to invest directly in some export industries, as the Korean government has done, but not to undertake all or even most investment decisions directly. All governments act as investors, but the scope, and hence the problems, of that role can be limited when investment is induced by demand. Countries are very differently situated, therefore, with respect to the dimensions of the investment planning problems they face.

The Korean case illustrates these points concretely. A comparison by the UNCTAD secretariat of fifty LDCs for the 1950-65 period ranked Korea forty-ninth in the ratio of gross domestic savings to GDP (it averaged only 3.5 per cent for the period, largely because of the Korean war and its aftermath), far below international averages. However, the marginal savings ratio increased steadily during the same period and growth rates in GNP were substantial, growing at an average annual rate of 5.1 per cent.[3] By 1966-68, gross fixed capital formation in Korea was 26.9 per cent of GDP, the highest for any of the thirty-nine LDCs examined in a later UN study. Korea therefore moved from a low-saving/moderate-growth pattern to a high-saving/high-growth one in less than twenty-five years. Comparatively speaking, it moved in savings from among the lowest to the highest of LDCs. The growth rate of GNP for 1963-65 averaged 7.8 per cent annually, while investment rates never exceeded 11 per cent of GNP in any prior year. Since 1967, expenditures on gross fixed capital formation have exceeded 20 per cent of GDP in all years and were in excess of 25 per cent in both 1973 and 1974. Recent expansions in real GNP have kept apace: average annual growth was 10.8 per cent for the 1965-69 period and 9.8 per cent for 1970-74.[4]

The role of government in savings and direct investment has not, however, grown proportionately; in fact it may have decreased. In 1974, government enterprises (including the national railway, postal, telephone and telegraph systems, grain management, general government procurement, a life insurance company, and the tobacco and ginseng manufacturing monopoly), accounted for 5 per cent of fixed capital formation, down substantially from the 12-14 per cent averages of the early 1960s. General government operations accounted for 12 per cent of fixed capital investment in 1974, a much smaller proportion than was true for most prior years (when 15-20 per cent levels were common). The fact that tax rates were increased during the same period, the revenues from which were used to increase social overhead investment, may have maintained the government's position as an overall, if not direct, investor.

Private and public enterprises (the government holds stock in a number of firms, most of which also have private shareholders) accounted for 82 per cent of fixed capital formation in 1974, up generally by 5-15 per cent over the years of the early 1960s. Since 1966 the government has disposed of many of its holdings in firms able to meet market tests and has invested directly in certain capital intensive, import-substituting activities, especially petrochemicals, not in competition with private industry.

The policy of divesting itself of holdings in some industrial (e.g., Inchon Heavy Industry, Dai Han Iron Mining, Han Kuk Machine Industries) and transporation (e.g., Korea Express, Korea Airlines and Korea Shipping) enterprises and of selling shares in others has reduced the government's decision costs, attracted savings and investment and increased growth and equity (the latter by eliminating subsidies never calibrated precisely to need).[5]

Unfortunately, international comparative data on governmental divestiture policy are not available, but the strongest suspicion exists that a policy similar to Korea's is altogether rare. In many LDCs (and increasingly in "developed" countries as well) government-held firms operate at a loss as a matter of policy, producing short term political gains, perhaps, but creating less efficient capital allocations, often subsidizing non-meritorious welfare activity, generating intense pressure on the public revenue system, and frequently encouraging corrupt administrative and political practices.

The devolution of economic decision-making in Korea from government to firms and individuals is reflected in patterns of ownership of common stocks. The absolute growth in stock issues increased phenomenally from 1966 (when 43 million shares were held) to 1974 (501.4 million). During that period, the proportion of total stock owned by government and government corporations declined from 63.3 per cent to 15.4 per cent, while the proportion held by individuals rose from 15.1 per cent to 57.8 per cent.

Private corporations increased their share of stocks owned from 14.8 per cent to 20.3 per cent.[6] The maturing of the Korean capital market -- some 250 firms are now listed on the Seoul stock exchange -- and the devolution of government ownership have altered dramatically the burden of governmental decision-costs and undoubtedly improved investment efficiency while doing so. Broad international comparisons are difficult, but it is widely acknowledged that underdeveloped capital markets are a key problem in increasing savings and investment. It is less widely accepted that government's role in the economy should be limited and that of others expanded in certain ways. The Korean example suggests that the facilitation of capital market efficiency and limited government involvement in direct investment can be beneficial to growth.

The public policy decision to move the pricing of public enterprise products and services to levels that yield returns similar to those obtainable in alternative uses (opportunity cost pricing) has encouraged additional savings, investment and growth. Just as importantly, it has reduced demands on the political system by obviating the need for public administrators themselves to make specific allocative choices, and by reducing access to valued goods and services on the basis of particularistic and ascriptive claims and relationships. It has also meant that it has been possible to expand production without making heavy demands on the public budget.[7] Ideological rigidity (manifest in the uncritical bias among elites in many LDCs toward public sector expansion) and political expediency have meant, in many countries, that divestitutre and opportunity cost pricing policies have received inadequate attention in developmental strategies.

In seeking to explain rates of private saving in LDCs, the motives of individuals are crucial. Impressionistically, it might be thought that the propensity to save (for retirement and other future needs) would increase with the level and rate of growth of per capita income, a point to be addressed momentarily. Business savings from earnings in LDCs tend to be high (capital markets tending to be underdeveloped) when market expansion and increased earnings are perceived as likely. Unfortunately, aggregate savings data for most LDCs are not sufficient to distinguish between these motivations. The UNCTAD study of development effort, using proxy measures for each set of presumed motivations (level and rate of growth of per capita GNP and the size of the export sector), found that, for some 50 LDCs over the 1950-65 period, these variables served to explain 30 per cent of the cross-national variations in the average rate of savings. For the 1960-65 period, 50 per cent of the variation was so explained.[8] In the short run, individual countries have little control over these structural conditions. Consequently, structure rather than "effort" may account for large parts of whatever rates and levels of savings exist at a given point in time: high savings reflect high profits which themselves reflect growth in production and exports. Increased savings, the UNCTAD analysis consequently suggests, may be "more in the nature of 'success' rather than a measure of a country's conscious and deliberate effort to contain consumption so as to free resources for development."[9]

There is an element of question begging in this observation, however, for structural circumstances themselves need not be immutable conditions but consequences of government policy. If development goals are based on an inappropriate import-substitution strategy, which is often the case in LDCs, policy itself may shackle the propensity to save and invest. Moreover, the variables analyzed in the UNCTAD study leave most cross-national variation in levels of saving unexplained, variations which surely have to do with other aspects of public policy – for example, the tax system, interest rates, inflation management, government pricing policies and, very importantly, the stability of the regime and its attitude toward economic activity. In the case of Korea, policies and attitudes on all fronts have served to increase levels and rates of savings and growth. Perhaps development is less a matter of effort -- one may grant that everyone tries hard -- than of making the right decisions.

International comparisons for the sectoral distribution of capital formation are inhibited by profound data problems. In Korea, investment in manufacturing, while increasing dramatically in absolute terms, actually declined somewhat during the 1960s in proportionate terms. Thus, manufacturing, which accounted for an average of 27 per cent of investment during 1960-1966 declined to 23 per cent in 1967-69. Agriculture, which received 12 per cent of total investment in the earlier period, received 1 per cent in the latter. No change occurred in the service sector (27-28 per cent for the two periods), but infrastructure (electricity, gas, water, construction, transport, storage and communications) moved from 32 per cent of all capital absorption to 42 per cent. Interestingly enough, similar tendencies -- a movement of capital formation from manufacturing to infrastructure--occurred in five of the six LDCs (Bolivia, Kenya, Mauritius, Korea, Southern Rhodesia, Tunisia, Venezuela) for which data were available. Korea ranked highest of all six countries in proportion of capital allocated both to manufacturing and infrastructure and last in the proportion allocated to services.[10]

Efforts to generate savings and to mobilize them for investment may take a three-fold focus: internal private, government, and foreign sources. As noted in the previous chapter, Korean developmental strategy recognized in the early 1960s that the generation and mobilization of internal saving, although indispensable, would by themselves be inadequate for the launching of sustained growth, with the result that policy was adjusted to encourage foreign investment, both private and official, in the Korean economy. Such policy took several forms, including the granting of tax concessions, guarantees on the repatriation of principal and earnings and against expropriation, the establishment of a free import industrial zone, government investment in infrastructure, some direct public investment, and, perhaps most importantly, the successful if politically difficult normalization of relations with Japan in 1965.

A number of structural circumstances attracted foreign investment and assistance -- political stability, geographical proximity to Japan, skilled but inexpensive labor (about 20 per cent of U.S. labor costs), improved global communications and transportation, product standardization -- as well as international policy developments (e.g., enlarged official international banking and monetary institutions, the generalized system of preferences, U.S. tariff regulations such as item 807.00 which encouraged multi-national firms to add value off-shore at the intermediate stage of the product cycle), combined to encourage capital movements to Korea. (See endnote 23.) Official donations from abroad have come largely from American sources, where they were often justified in terms of U.S. national security, and where a viable Korean economy was thought to be essential to general stability in Northeast Asia.

The relative success of the strategy of attracting foreign savings for local investment can be judged from a cross-national comparison of external resource flows to the LDCs during the critical 1960s. In 1965, Korea received $155 million in long-term capital and official donations from abroad, an amount exceeded only by Brazil ($320 million), Mexico ($215 million), Peru ($175 million), Nigeria ($222 million), Egypt ($159 million), India ($1,262 million), Indonesia ($271 million), Israel ($285 million), Pakistan ($604 million), and South Viet-Nam ($384 million), among fifty-five LDCs. It will be noted that, on a per capita basis, the Korean receipts were greater than several of these countries. Two years later, in 1967, Korea's relative position had improved still further. In that year, Korea received $347 million in long-term capital and aid from external sources (a doubling of the 1965 figure) and ranked fifth in the world among LDCs in absolute terms, behind only Mexico ($518 million), India ($1,273 million), Pakistan ($596 million), and South Viet-Nam ($384 million). (See Table 3-1.)

Foreign savings-investment flows to Korea rose from 5.2 per cent of GNP in 1954 to 11.7 per cent in 1968 and averaged 8.4 per cent per annum over 1954-68. In 1953, private domestic savings were 6.1 per cent of GNP, somewhat less than the 7.1 per cent average maintained over 1953-67. Government savings following the Korean War were negative (–2 to –3 per cent of GNP, 1953-63) until 1964, and averaged 2.3 per cent of GNP over 1964-67. By 1971, government savings-investment rose to 5.8 per cent of GNP; local private savings-investment rose to 8.6 per cent of GNP; while foreign savings-investment declined to 5.5 per cent of GNP.

Table 3-1

Developing Countries: Net Inflow of Resources, 1965-1967
(millions of dollars)

Region and country	Net receipt of long-term capital and official donations 1965	1966	1967
LATIN AMERICA (twenty-three countries)	1,449	1,861	1,613
Argentina	- 95	154	74
Bolivia	50	34	37
Brazil	320	327	207
Chile	132	95	26
Colombia	77	171	37
Costa Rica	35	46	(41)
Dominican Republic	77	32	40
Ecuador	25	33	45
El Salvador	29	32	30
Guatemala	47	13	45
Haiti	7	2	4
Honduras	15	14	22
Jamaica	20	74	(68)
Mexico	215	330	518
Netherlands Antilles	15	7	1
Nicaragua	22	51	34
Panama	32	33	16
Paraguay	14	19	23
Peru	175	185	148
Surinam	50	19	17
Trinidad and Tobago	77	30	28
Uruguay	31	12	(1)
Venezuela	79	148	151
AFRICA (fifteen countries)	1,026	797	613
Ethiopia	42	46	25
Ghana	143	88	50
Ivory Coast	62	31	31
Kenya	47	51	40
Libya	- 21	-45	-135

Table 3-1 Cont.

	1965	1966	1967
Malawi	35	27	28
Morocco	101	60	63
Nigeria	222	214	159
Sierra Leone	22	11	14
Somalia	14	21	14
Sudan	32	32	35
Tunisia	163	109	134
United Arab Republic	159	134	87
United Republic of Tanzania	13	19	33
Zambia	-8	-1	35
ASIA (seventeen countries)	3,650	3,122	4,118
Burma	21	12	10
Ceylon	17	32	42
China (Taiwan)	68	42	127
India	1,262	916	1,273
Indonesia	271	71	(230)
Iran	149	180	160
Iraq	-38	73	33
Israel	285	190	251
Jordan	81	101	149
Malaysia	142	85	29
Pakistan	604	401	596
Philippines	152	28	153
KOREA	155	336	347
Republic of Viet-Nam	259	398	384
Saudi Arabia	121	144	156
Syria	–	23	30
Thailand	101	90	148
Total for fifty-five developing countries	6,125	5,780	6,344

SOURCE : *External Financing of Economic Development: International Flow of Long-Term Capital and Official Donations, 1962-1966* (New York: United Nations Department of Economic and Social Affairs, 1968), pp. 96-97.

In 1968, domestic capital investment (private and governmental) was 51 per cent of gross domestic investment (i.e., Korean plus foreign investment), a ratio which has increased significantly in recent years. In 1969, domestic sources accounted for 58.8 per cent of gross domestic investment; in 1970, 60 per cent; in 1971, 56.9 per cent; in 1972, 71.7 per cent; in 1973, 84.3 per cent; in 1974, 62.7 per cent. Thus, the Korean economy has become increasingly self-sustaining as a consequence of its enlarged capacity to generate and mobilize internal savings. The ratio of foreign savings in gross domestic capital formation has fallen accordingly from the 50-80 per cent levels of the 1955-64 period to the more modest levels of recent years (35 per cent average over 1968-74). Also noteworthy is the fact that, in 1972, private internal savings-investments for the first time provided more than half of gross domestic investment (53.1 per cent), increased to 66.9 per cent in 1973 (a year when foreign savings flows fell to 17.4 per cent) and were 52 per cent in 1974. The important role of government in capital investment has continued, but has in recent years fallen sharply relative to private activity: in 1972, government's share was 18.6 per cent of gross domestic investment; it was 17.4 per cent in 1973 and 10.1 per cent in 1974.

Direct foreign investment has increased rapidly over the last decade, growing from only $9.8 million in 1967 to $324.1 million in 1973. Table 3-2 shows the growth trends in direct foreign investment by source, where, it will be noted, investment from Japan exceeded that from the United States beginning in 1971.

Foreign economic aid has also been mobilized on a large scale, although it is no longer available in significant amounts. From 1951 to 1974, Korea received over $3.84 billion in

Table 3-2

Foreign Direct Investment in Korea, 1967-73
(millions U.S.$)

	1967	1968	1969	1970	1971	1972	1973
United States	7.6	10.8	6.0	46.4	16.3	32.6	12.6
Japan	.1	2.1	4.8	13.5	18.3	78.5	295.2
West Germany	–	.6	–	.1	–	3.8	–
Panama	–	3.5	1.4	–	.5	–	–
Netherlands	–	.1	.4	4.9	.9	–	–
Hong Kong	–	–	–	–	—	–	2.6
France	–	–	–	–	–	–	2.6
Others	2.1	.1	.3	.2	1.9	2.2	1.1
Total	9.8	17.2	12.9	65.1	37.9	117.2	314.1

SOURCE: *Korea Annual,* various years.

assistance almost all of it from the United States. In the late 1950s and early 1960s, over $200 million in American donations were received annually. Of total foreign aid received over 1951-74, some $8 billion consisted in food shipments from the United States under the PL 480 program (in which normal participation ceased in 1971) and $122 million from the United Nations Korean Reconstruction Agency (ending in 1960), most of which was contributed by the United States. The remainder, some $3.7 billion was from the U.S. Agency for International Development (AID) and its predecessor agencies for both project and nonproject assistance. In 1974, less than $1 million was received from AID for project assistance. All AID nonproject assistance was ended in 1972. PL 480 donations, although ending in 1971, were resumed on the basis of a U.S./Korean agreement which traded Korean restraint on textile exports to the United States for a total of $776 million in PL 480 shipments, 70 per cent of which was to be concessional assistance. The United States was in arrears in 1976, although efforts were being made over some congressional opposition (it being argued that needs were greater elsewhere) to fulfill the agreement. Grants from official foreign sources have steadily declined in recent years, reflecting the general withdrawal of AID funds, from 104 million in Special Drawing Rights (SDR 1 = US$1.04 average over 1967-73) in 1969 to 30 million SDRs in 1973.

On the other hand, loans from official foreign sources have expanded greatly since the late 1960s. In 1967, the central government received loans from external official sources of some 10 million SDRs; 213 million was received in 1970; 300 million in 1971; 98 million in 1972; 310 million in 1973. (See Table 3-3.)

Table 3-3

Foreign Grants and Loans to Korea, 1967-73
(in million of SDRs)

	1967	1968	1969	1970	1971	1972	1973
Grants (official)							
United States	96	88	68	50	41	8	2
Japan	37	30	32	28	16	28	19
Other	3	5	2	5	6	10	9
Loans							
Official	110	72	219	213	300	298	310
Private/private	142	345	335	210	174	123	85

NOTE: 1967-71 SDRs were at par with US$. For 1972, SDR1 = $1.086; for 1973, $1.189. Official loans net of repayment.

SOURCE: International Monetary Fund, *Balance of Payments Yearbook*, various years.

The bulk of these official loans have come from the United States government, with significant participation from Japan and the European OECD members. Drawings on long-term loans received by the Korean private non-monetary sector have gradually increased as well over the same period, from 31 million SDRs in 1969 to 89 million in 1973. These latter loans were from diverse foreign official sources -- mainly from the Asian Development Bank and European, Japanese and American governments. Long-term loans from foreign private sources to private Korean borrowers have tended to decline in recent years (142 million SDRs in 1967; 345 million in 1968; 335 million in 1969; 210 million in 1970; 174 million in 1971; 123 million in 1972; 85 million in 1973) as direct investment has expanded, and as domestic savings have increased.

Capital flows to Korea from both foreign official and private sources have therefore increased greatly from the early 1960s forward. It is not too much to say that without the successful implementation of the strategy to attract foreign savings, the Korean economic expansion could not have occurred. It seems likely that, along with two or three other countries, Korea's effort to mobilize foreign capital was among the most effective in the less developed world. Two related observations should be emphasized at this point: (1) the internal mobilization of capital increased rapidly as well when public policy was altered to offer attractive opportunities to investors; (2) export expansion and foreign capital flows, while mutually reinforcing, were themselves contingent upon a host of other developmentally-relevant decisions affecting other aspects of economic and social life, some of which are discussed in this and following chapters.

Investment Efficiency

In addition to the generation and mobilization of resources (savings), economic development requires that such resources be put to effective uses. In fact, it is questionable whether there is any real test of effectiveness or efficiency of investment beyond growth itself. It is sometimes suggested, however, that the incremental capital output ratio (ICOR) might usefully be regarded as a measure of performance in so far as it reflects the efficiency with which capital is being utilized. Leibenstein has shown, however, that movement in a country's ICOR can usually be predicted accurately from changes in its rate of growth, raising the question as to whether knowledge of ICORs contains any information not more accessible elsewhere.

Fast growing countries are expected to have low, and slow growing countries high, ICORs.[11] Apart from this, countries have very different patterns of production. ICORs will ordinarily be high when the needs for basic infrastructure are deemed paramount and lower when investment with emphasis on plant and equipment is possible, or investment which will usually yield greater growth in the short run. At this time, there is no entirely satisfactory method by which to correct for these cross-national variations in production patterns for comparative purpose. In these circumstances it would be a mistake, even putting measurement error aside, to regard an international comparison of ICORs as very informative. Even for purposes of national planning, the usefulness of sectoral ICORs is limited, sectoral growth rates again being associated with such ratios.

It is at least interesting to note, however, that ICORs, while related inversely to rates of growth, are not necessarily related to levels of development. This is mildly surprising, since higher ICORs might be expected in poorer countries preoccupied with needs for investment in infrastructure. Countries at more advanced stages of development, with considerable infrastructure in place, might be expected to have lower ICORs. If the LDCs are grouped according to the previously cited *World Bank Atlas* classification of lower, middle, and higher-income developing countries and compared, where data are available, in terms of the average ICORs for each of these groups of countries, no such relationship is apparent. A recent United Nations study has calculated ICORs for a large number of LDCs, making it possible to compare levels of development with capital efficiency. For the ten lower-income developing countries compared, the average ICOR (for, roughly, the 1960s) was 2.8, a surprisingly low index. (Since the World Bank study placed thirty-five nations in this group, the missing cases might, if included, change the ratio considerably.) For twelve middle-income developing countries (twenty-three cases in the World Bank classification), the ICOR averaged 3.4 for the decade of the 1960s. And for fourteen higher-income developing countries (the World Bank universe contained twenty-nine observations), the average ICOR for the same period was also 3.4. For Korea, the ICOR was 2.3, lower than the average for each group of LDCs. Indeed, no country in the entire group had a significantly lower ICOR, although several richer countries, including Guatemala (2.3), Nicaragua (2.2), and Zambia (2.2), approximated the Korean rate, as did Bolivia (2.3), El Salvador (2.0) and Thailand (2.4) among middle-income LDCs, and India (2.5), Malawi (2.4), and Sierra Leone (2.3) among lower-income LDCs.[12]

Table 3-4

Incremental Capital-Output Ratios in Selected LDCs
(circa 1960s)

Higher Income Developing Countries (over $375 per capita, 1972)	ICOR
Barbados	4.8
Brazil	3.6
Chile	3.3
Colombia	3.7
Cyprus	3.2
Dominican Republic	4.1
Guatemala	2.3
Jamaica	4.3
Mexico	2.4
Nicaragua	2.2
Panama	2.3
Peru	3.3
Tunisia	5.6
Zambia	2.2
Middle Income Developing Countries ($200-$375 per capita, 1972)	
Bolivia	2.3
Congo	5.6

(Table 3-4 Cont.)

El Salvador	2.0
Ghana	6.8
Honduras	2.7
KOREA	2.3
Mauritius	3.6
Morocco	3.2
Paraguay	3.2
Philippines	3.7
Thailand	2.4
Lower Income Developing Countries (under $200 per capita, 1972)	
Ethiopia	2.6
India	2.4
Kenya	2.5
Malawi	2.4
Pakistan	2.8
Sierra Leone	2.3
Sri Lanka	2.9
Sudan	3.3
Tanzania	2.5
Yeman Arab Republic	4.5

NOTE: ICORs computed by $C = y/\frac{I}{Y}$ where C = ICOR; y = growth rate of GDP; I = gross fixed capital formation; Y = GDP.

SOURCE: UNIDO *Industrial Development Survey*, v. 5 (New York, 1973), pp. 106-7. Country groupings by *World Bank Atlas, 1974* classification.

Pannonia to Constantinople, a city reached after about one month's travel from Dubrovnik. Communities of traders developed at various points, as at Sofia or Sremska Mitrovica where a flourishing settlement enjoyed the protection of the King of Hungary. At Prizren Dubrovnik merchants established their chief commercial 'factory' for Albania. Another important station was provided at Drijeva, including a salt store for the Bosnian trade (for Dubrovnik controlled the salt pans at the mouths of both the Bojana and Neretva). Settlements were also established inland in Bosnia at several places, including Borac, Foca, Jajce and Kresovo, in addition to the principal ones at Fojnica and Visoka. Some merchants were permanently resident in these places while others stayed for only short periods. For the Serbian trade overland routes took off from Bar and Kotor to Ribnica, Brskovo (with its 'colony' dating to the fourteenth century) and Péc. As regards commodities obtained from the Balkan interior minerals deserve special mention for they were important in dealings with both Bosnia (Kamenica, Olovo and Srebenica) and Serbia (Novo Brdo and Ridnik), especially in the hundred years 1360-1460. Most important was silver (Novo Brdo and Srebenica), followed by lead (Olovo and Kamenica) and copper (Ridnik).

In the reverse direction there was a considerable trade in textiles, some of which originated in northern Europe, though most came from Florence whose trading axis to the east connected Ancona and Dubrovnik with Constantinople. The trade was not without its difficulties, however. Competition was maintained in the Bosnian market by other Dalmatian trading towns as well as by traders operating from the Black Sea coast through Wallachia and Transylvania. Partly in response to these difficulties there were attempts by merchants to manufacture their own cloth in Dubrovnik, an initiative well supported by the town authorities through removal of customs duties on imported raw wool (1440) and the imposition of the same on imported cloth or exports of raw wool.[55] It is evident that steps were taken to find the best wool in the Balkans (Bulgaria and Serbia rather than Bosnia and Hercegovina) and further afield in Italy, while skilled textile workers from Florence were invited to settle in Dubrovnik. The transit trade offered a particularly good opportunity in the early sixteenth century when Venice was temporarily unable to retain complete control over Adriatic commerce. But it was always an uphill struggle to improve quality and the local industry finally dwindled in the late sixteenth century with a sharp decline in local enterprise. The transit trade continued, mainly in the hands of Jewish merchants who had good connections in both Italy and the Balkans and little personal interest in the Dubrovnik's own woollen industry.

Much more successful, however, was the shipbuilding industry for which Dubrovnik was famous throughout Dalmatia. There was already a strong merchant marine by the end of the eleventh century, arising out of participation in some of the struggles of the Byzantine Empire, but further expansion occurred after 1358 when Dalmatia came under Hungarian rule and Venice retreated, along with her shipping. New shipyards were now commissioned in the town and the tonnage of merchant shipping began a significant rise to reach some 40,000 tons by 1582. Timber was still available locally (the islands of Lastovo and Mljet), though with some deliveries from Albania and Bosnia, while cordage came from Dubrovnik itself. But canvas was obtained from Ancona and iron from either the Balkan interior or Venice. In addition to these major industrial initiatives there were of course various handicrafts represented: workers in furs and precious metals as well as the usual run of blacksmiths, carpenters, shoemakers and tailors. And agriculture should not be overlooked, for there were significant land resources available through the territorial growth of the fourteenth century (Peljesac 1333 and Mljet 1345) culminating in Terre Nove 1399 and Konavli 1418, which pushed Dubrovnik's limits towards the Neretva and Bay of Kotor respectively. In addition to the livestock raising already mentioned there was some development of viticulture but the crucial consideration was cereal growing. Since supplies were usually adequate only for about one third of the year imports were essential, from a very wide area extending to the Middle East and the Black Sea coastlands as well as Greece and Italy.

After 1500 there seems to have been a considerable decline in Dubrovnik's trade, the result of several different factors which had an important cumulative effect. Competition with other Dalmatian trading centres resulted in the decline of the salt trade with Bosnia as local traders in the province were encouraged by the Turks to deal with places like Gabela and Pocitelj in the lower Neretva valley. This could have been one result of a growing Levantine conflict between Turkey and Venice (with which Dubrovnik was associated). Another result was Turkey's growing interest in the minerals of Bosnia in connection with its own war machine as well as its desire to deny the resources to Venice. Dubrovnik found some compensation through distancing itself more from Venice and concentrating on the Balkan hinterland where the Turks appreciated the essential commercial nature of her activities.[56] Helped by a lack of interest in trade by the Turkish nobility and by trade concessions from the Ottoman government Dubrovnik was able to build up a virtual monopoly in Bulgaria and Serbia if not in Bosnia and Hercegovina. Skins, wax and wool were particularly important commodities at this time. Basically the Ottoman attitude was favourable to Dubrovnik and independence of Venice made it a particularly acceptable outlet for Balkan produce. Earlier trading rights were renewed by the Turks and although placed under Turkish protection in 1458 Dubrovnik was the only vassal state whose territory was never invaded and in whose internal affairs the Turks did not interfere. In return for economic services the city was allowed not only to maintain consuls in Ottoman cities but also in foreign countries, with rights to negotiate treaties abroad and sail ships under her own flag.

Ottoman influence

The Ottoman advance was initially unfavourable to town development with the exception of principal military depots like Belgrade and Smederovo where large forts were built. However, the revival of trade was a significant factor in town development. Military routes became commercial highways and the simple fort (*palanka*) often blossomed into a town with its complement of craftsmen and its caravan station (*han*). Examples of such development in the sixteenth century include Kharmanli and Pazardzhik on the road from Edirne to Nis; also Lom, Ruschuk (Ruse) and Svishtov on the Danube. Most growth, however, occurred in the principal administrative centres like Monastir (Bitola), Sarajevo, Sofia and Usküb (Skopje). T. Stoianovich has referred to three concentric zones in the Ottoman town: 'the first ring was the nucleus of power, the second was the host of wealth and talent and the third was the hem of poverty and despair'.[57] The core comprised several different elements. The citadel (*kastron* to the Byzantines and *grad* to the Slavs) and old town (*agrora*) were complemented by a lower town (*carsi*) which gradually attracted market functions and became known first as *targ* and later (by the sixteenth century) as varos. Industry and commerce focussed on the bazaar (bedestan) where there were merchants and craftsmen. The merchant might be either a tüccar, handling long-distance and even international trade, or an esnaf concerned only with the local market. The craftsmen operated within a guild system which was supposed to ensure adequate production while maintaining a monopoly to ensure a satisfactory living for the members. But it has been argued that Ottoman guilds were more rigid than their western counterparts and by maintaining a set number of masters in each guild production could not be increased to meet any rising demand and economic growth was thereby hampered. The industries were important to the government as a source of taxation, levied on houses, workshops and on raw materials. Indeed the muhtesib who levied taxes on goods entering the cities, collected market dues, maintained quality controls and checked weights and measures, was a key figure - a state-appointed economic master.

The two outer zones comprised various autonomous residential quarters (mahalla), giving rise to the comment by P.F. Sugar that the Ottoman city 'was really nothing more than a conglomeration of more or less self-contained boroughs grouped around a common core'.[58] They were usually separated by natural obstacles or by walls. Each suburb consisted of some twenty-five to fifty families with the same occupation and religious affiliation and supervised by a headman. The larger suburbs might have their own market, bath, coffee house and place of worship, although these installations would not completely supplant the complex of centrally-placed facilities around which the various quarters were arranged. The outer band of poor quarters of course contrasted strongly with the more desirable neighbourhoods in the middletown districts. This was particularly evident in the seventeenth century when there was a great increase in the numbers of Christian migrants to the towns, representing the rise of a proletariat. It brought a substantial change in the ethnic character of Turkish towns since the immigration coincided with the departure of many Jews in search of better opportunities. The urban population was, therefore, somewhat unstable and the commercial importance of the fairs reflected the frailty of the urban system which was always vulnerable to war and plague. Another factor in the decline of population was plague. This was a permanent fact of life in the Balkans but there appears to have been an exceptional pestilence every dozen years or so in the Ottoman Empire in the seventeenth and eighteenth centuries which could carry off more than one fifth of the urban population. Less severe epidemics, experienced every third, fourth or fifth year, might account for a tenth of the population compared with just about one percent under the most favourable circumstances. The threat was greatest in the larger cities and ports, though all settlements in the plains were vulnerable, in contrast to the mountains where a healthy environment went hand in hand with greater personal security. Plague was actually a hazard in the Balkans every summer but it was more easily communicated under certain meteorological conditions and especially when these 'coincided with the time of collective travel of merchants, soldiers, pilgrims and seasonal labourers'.[59] Thus cities were subject to a continual threat of ruralisation and could only maintain their populations with a constant flow of immigrants from the countryside.

NOTES

1. N.J.G. Pounds 1974, 279-337. See also M.M. Postan 1972, 'The Medieval economy and society' (London: Weidenfeld & Nicolson).
2. M. Malowist 1966, 'The problem of inequality of economic development in Europe in the later Middle Ages' Economic History Review 19, 15-28.
3. N.J.G. Pounds 1974, 92.
4. Ibid. 175. See also J.H. Mundy 1973, 'Europe in the High Middle Ages' (London: Longman) 25-74.
5. C.T. Smith 1967, 179.
6. F.L. Carsten 1941, 'Slavs in northeastern Germany' Economic History Review 11, 61-76.
7. B. Zientara 1982, 'Melioratio terrae: the thirteenth century breakthrough in Polish history', J.K. Fedorowicz et al., 31-48. See also B. Zientara 1970, 'Nationality conflicts in the German-Slavic borderland in the thirteenth and fourteenth centuries and their social scope' Acta Poloniae Historica 22, 207-25.
8. B. Zientara 1982, op. cit., 45.
9. Ibid.
10. F. Graus 1970, 'Slavs and Germans', F. Graus et al. 'Eastern and Western Europe in the Middle Ages' (London: Thames & Hudson) 15-42 (quote p. 36).
11. H. Szulc 1972, 'The development of the agricultural

landscape of Poland' Geographia Polonica 22, 85-103; H. Szulc 1978, 'Regular green villages in Pomerania' Ibid. 38, 265-70.

12. C.T. Smith 1967, 264-8. For contextual matters see pp. 191-259.

13. G. Demidowicz 1985, 'Planned landscapes in northern Poland: the Suraz estate 1550-1760' Journal of Historical Geography 11, 21-47. H. Szulc 1983, 'Morphogenetic typology of villages and their regulation in Poland: a case study from Silesia and Pomerania', B.K. Roberts and R.E. Glasscock eds. 203-15.

14. T. Dunin-Wasowicz 1975, 'Climate as a factor affecting the human environment in the Middle Ages' Journal of European Economic History 4, 691-706.

15. M. Linke 1983, 'Medieval deserted fields and deserted villages in the Lower Harz Mountains: an interim report', B.K. Roberts and R.E. Glassock eds. 293-305.

16. M. Bogucka 1980, 'The role of Baltic trade in European development from the sixteenth to the eighteenth century' Journal of European Economic History 9, 5-20.

17. W.G. East 1966, 166. See also J.V. Thirgood 1981, 'Man and the Mediterranean forest' (London: Academic Press).

18. H.H. Stahl 1980, 'Traditional Romanian village communities' (Cambridge: Cambridge University Press).

19. F.W. Carter 1977, 'Brac island Dalmatia: a case for sequent occupance?', F.W. Carter ed. 239-70. For further work by the same author see F.W. Carter 1984, 'Eleventh century Poljica: an analysis of its historical geography', E. Pivcevic ed. 'The cartulary of the Benedictine Abbey of Gumany (Croatia) 1080-1187' (Bristol: David Arthur & Sons) 23-37 (describes transhumance).

20. Ibid. 246.

21. E. Carus-Wilson 1952, 'Woollen industry', M. Postan and H.J. Habakkuk eds. 355-428. F.F. Mendels 1972, 'Proto-industrialisation: the first phase of the industrialisation process' Journal of Economic History 32, 241-61. See also K.H. Wolff 1979, 'Guildmaster to millhand: the industrialisation of linen and cotton in Germany to 1850' Textile History 10, 7-74.

22. H. Kisch 1959, 'The textile industries in Silesia and the Rhineland: a comparative study in industrialisation' Journal of Economic History 19, 541-64.

23. N.J.G. Pounds 1973, 292-4, 395-8. See also J. Brutzkus 1941, 'Trade with Eastern Europe 800-1200'

Economic History Review 11, 31-41; J.U. Nef 1941, 'Silver production in Central Europe 1450-1618' Journal of Political Economy 49, 575-91; J.U. Nef 1952, 'Mining and metallurgy', M. Postan and H.J. Habakkuk eds. 429-92; B. Salvemini 1973, 'Transport and economic development' Journal of European Economic History 2, 747-61.

24. D. Molenda 1976, 'Investment in ore mining in Poland from the thirteenth to the seventeenth century' Journal of European Economic History 5, 151-69.

25. A. Keckova 1981, 'Polish salt mines as a state enterprise' Journal of European Economic History 10, 619-31.

26. R. Ludloff 1957, 'Industrial development in sixteenth and seventeenth century Germany' Past and Present 12, 58-75.

27. W. Hensel 1977, 'The origins of the western and eastern European Slav town', M.W. Barley ed. 373-90.

28. W. Jansen 1985, 'The origins of the non-Roman town in Germany', H.B. Clarke and A. Simms eds. 217-37.

29. W. Kuhn 1985, 'German town foundation of the thirteenth century in western Pomerania', H.B. Clarke and A. Simms eds. 547-80.

30. L. Leciejewicz 1985, 'Polish archaeology and the Medieval history of Polish towns', H.B. Clarke and A. Simms eds. 335-51.

31. A. Zbierski 1985, 'The development of the Gdansk area from the ninth to the thirteenth century', H.B. Clarke and A. Simms eds. 289-334.

32. M. Malowist 1966, op. cit. (note 2) 22.

33. E.A. Gutkind 1964, 135-230, 413-35; N.J.G. Pounds 1973, 263-75, 343-59; N.J.G. Pounds 1974, 223-78. See also G. Conzen 1945, 'East Prussia: some aspects of its historical geography' Geography 30, 1-10; R.E. Dickinson 1942, 'The development and distribution of the Medieval German town: the eastern lands of German colonisation' Geography 27, 47-53.

34. D. Molenda 1976, 'Mining towns in central-eastern Europe in feudal times: problem outline' Acta Poloniae Historica 34, 165-88.

35. Ibid.

36. Ibid. 177.

37. Ibid. 179.

38. B. Zientara 1976, 'Socioeconomic and spatial transformation of Polish towns during the period of location' Acta Poloniae Historica 34, 57-83 (quote p. 66).

39. Ibid. 71.
40. Ibid. 72.
41. Ibid. 81.
42. A. Wyrobisz 1976, 'Small towns in sixteenth and seventeenth century Poland' Acta Poloniae Historica 34, 153-63. For a context see J. de Vries 1984.
43. M. Bogucka 1982, 'Polish towns between the sixteenth and eighteenth centuries', J.K. Fedorowicz et al. eds. 135-52 (quote p. 136).
44. L. Kuklinska 1982, 'Central European towns and the factors of economic growth in the transition from stagnation to expansion between the seventeenth and eighteenth centuries' Journal of European Economic History 11, 105-15. See also W. Kalinowski 1966, 'City development in Poland up to the mid-nineteenth century' (Warsaw: Institute for Town Planning & Architecture); W. Kalinowski 1972, 'City development in Poland', E.A. Gutkind ed. 11-108.
45. K. Dabrowski 1976, 'Kalisz between the tenth and thirteenth centuries': P.H. Sawyer ed. 'Medieval settlement: continuity and change' (London: Arnold) 265-73.
46. B. Zientara 1982, op. cit. (note 7) 38.
47. J. Adamczewski 1973, 'In Cracow' (Warsaw: Interpress). F.W. Carter 1983.
48. J. Herrmann 1977, 'Research into the early history of the town in the territory of the GDR', M.W. Barley ed. 243-59. See also R.E. Dickinson 1945, 'The morphology of the Medieval German town' Geographical Review 35, 74-97.
49. C.T. Smith 1967, 321.
50. L. Gerevich 1977, 'Hungary', M.W. Barley ed. 431-55 (quote p. 442). See also L. Pereicyi 1972, 'Historical development of Hungarian cities', E.A. Gutkind ed. 361-428.
51. F.W. Carter 1977, 'Urban development in the western Balkans 1200-1800', F.W. Carter ed. 148-95.
52. F.W. Carter 1972. See also F.W. Carter 1968-9, 'Balkan exports through Dubrovnik: a geographical analysis' Journal of Croatian Studies 9-10, 133-59; F.W. Carter 1969, 'Dubrovnik: the early development of a pre-industrial city' Slavonic & East European Review 47, 355-68; F.W. Carter 1971, 'The commerce of the Dubrovnik Republic 1500-1700' Economic History Review 24, 370-94; F.W. Carter 1980, 'Ragusa: the city republic of Dubrovnik' History Today 30, 46-51; B. Krekic 1972, 'Dubrovnik in the fourteenth and fifteenth centuries' (Norman: University of Oklahoma Press); J. Roglic 1961, 'The geographical setting of Medieval Dubrovnik', N.J.G. Pounds ed. 1961, 141-59; L. Villari 1904,

'The republic of Ragusa' (London: Dent); F. Violich 1972, 'An urban development policy for Dalmatia' Town Planning Review 43, 151-65; 243-53.

53. F.W. Carter 1972, 86. See also H.C. Darby 1932, 'The Medieval sea state' Scottish Geographical Magazine 48, 136-49.

54. S.M. Stuard 1981, 'Dowry increase and increments in wealth in Medieval Ragusa' Journal of Economic History 41, 795-813.

55. F.W. Carter 1971, 'The woollen industry of Ragusa (Dubrovnik) 1450-1550: problems of a Balkan textile centre' Textile History 2 (1), 3-27.

56. N.H. Biegman 1967, 'The Turko-Ragusan relationship' (The Hague: Mouton).

57. T. Stoianovich 1970, 'Model and mirror of the premodern Balkan city', N. Todorov ed. 'La ville balkanique XVe-XIXe siecles' (Sofia: Bulgarian Academy of Sciences, Institute of Balkan Studies) 83-110 (quote p. 102).

58. P.F. Sugar 1977, 75.

59. T. Stoianovich 1970, op. cit. (note 57) 107.

6

The Trade Routes

Eastern Europe was drawn into a continental trading system which focussed on the Champagne fairs in the early Middle Ages and, more importantly in the fourteenth and fifteenth centuries, on Frankfurt am Main.[1] In the early Medieval period the principal trade routes were by sea, linking Byzantium with Italy and the Baltic lands with the Low Countries, and these had only a marginal impact on Eastern Europe through the tapping of Dalmatia by Venetian ships (at Ragusa and Zadar for example) and the Viking expeditions up the Oder and Vistula. But there seems to have been a significant growth in Baltic trade in the tenth century for the number of coastal centres increased as Kołobrzeg (Ger. Kolberg), Mecklenburg (near Wismar), Raiswiek, Wolgast and Wolin (Ger. Wollin) were supplemented by Demmin, Gdansk (Ger. Danzig), Rostock, Szczecin (Ger. Stettin) and Usedom. Gdansk was particularly significant as this new economic centre of 980 eclipsed the old Prussian market of Trusno near Elblag (Ger. Elbing). And after 1100 however the Genoese were able to take advantage of the Crusades and open up trade hinterlands in the east complementary with those of Venice: by the late thirteenth century the Black Sea had been drawn into their orbit although the main thrust of their activities was aimed at the exotic products of Central Asia.

Most of the ports lay beyond the limits of Eastern Europe, on the Crimean coast (like Caffa) or else on the rivers Don, Dneiper and Volga, but Moldavian outposts such as Cetatea Alba (Belgorod Dnestrovsky), Chilia and Tighina also featured in the picture and stimulated some grain production along the Black Sea coastlands. The shipping lanes were, however, complemented by overland trade which was initially most important along the route from Mainz to

Kiev. The traders went to Bamberg (situated on the Main and one of Charlemagne's 'ports of entry') and eastwards to Prague, Olomouc, Krakow, Przemysl and Lwow (Lvov). Branches off this main artery brought in the towns of central Poland, like Gniezno, Poznan and Wrocław (Ger. Breslau) while the extension of Christianity to Hungary in the eleventh century opened up an alternative route to the east through Regensburg, Esztergom and Buda with navigable rivers offering some relief from dependence on pack animals and carts. Indeed before the Turkish conquests the overland routes continued on the Black Sea. Spices featured among the leading commodities but as the exotic element faded forest products, livestock and minerals predominated.

THE BALTIC

Trade was not usually handled to any extent by the indigenous population of Eastern Europe. Jews were prominent (Przemysl for example had a large Jewish community, as did Vienna after 1221 when the Danube trade route was closed to foreigners) while Scandinavian people operated in the Baltic and Italians gradually asserted themselves in the Adriatic. However in the Baltic the period opens with a considerable Slav involvement for 'the Slavonic peoples of the southern coast of the Baltic Sea now not only supplied raw materials to foreign merchants but themselves became producers and traders'.[2] This trend was doubtless associated with the emergence of a Polish state, under the Piast dynasty in the tenth century, and its consolidation through the conquest of Pomerania by Bolesław III in the twelfth century (Figure 6.1). Polish traders (including a significant professional element by the twelfth century despite the important commercial role of the upper classes) acted as brokers for merchandise sent north from the Czech Lands, Hungary and Byzantium, some of it destined for re-export to Russia and Scandinavia. The decline of German colonisation in the east may not have affected the volume of trade but it almost certainly weakened the position of German merchants, especially with the growth in the power of Slav states well-illustrated by the Polish victory over the Teutonic Order in 1410. Nevertheless the German influence remained substantial and Baltic trade must inevitably be studied in the context of the Hanseatic League, which is one of the many ramifications of the eastward movement of

Figure 6.1: Medieval Poland. Inset: growth areas of Medieval Europe

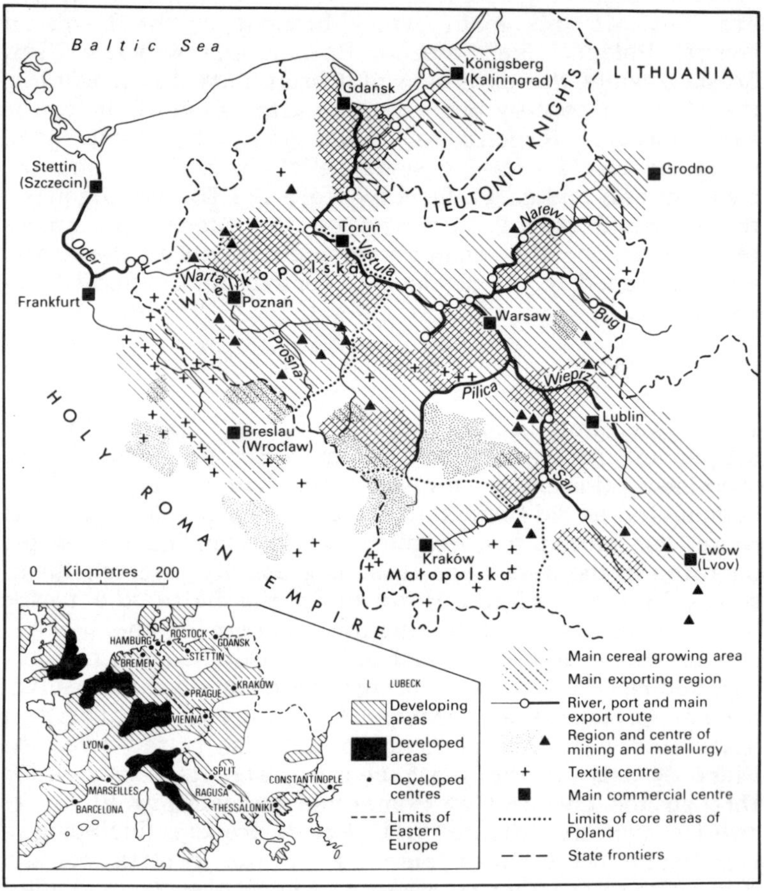

Sources: J.K. Fedorowicz et al. 1982; N.J.G. Pounds 1974.

German settlement in the early Medieval period. Merchants, based at a string of ports along the coast, followed in the wake of the first settlers and were given considerable opportunity through the activities of the Teutonic Knights. Evidently the latter found Poland more congenial than Transylvania, where they had previously operated, and by the middle of the century they had conquered Prussia, absorbed the Brethren of the Sword (originally sent by the Archbishop of Bremen against Lithuanian and Livonian tribes) and become a threat to their Polish hosts. There were strong commercial undercurrents through urban expansion and the forging of overland trade links with Russia.

The German penetration was not a particularly coordinated one and the Hanseatic League was a somewhat enigmatic organisation. Although it was a formally-constituted body, with its diet or Hansetag, initiative lay largely with the merchants of Hamburg and more especially Lübeck. This arose from settlement between 1143 and 1159 in connection with loading or unloading operations on either side of the Jutland peninsula. Trade between Hamburg and Lübeck, avoiding the open sea, became more important as the old Schleswig portage was superseded and the Streknitz Canal (1398) between the Elbe and the Trave was opened. Lübeck gained further importance from exploitation of the fishing grounds off southern Sweden and was poised to play a predominant role in Baltic trade, eventually becoming informal capital of the Hanse. 'For the first time the German presence, until now limited to merchant colonies situated in the midst of Slavonic or Scandinavian surroundings, obtained a convenient base for further expansion'.[3] The supply of West European commodities to the Baltic was now progressively taken over. However, many of the eighty towns listed as members in the fourteenth century, when the League was most powerful, were small places affiliated only through convenience. Ports despatching goods westwards had little interest in the ownership of the vessels and as competitors appeared in the form of Dutch and non-Hanseatic German traders there was no sense of obligation towards the merchants of Lübeck. The competition arose partly through increased movement overland and partly because of the Umlandfahrt, circumnavigation of the Jutland peninsula, which avoided any need for trans-shipment and allowed direct voyages from the Baltic grainlands and forests to the Low Countries. Being so crucial to the industrial and urban development of the west it was inevitable that any opportunity for competition would be taken and equally inevitable that there would be competition between the Baltic powers for control of the straits. Thanks to their advance as a maritime power in the fourteenth and fifteenth centuries the Dutch (and to a much lesser extent the English) were able to break the German monopoly. With the rise of Dutch trade the Baltic operations became particularly well-organised and much of the capital of the Amsterdam merchants was tied up with this lucrative business. Full advantage was taken of an early and fortunate alliance with the Danes to make use of their skills in bulk trading and the Dutch lead survived into the eighteenth century.[4]

It was at this time that representatives of the German towns met in Stralsund (1367) and converted their informal association into an overtly political organisation, though such a change could not alter the fundamental spatial realities and desperate measures to bolster the League's flagging fortunes probably served only to divert further trade to alternative routes. The princes of Poland did not hesitate to encourage competition in order to limit the League's economic and political power while the Hanse lost an important protector with the collapse of the Teutonic Order. The League survived until the seventeenth century but their monopoly was lost two hundred years before: in the late fifteenth century Lübeck accounted for almost a third of all the vessels visiting Gdansk but the proportion dropped to just two percent by 1530 and it required the shipping of all German ports together to reach the earlier figure. Further lack of cohesion arose from Stapelrecht or staple right, a privilege that required ships to stop and offer their goods for sale, proceeding only if there was no local demand. Although these rights were more important in the west there was, for example, the case of Frankfurt/Oder where exercise of the privilege disrupted trade on the river: in effect goods could not flow from the upper reaches (Silesia) through to the Baltic and Stettin was thereby denied access to part of its natural hinterland. In summary, therefore, H.A. Miskimin considers that 'failure to preserve discipline among the Hanse towns, resentment of prior German success, political change in the Baltic region and even the disrupting impact of the Reformation in Germany weakened the organisational structure of the Hanse and its ability to act in concert'.[5]

Although trade was substantial it was not characterised by luxury goods and hence the phrase 'poor man's Mediterranean' has been coined to emphasise an important distinction between the two basic sea routes. Outgoing cargoes of fur, flax and hemp, tar timber and wood-ash, in addition to the all-important cereals, were balanced by imports of cloth, wine and colonial products. Trade appears to have been quite well balanced, although the period of closest contact with Flanders (early fifteenth century) seems to have been one of substantial deficit. But while grain was carried by boat, livestock used the overland route as did some of the textile imports to Poland. With the growth of the Christian practice of fasting fish became a more important food commodity and there was considerable overland movement of herring from the Baltic coast southwards through Poland and even into Silesia and the Czech Lands. Salt too was carried inland from the coast and several monasteries are reported as having an interest in the industry at Kołobrzeg. But further supplies had to be brought in from the west: some were sent from Lüneburg via Hamburg but massive shipments of salt from the Bay of Biscay were being made by the fifteenth century. On the whole, however, the emphasis was on the movement of primary produce from the Baltic in exchange for manufactures. The trade was mutually beneficial, but in several respects it was damaging to Baltic interests. On the one hand there was the permissive influence of these new resources on the development of shipbuilding in the west, paving the way for the age of discovery. The flood of cheap grain also provided opportunities in the west: where regular imports of cereals were not needed to avoid famine they could be used in manufacturing, particularly brewing. On the other hand the competition discouraged industrial growth in the Baltic and corresponding changes in settlement patterns and social structure.[6]

It is interesting to note the progressive widening of the trading area focussing on the Baltic ports. In 1250 the combined hinterland embraced Brandenburg, Livonia, Masovia, Mecklenburg, Pomerania and Prussia, but by 1400 it had extended to include the whole of Poland, along with the Czech Lands and Slovakia and after another century took in Podolia and the northern parts of Hungary and Moldavia. Subsequently the Ukraine and Volhynia were drawn into the cereal trade of the Baltic. Trading ships were of sound construction with broad beam which was conducive to handling bulky and heavy cargoes and with shallow draught which made them suitable for navigating the estuaries and lower reaches of rivers. Indeed while most Hanseatic towns were on the coast not a few of those situated in the territories of the GDR and Poland were river towns on the Elbe (Wittenberge), with its tributaries the Havel (Brandenburg and Rathenow) and Saale (Bernburg and Weissenfels), the Oder (Breslau) and Vistula (Krakow and Torun/Thorn). By no means would all these places have been accessible to sea-going vessels. Boats intended purely for river navigation must have been very crudely constructed with very shallow draught in view of the limited depth of water on some sections of the rivers. Boats may well have been knocked together for a single journey to the estuary, with timber sold for building or fuel once the grain had been transferred to the coasters.

Development of the feudal system

Profits obtainable in the grain trade stimulated East European feudal landowners to increase the obligations of the peasantry. Labour dues increased and set off an evolution process which was to reach its peak in nineteenth century latifundia. The transformation has been outlined in general form by E.J. Hobsbawm who points to great improvement in the relative advantage of the West European economies in well-integrated home markets and ease of communication (by sea) with their colonies and each other.[7] Eastern Europe was in an inferior position and consequently the aristocracy extended the process of specialisation in agriculture which had first started to become evident in the fifteenth and sixteenth centuries. A system of Gutherrschaft involving financial gain from serf labour in agriculture was substituted for the traditional Grundherrschaft in which the lord received income in money and kind from dependents. By the change the position of the peasant deteriorated but the elite was able to enjoy the levels of affluence of West European counterparts despite their countries' overall economic weakness. In Prussia and Saxony after the Thirty Years War there was even a system of Gesindezwangdienst under which young peasants were required to work more or less full-time for the landowning nobles (the future Junkers) for a prescribed period and for very low wages. This was virtually a forced labour regime which demonstrated the importance both states attached to the landowning class for stability and development.[8] This system was later weakened by the growth of industry in the countryside although the lords did their best to prevent this competition for labour from endangering the system of servile relations.

Why did trade lead to such a gross exploitation of the feudal system in the east? Arguments like those of I. Wallerstein which stress the market opportunities for East European estates may be combined with the Marxist approach of R. Brenner who emphasises the weakness of peasantry in the face of the capitalistic designs of the nobility.[9] However, this leaves unanswered the intriguing behavioural question as to <u>why</u> the aristocracy was motivated to establish their manorial systems: 'why was it inclined to take advantage of existing objective circumstances such as the subordination of the peasantry which the nobility's political power made possible or the favourable markets for agricultural products?'[10] It may have been that inability to compete in manufacturing gave rise to an attitude among the elite which valued exotic manufactures (military hardware as well as consumer luxuries) and sought their acquisition through maximum output of grain and any other staple commodity saleable in the west. Hence the urge to exploit the peasant, an urge that would be easy to express through the powerful position of the feudal authorities in Eastern Europe in relation to central governments. Inevitable government support for aristocratic interests seems to have ruled out any significant programmes of social reform while the more or less passive acquiescence in Western Europe's industrial dominance removed the possibility of a rising middle class modifying the polarisation of economic and political power. Eastern Europe did not share in the trend towards greater social mobility evident in Western Europe in the later Medieval period, when speculation in land and commodities was rife and when acquisitive and unscrupulous peasants could acquire considerable holdings and aspire to the ranks of the gentry. A fundamental consideration may also be the less severe impact of the Black Death, with the relative abundance of labour justifying a harsher regime. Any fall in prices tended only to strengthen the grip of the state with heavier pressures on the peasants to maintain the total value of exports through higher output.

The peasants were not altogether docile and there are various cases of revolt, as in 1525 when the Prussian peasantry, subjugated by the Teutonic Knights in the thirteenth century, joined with the Germans to contest the subordination of Prussia to the Polish crown.[11] But to a surprising degree the peasants apparently tolerated the conditions of the new serf status, perhaps because, in the words of W. Kula, 'they were tolerable'.[12] The area to be worked by one peasant did not necessarily increase and the production available to the family may not have been any smaller. The prevailing inflationary trend meant that the peasant, even if he had less to sell, could trade at price levels that were more favourable to him. 'The only difference was that it was now known which plot would yield the harvest to be deposited in the peasant barn and which the harvest that could go into the lord's granary'.[13] Some difficulty apparently arose over the value of labour with and without draught animals. Since many peasants believed that the conventional ratio of two to one was unreasonable they tended to dispense with animals rather than furnish draught labour, notwithstanding the fact that they might need animals to cultivate their own holding.

Feudalism in Poland

H.A. Miskimin argues that the relative mild incidence of plague in Poland allowed migration and colonisation to continue into the late Medieval period. Domestic trade sustained the towns as market and manufacturing centres while technological innovation was evident in metallurgy and in the application of water power to industry. But when population and purchasing power recovered in the West the scope for grain exports encouraged landowners to oppose further economic progress. 'Trade within the region was open to all and gave less advantage to the great nobles than long-distance trade, and by sustaining the towns it deprived the large landlords of the labour necessary to expand their grain output and to capitalise on rising demand'.[14] After all the prospects were particularly good in view of the great agricultural potential of the temperate plains drained by a series of major rivers that were already major commercial highways, while the Baltic ports were well-organised for trade and voyages to Western Europe and relatively free of natural and political hazards. But from the late fifteenth century the nobles continually sought to regain control and reassert feudal authority over the peasantry, especially in 1518-20 when grain prices began to rise steeply. The nobility also asserted their privileged position to the extent of being exempted from toll payments on the Vistula in respect of agricultural and forest products grown on their estates: this concession was, of course, exploited to avoid payments on goods purchased from other lands and non-privileged merchants were thereby undercut. The urban economy was eroded, for the merchants were gravely disadvantaged (in 1565 there was an outright prohibition on their exporting of domestic products) while labour demands reduced the purchasing power of the peasantry and damaged the market for manufactures. 'Out of self-interest the nobles successfully contrived to reserve for themselves the rich grain trade and to assure adequate supplies of agricultural labour for the maximum exploitation of their estates'.[15] Landlord interests were all the more prominent because of the weakness of the monarchy and in 1496 the king had to buy support for his campaign against the Turks by allowing a reimposition of serfdom and a denial of landownership to townspeople. Hence the growth of the estates and the restriction of grain surpluses almost exclusively to the granaries on such large properties.

However it is significant that the campaigns by Kazimierz to win territory from the Teutonic Knights preserved many local arrangements so that the merchants of Elblag and Gdansk retained their trading privileges after the Peace of Torun (1466) and remained the dominant force in the grain trade of Prussia. This was particularly significant since these two towns controlled the Vistula basin which accounted for some four fifths of the Baltic grain trade. Cereal exports from the two ports together amounted to only 35,000 tonnes in 1585 but rose nearly six-fold to exactly 200,000 in 1618. But generally speaking the new trends had a depressing effect on industry and commerce. Of course craftsmen who catered for the luxury market (such as builders, goldsmiths and paper makers) could find plenty of work and for a time the demand for tools in agriculture helped to maintain growth in the iron industry, whose furnaces fell under noble control and were kept working with servile labour. There was also a demand for armaments which helped the iron industry as well. But the prevailing trend in Polish industry in the sixteenth century has been summarily described as a downward spiral, largely the result of the specialisation in grain production imposed by the nobles. Finally it is worth noting that while cereals dominated the export trade there were also other staple products in demand in the west which helped to underline the colonial relation that developed. The growth in shipbuilding required not only special timbers (which came more from Scandinavia than Poland) but also tar, while wood-ash, often refined to potash, was important in many industrial processes. Shipbuilding again created demand for flax, to be made into sailcloth, and hemp, to provide rigging, rat lines and hawsers.

In the early stages it was demand in the heart of Poland that encouraged the landowners to take agriculture on their estates more directly 'in hand'. L. Zytkowicz has shown that 'it would be wrong to assume that big farms producing for the international market developed first where the best communications existed', for estates in Pomerania, nearest to Gdansk, were the last to develop a strong export trade.[16] Further south the landlords could secure holdings on abandoned land or else use fallow and permanent pasture. It was not necessary to expel peasants, but only to resettle them on other land or perhaps reduce the size of their farms. It was not necessary to purchase sołectwo (lands owned by the village sołtys, hereditary chiefs of village assemblies) although some land may have been obtained in this way. Important social changes could be forced through to extend the serf labour system. 'The serf-labourer worked on the folwark with his own tools and beasts of burden and the farm installations could be built and repaired without spending any money'.[17] If wage labour had been employed profitability would have been reduced by low productivity and by landlord obligations to look after animals, buildings and equipment. Paid labour was used in some cases, as at Malbork and Poznan where the greater strength of the market and the low transport costs made this system possible. And again on the lands owned by the cities of Elblag and Gdansk the tenant farming system continued to operate with money rents paid from the proceeds of local marketing, as it also did in areas that were either remote from the trade routes to the Baltic ports or physically unsuitable for cereal growing. Here the large farms of landowners were slow to appear and when they did their inaccessibility tended to place emphasis on the sale of spirits rather than cereals. So whereas the general reduction in the size of peasant farms meant that the prominence of independent peasants (kmiecje) decreased from 67.5 percent (1564) to 33.0 (1660) in the central part of the Krakow region the decrease in the mountainous southern part was much less marked: from 74.7 percent to 56.6. The balance was made up of zagrodniki (peasants holding the usufruct of only a small plot of land around a house), chałupniki (peasants with only small kitchen gardens besides their houses) and komorniki (labourers living in rented cottages).

Where the folwarki emerged the peasant suffered, for he no longer had the opportunity to produce much for the market on his own land and only peasants with large farms were able to enjoy the benefit of rising cereal prices. Moreover the peasantry saw their political power whittled away as the landowners, whose influence in government was essential in the first place to get approval for the binding of the peasants to the land (glaebae adscriptio) in 1496, were able to lobby the Diet into passing laws against escapes: the fact that suits brought by peasants against landowners disappeared from the royal courts of justice in the late fifteenth century shows how the lords enjoyed full power by this time. The full extent of the serf's obligations is difficult to assess but Zytkowicz claims that 'from the end of the sixteenth century the peasant-serf with a self-sufficient farm was obliged to keep a labourer and a beast of burden to perform his duties on the landlord's property, especially during the harvest season when these duties were heaviest'.[18] He would also have to give his landlord some fifteen percent of his production in rent, to say nothing of dues to church and state and landowner monopolies over corn milling and the production of liquor (the propinatio, covering the manufacture and sale of beer and brandy). Indeed the granaries on the great estates were probably filled as much through the deliveries from peasants, as payment of rents and milling dues, as they were from the production of the landlord farms, but one way or another the landowners controlled a large part of the peasants' capacity to produce. Only the large peasant farms (decreasing in numbers in the sixteenth and seventeenth centuries) were able to generate a significant grain surplus: the smaller producers would have livestock, dairy products, vegetables and forest products to sell at local markets.

The stimulus to produce more agricultural commodities did not last throughout the period and there are clear signs of depression in seventeenth century Poland. A decline in production in Poland is well-documented through records relating to the estates of the Archbishopric of Gniezno where a slight growth in the total area cultivated during the sixteenth century was followed by a sharp fall during the next hundred years (forty percent from 1600 to 1685), so that a slight recovery during the eighteenth century still left more land uncultivated in 1800 than was the case in 1500. It seems clear that the reduction in the cultivated area was not compensated for by increased yields: in fact the reverse was true in the early seventeenth century and this is borne out not only by evidence from Gniezno but also from crown lands in Sandomierz and farms belonging to the town of Poznan. Moreover there was a fall in production on peasant farms considerably greater than the contraction on the large estates. It was also on the peasant farms where the concurrent decrease in stock breeding was most noticeable. J. Topolski therefore assesses the overall reduction in cereal production and stock breeding at one third during the seventeenth century.[19] Regressive tendencies were noted earlier in some parts of Poland than in others. In Masovia (well-integrated through river transport with the Baltic trade route) the fall dates to the turn of the sixteenth century with a reduction in the area cultivated (and in the total number of farms) and a decline in industrial production from both country mills and urban-based crafts. Early depression was noted too in Sandomierz but in Pomerania (and particularly Gdansk) the timing was different. Both farmers (peasants as well as nobles, employing mainly day-labourers) and merchants maintained their positions in this prosperous grain country until the war of 1626-9 where there was great destruction from which the region had still not recovered when it was again ravaged by the Swedish invasion of 1655-60. The Thirty Years War was also damaging and brought decay to the previously buoyant Silesian economy, as well as accelerating the decline in Masovia where one third of all towns were now razed to the ground. In particular the exchange of Polish livestock for Silesian textiles was gravely disrupted. However there is some disagreement on the timing of depression for while a conventional view sees 1618 as the peak year for cereal exports, research on Vistula trade at Warsaw suggests 1641, with growth right up to the mid-seventeenth century wars.[20]

'It is not to be doubted that frequent and prolonged wars caused serious damage to the country's economy and heavy losses in population both of which contributed to economic decline'.[21] Yet Gdansk and Pomerania recovered from devastation relatively quickly and it cannot therefore be argued that wars inevitably brought long-lasting economic decline. It may be significant that in these areas the agriculture was organised on the basis of cash payments, either as rents delivered by tenants to landowners or wages paid to day-labourers. Little use was made of servile labour, in sharp contrast to the rest of Poland where the cereal surpluses directed to Western Europe were based on the labour of peasant-serfs. Elsewhere landlord oppression through rising demands for labour and reductions in the amount of land that peasants could cultivate for their own profit threatened the potential of the small peasant farms while the growth of the towns was prejudiced by the limitation of the home market and the nobility's control of foreign trade, exemplified by Radziwiłł's virtual monopoly on trade with Königsberg in the seventeenth century. In short, in most of Poland depression was aggravated by war but it was not caused in the first place by the outbreak of hostilities since 'the development of noble landed property at the expense of the peasants had begun to have harmful effects from the first half of the seventeenth century'.[22] At the same time, as M. Bogucka points out, the rapid growth of West European demand was coming to an end not only because of war and plague but because of intensification of domestic agriculture.[23] English grain exports were rising in the late seventeenth century while new crops like maize and rice were being introduced.

Bohemia

In Bohemia the growth of population in the late fifteenth and sixteenth centuries and the consequent increase in the demand for food encouraged the nobility to exploit the strong position in which they had found themselves at the end of the Hussite Wars. Laws enacted between 1487 and 1500 bound the peasant to the soil and subordinated him to manorial jurisdiction, but over the next century the weight of serfdom tended to increase. An important factor in the process was the successful competition of the nobility with the towns over industry and commerce: after successful competition with the royal cities for brewing and trading rights the number of markets and towns controlled by the nobility increased. There was every incentive for the nobility to develop their farming activities: hence the increases in labour obligations (robota) and the engrossing of peasant-held land to produce extensive demesnes free of the constraints of open-field farming. It was not only cereal growing that generated high profits for the landlords: hops, flax, fruit and vines were also important. Nevertheless despite the political power of the nobility (with a lack of any involvement by the crown in the countryside in defence of peasant interests) and the strong commercial stimulus, the burdens of serfdom on the peasantry were not excessive at the end of the sixteenth century and the traditional fish-pond economy (which triggered the original demands for peasant labour) was still very important.

The Thirty Years War had a most devastating effect because the old Bohemian aristocracy 'which had accepted the restraints of custom and law and had exhibited a certain degree of paternalism in their relations with the peasants' was largely replaced by a new elite of conquering foreigners anxious to discipline the serfs and command more of their labour since depopulation had made it an even more precious commodity than before.[24] More peasant land was incorporated into landlord demesne: it might be purchased compulsorily at a nominal price or exchanged for a less desirable holding since the prospect of resistance was minimised by the difficulties inhibiting the airing of peasant grievances at a higher level than the manorial court. Of course the system was inefficient and the peasant made sure that the lord's gain was not as great as his own loss: 'peasants went to discharge their robota obligations with a notable lack of enthusiasm, brought their worse tools, drove their oldest animals, malingered at work as much as possible and generally performed at a level far below their potential'.[25] But the system brought political and social advantages for the lord enjoyed high status in the community and considerable power in dealing with the state government, until such time as the latter realised that the whole country as well as the peasantry was being disadvantaged by such inefficiency and summoned the political will to introduce reform.

Hungary

Hungary too was drawn into the trading orbit of Western Europe, though with livestock rather than cereal production as the dominant enterprise. Rents were converted to cash payments and arbitrarily increased while labour dues also became more burdensome. At Pozsony (Bratislava) they increased from seven to sixty days during the sixteenth century.[26] The old privilege giving the lords exclusive right to sell wine was revived in order to eliminate the merchants and remove all risk of competition from peasant producers. Further privileges exempted nobles from export taxes on their own livestock and, as in Poland, this concession was greatly abused so that additional stock purchased by the lords also avoided tax, thereby eliminating all non-noble competition. The cattle trade from Eastern Europe was also very buoyant in the fifteenth and sixteenth centuries. Cattle from Transylvania and Pannonia were driven through Buda and Vienna to the towns of southern Germany (sometimes even the Rhineland) while livestock from Podolia and the Ukraine travelled through Lublin and Krakow and on the Leipzig and Frankfurt (with some heading through Bohemia to Bavaria). The Polish cattle trade was more important than the Hungarian despite the fact that Poland also exported large quantities of cereals and furs. The Hungarian trade was more open to disruption by war as well as interference by privileged cattle trade companies while the eclipse of the south German towns reduced the markets available.

THE BALKANS

Initially the main trade route ran from Constantinople northwards by the Black Sea and Dneiper river to Kiev. Movement into Pannonia was limited at first by the Magyar incursions but in any case the overland routes by the Morava-Vardar and Morava-Maritsa seem to have been preferred to the Danube, which was little used for commerce. The lowest section of the river was important in view of the Bulgarian settlements of Great and Little Preslav which deferred only to Constantinople in the Balkan context. But the Iron Gates posed a substantial physical barrier to say nothing of the distinct possibility that extreme climatic conditions in the thirteenth and fourteenth centuries exacerbated problems of both freezing and flooding. Further difficulties certainly arose through the boatmen's guilds, claiming the right to tranship goods reaching their ports, and the holding of boats to ransom through abuses of feudal power. But their significance in discouraging through traffic is hard to assess. Even when conditions became more stable in Pannonia the Danube river route must have seemed rather indirect for travel to the Orient via the northern shores of the Black Sea and even more so in the case of Constantinople. 'Evidence available from the twelfth century shows that the river was used along certain sections rather than as a continuous through route. Wine from Hungary was exchanged for salt from Wallachia by river, but the shipments of oriental commodities along the upper river is no indication that the Danube was the channel of importation from the east since these commodities were carried overland from Italian ports to Ulm, Regensburg and Vienna'.[27] This comment draws attention to a further disadvantage of the Danube: it was easily overshadowed by the sea route from the Black Sea through the Mediterranean to Italian ports.

A new chapter in Balkan commerce opened in 1261 when the Treaty of Nymphaiou gave Genoa exclusive right to export cereals from the Byzantine Empire, thereby ousting the Venetians who have previously been in the ascendancy. Bases were established at the mouth of the Danube, notably Chilia, and from these places overland trade routes led in Transylvania (Tirgoviste-Brasov) and Ukraine (Suceava-Lwow). Spices and textiles for the nobility and wealthy townsmen were exchanged for such staples as cereals, fish, hides, honey, salt and timber. Some use was made of the Danube with navigation upstream to the Iron Gates, until the Ottomans put an end to the Bulgarian state in 1393. The Genoese had stations right up to Calafar and they are thought to have been responsible for the castle at Giurgiu. A document of 1349 tells of permission granted by Louis the Great of Hungary allowing the merchants from Genoa to continue their journeys overland from Orsova through Temesvar (Timisoara) to Buda.[28] Of course in these northerly markets Lombard cloth brought by the Genoese ran into competition with Flemish textiles coming in through Prague, but the trade was evidently valuable enough for them to continue to reach Buda after the Turkish conquests using routes across the Dinaric Alps from Zadar. However, the Danube trade was really just a branch of the Black Sea commerce with the Crimea and Sea of Azof where local resources (fish, olives, timber and vines) were supplemented by locational advantages in relation to caravan traffic to Persia and beyond which the Tartars carefully preserved. The Genoese also supplied wheat to Constantinople from Cetatea Alba and other ports with hinterlands extending into the steppes. And timber must have been a particularly important commodity during the rise of Turkish power in the fourteenth and fifteenth centuries for the city states had to turn to their defences against this new sea power. More ships were needed, to cover the needs of war as well as commerce, and reduced life of vessels on account of rising hostilities would have prolonged the increased pressure on the forests.

Genoa lost its maritime empire in the Black Sea with the rise of the Ottoman Empire and although there was some compensation in New World trade the functions of the port were reduced increasingly to local shipping. Ottoman trade policies reflect the government's understandably ambivalent attitude. With a rising population (which may have numbered eight million in the Balkan territories alone in the sixteenth century) it was essential that home demand for food and manufactures should be given priority. But the simultaneous rise in demand in other parts of Europe, coupled with the persistent crop failures in the western Mediterranean, created a great incentive for cereal producers to export despite Ottoman attempts to retain all surpluses for the home market. The rapid growth of cereal exports from the Greek lands provided wealth for the purchase of western manufactures, but it also resulted in a shift of the grain supply area for Istanbul eastwards to the Black Sea coastlands where trade could be more easily controlled. Only if production from Bulgaria and the Romanian Principalities was insufficient would grain from Anatolia and Greece be required. However it became clear during the seventeenth century that the inability of the empire to compete with western manufactures gave rise to the necessity to export cereals and also precious metals from the mines of Bosnia and Serbia. Hence the marked reluctance of the Turks to deal with infidel western traders, a feeling reinforced by the first defeats suffered at the hands of western forces which disturbed the Ottoman sense of confident superiority. To cope with the situation European traders recruited assistants as their agents in Istanbul and in this way the commercial role of Greeks and Jews was consolidated.

The stimulus to trade with the west had one very significant consequence for the agrarian organisation of the empire, for in the seventeenth century (continuing with more emphasis in the eighteenth) there was a development of the landed estate in the form of a quasi-private property: ciftlik. On account of indebtedness and depopulation, along with the connivance of civil servants, many old timar properties (military fiefs) were converted into private estates through the sale of usufruct rights. Peasants were now bound to these lands and their cooperation with this exploitative system assured through the employment of the kirjalis (armed irregulars). T. Stoianovich demonstrates how the system went hand in hand with a growth of cash cropping (cotton and maize most notably) and with continuing urban stagnation on account of the concentration of investment in the rural areas.[29] The system did not appear in Moldavia and Wallachia but a distinctive form of latifundia system did of course emerge in the Principalities in the nineteenth century. The creation of the estates led to some changes in settlement patterns. There was a movement of peasants to the mountains to escape the heavier feudal demands that were now made of them. This led to new dispersed settlement on the high ground with an economy based on banditry and the cultivation of free soil. On the other hand defections created a need for tighter security on the estates. 'The manor house which now made its appearance often looked like a manor fortress and was frequently defended by the lord's private troops'.[30] People had to be moved into the protected areas and villages might therefore be resited closer to the manor house. But it was also significant that the labour contracts (enforceable through the courts) were imposed on the whole community group and defections were restrained by the knowledge that the remaining members would have to assume greater burdens. Arguably therefore 'it was the ciftlik system that gave the traditional zadruga its final form and full power over the lives of its members'.[31]

It has been argued that the seventeenth century ciftlik was an important innovation that could have regenerated the empire. Yet Stoianovich considers that this 'crude para-military internal colonialism' was hardly a promising vehicle for further evolution towards a modern capitalist economy and in that sense the Ottoman experience may offer contrasts with the rest of Eastern Europe.[32] However the ciftlik cannot be accepted too readily as a manifestation of capitalist agriculture despite the clustering of estates around the main commercial centres in the cereal, cotton and tobacco growing areas of Bulgaria and Macedonia. There was no system of leases on the British model and 'ciftlik owners were also unwilling to furnish any but the most rudimentary equipment or consolidate cultivation, let alone introduce crop rotation and other improved methods'.[33] The rather primitive sharecropping system in any case applied to only about one fifth of the land, even in areas where it was widespread and in Bulgaria as a whole only about one tenth of the peasantry faced ciftlik obligations. Many peasants were disposed to migrate into the uplands and concentrate on cattle rearing organised around extended family farms which would enjoy a measure of security. Livestock were subject to lower taxes and could easily be hidden on the few occasions when the collectors actually penetrated the remoter lands.

NORTH-SOUTH TRADE IN EASTERN EUROPE

It would be a gross oversimplification to suppose that Eastern Europe as a whole was tied into a satellite relationship with the west without developing internal trading relationships of its own. Although both the Ottoman Empire and Poland were exporting to the west such primary products as cereals, livestock and livestock products there was also a considerable trade with each other. The excellent archival material available at Krakow reveals close contacts between the city and the Balkans at the turn of the sixteenth century (a time of rapidly rising industrial prices in the Ottoman Empire) despite the loss of the city's function as Polish capital.[34] The most important commodity was textiles with cloth manufactured locally in Silesia sent south, along with other material of British origin. In the opposite direction there was silk and cotton collected in Istanbul from the Orient. Poland was also exporting minerals (copper, lead and salt) while livestock, spices and wine travelled northwards. There was a thriving cattle trade from Moldavia and the Ukraine to Lwow, Krakow and various destinations in the Czech and German lands, while spices could still be taken more cheaply overland to southeastern Poland than they could be supplied by sea through Gdansk. Wine became an important commodity with the decline of viticulture in Poland and when supplies from the Mediterranean via the Danube delta were cut off by Ottoman-Venetian conflict alternative supplies were drawn from Pannonia and Transylvania which had previously been more important for the export of cattle. Various groups of people were active in this trade, including Greeks, Italians and Ragusans, but Armenians specialised in the exchange of spices for handicraft goods and Jews were prominent on the trade routes through Lwow. Two routes seem to have been particularly important: one across the Tatra Mountains (via Bochnia, Nowy Sacz and Presov) and thence to Kosice, Oradea, Cluj, Sibiu and Brasov to the Danube at Ruse and across the Balkan Mountains to Shumen, Edirne and Istanbul. The other avoided the high ground and the terrible hazards of brigandage in the Carpathian passes by following the Vistula and San upstream to Lwow and then southeastwards to the tidewater on the Danube at Galati and Chilia via Kamieniec Podolski, Dorohoi, Iasi and Bîrlad with the journey completed either by sea or by the overland route through Silistra, Burgas and Edirne. Various alternatives were available on the second route for Iasi could be reached through Lwow, Siret and Suceava and an alternative tidewater to the Danube delta was the Dniester estuary at Cetatea Alba, accessible from Iasi via Bendery.

Journeys were long and caravans would be on the road for two to three months between Krakow and Istanbul; and with additional time for trading en route probably one return trip would take the whole year. There were, of course, great variations in speed between different legs of the journey and seasonal factors were also important. Only the more expensive goods could stand the inevitably high transport costs, although it was a great boon to Polish merchants when they were excused customs duties in Ottoman territory under Mehmet II (1596-1603). Given this type of trade with occasional appearances by caravans along extremely lengthy routes (along with the importance of the estate for much local trade) it is understandable that the periodic fair should handle much of the business arising from interaction between the long-distance traders and local producers. At the northern end major fairs were held three times each year in Kosice and Krakow while in Ottoman territory the relative importance of the fair was even greater. It has also been demonstrated that in the Balkans the monasteries assumed a modest commercial role especially when they were situated on the trade routes. However, Krakow certainly did not enjoy a monopoly of trade with the southern parts of Eastern Europe and it is important to recognise the growing commercial power of Leipzig which arose in part out of the Thirty Years War. The fluid situation in the early seventeenth century made for considerable changes in fortune and on the positive side the growth of Leipzig stands out. No town suffered more through prolonged fighting yet Leipzig emerged as a leading German trade centre, second only to Hamburg and now far ahead of Frankfurt, Köln and Nürnberg. During the war the bi-annual Leipzig Fairs established themselves as the meeting points for Europe's wholesale and retail traders, and the city also gained its particular reputation for the publishing and distribution of books and for the processing of Russian furs.

CONCLUSION

In the light of the economic structure it is useful to look again at the political geography of Europe and note how the Medieval nation states appear as a necklace with particularly clear eastern and western groupings on either side of the European heartland. This pattern has been interpreted by S. Rokkan through correlating the centre with a broad trade route belt and a well-developed system of cities which was at the same time the stronghold of the Catholic Church: it was not possible for core areas to emerge as lynch pins of a strong territorial system and attempts at unity through the Holy Roman Empire were not conspicuously successful since the emperors tended to be mere figureheads, frequently undermined by shifting electoral alliances.[35] By contrast the core areas in both east and west could develop with less competition from established urban centres, commanding resources lying far away from the cities of the central trade belt. Of course a 'great paradox of European development is that the strongest and the most durable systems emerged at the periphery of the old Empire, the heartlands and the Italian and German territories remained fragmented and dispersed until the nineteenth century'.[36] But this arises from the subordination of Eastern Europe to the growth of capitalism in the west in the late Medieval period. Indeed Z.P. Pach argues that the trading empires of the colonial powers of Western Europe were anticipated by the trading relations emerging between the two halves of Europe. For in the initial development of a modern world economy 'it was not yet the overseas colonies but rather the countries of Mid-Eastern Europe that were joined to the economy of Western Europe in the sense of a modern market, by exports of mass-consumption foodstuffs and imports of mass-consumption manufactures'.[37] This economic relationship constrained the growth of the urban system in Eastern Europe: cities there were relatively weak and could not generate major resources for building up military machines. 'This contrast in resource bases for political consolidation goes far to explain the difference between the western and eastern systems in their internal structure and in the character of the later transition to mass politics'.[38]

Social change was also inhibited for whereas some governments allied themselves with non-agricultural interests, to gain independence of action from serf owners, this did not happen in Eastern Europe for a very long time: indeed serfdom was extended in the sixteenth and seventeenth centuries on such a scale that it has sometimes been seen in retrospect as a 'reintroduction'. Whereas in the west the serf enjoyed some protection from arbitrary change through manorial custom, the power to make unilateral changes in the contract meant that the East European serf became de facto a slave. And while there were sound economic reasons for this, the power of the state (and the primacy of noble interests) meant a perpetuation of the system into economically adverse periods. 'It was able to shift the impact of declining incomes onto the serfs and to keep the majority of them at a subsistence level for extended periods. In the process of preserving the institution of serfdom intact not only did the serf owners become brutalised but the whole body politic became dehumanised and permeated by elements of lawlessness'.[39] So when serfdom was abolished in the nineteenth century by modernising governments anxious to break with the institutions of the past the legal system and the social attitudes underpinnings took a long time to adjust. Indeed some East European analysts would see 'neoserfdom' implicit in certain government attitudes and policies in the twentieth century.

It may seem that lack of interference from the west would have allowed a more rational development in the east. Put another way, the west may be held responsible for the backwardness of Eastern Europe. But such an argument can hardly be advanced by scientific analysis. While the social system was hardly progressive this system was not created simply by the trading system and a fairer distribution of the wealth created by specialisation in agriculture should not be regarded as inconceivable. It is also worth asking how far the process of urbanisation and industrial development could have continued in the east if the flow of manufactured goods from the more advanced external producers had been arrested. Agricultural yields were too low to allow the growth of more than a few strategically-placed cities of West European proportions. Then as now, the issue would appear to be not so much the legitimacy of capitalism as the distribution of power in the various sectors of this global system.

NOTES

1. N.J.G. Pounds 1974, 338-402; N.J.G.Pounds 1979, 297-305; 402-32. See also M. Postan 1952, 'The trade of medieval Europe: the North', M. Postan and H.K. Habakkuk eds. II 119-256.

2. K. Slaski 1979, 'Northwestern Slavs in the Baltic Sea trade from the eighth to the thirteenth century' Journal of European Economic History 8, 83-107 (quote p. 107). See also A. Attman 1973, 'Russian and Polish markets in international trade' (Goteborg: Goteborg University Institute of Economic History).

3. K. Slaski 1979, op.cit. 101.

4. C.T. Smith 1967, 430-44.

5. H.A. Miskimin 1977, 'The economy of later Renaissance Europe 1460-1600' (Cambridge: Cambridge University Press) 138. See also P. Dollinger 1970, 'The German Hansa' (London: Macmillan); W.G. East 1966, 323-47; J.K. Fedorowicz 1980, 'England's Baltic trade in the early seventeenth century' (Cambridge: Cambridge University Press).

6. M. Malowist 1958, 'Poland Russia and western trade in the fifteenth and sixteenth centuries' Past and Present 13, 26-41; Z.P. Pach 1970, 'The role of East Central Europe in international trade (sixteenth and seventeenth centuries)' Etudes Historiques (Budapest).

7. E.J. Hobsbawm 1954, 'The general crisis of the European economy in the seventeenth century' Past and Present 5, 33-53; 6, 44-65.

8. J. Blum 1957, 'The rise of serfdom in Eastern Europe' American Historical Review 52, 807-36; 62, 814-7.

9. R. Brenner 1976, 'Agrarian class structure and economic development in pre-industrial Europe' Past and Present 70, 30-75; I. Wallerstein 1975, 'The modern world system: capitalist agriculture and the origins of the European world-economy' (London: Academic Press).

10. J. Topolski 1982, 'Sixteenth century Poland and European economic development', J.K. Fedorowicz et al. eds. 70-90 (quote p. 89).

11. H. Zins 1959-60, 'Aspects of the peasant rising in East Prussia in 1525' Slavonic & East European Review 38, 178-87.

12. W. Kula 1980, 'Money and serfs in eighteenth

century Poland', E.J. Hobsbawm et al. eds. 'Peasants in history' (Calcutta: Oxford University Press) 30-41.

13. Ibid. 32.

14. H.A. Miskimin 1977, op.cit. (note 5) 57.

15. Ibid. 60.

16. L. Zytkowicz 1972, 'The peasant's farm and the landlord's farm in Poland from the sixteenth to the middle of the eighteenth century' Journal of European Economic History 1, 135-54 (quote p.138). See also W. Kula 1976, 'An economic theory of the feudal system: towards a model of the Polish economy 1580-1800' (London: N.L.B. Foundation of History Library).

17. L. Zytkowicz 1972, op.cit. 140.

18. Ibid. 148.

19. J. Topolski 1974, 'Economic decline in Poland from the sixteenth to the eighteenth centuries', P. Earle ed. 'Essays in European economic history 1500-1800' (Oxford: Clarendon Press) 127-42. See also A. Maczak 1976, 'Money and society in Poland and Lithuania in the sixteenth and seventeenth centuries' Journal of European Economic History 5, 69-104.

20. J.M. Malecki 1977, 'The Vistula and Poland's trade in the sixteenth and seventeenth centuries' Journal of European Economic History 6, 193-8.

21. J. Topolski 1974, op.cit. (note 19) 137.

22. Ibid. 139.

23. M. Bogucka 1980, 'The role of Baltic trade in European development from the sixteenth to the eighteenth century' Journal of European Economic History 9, 5-20.

24. W.E. Wright 1975, 'Neo-serfdom in Bohemia' Slavic Review 34, 239-52 (quote p. 245). See also W.E. Wright 1966, 'Serf seigneur and sovereign' (Minneapolis: University of Minnesota Press).

25. W.E. Wright 1975, op.cit. 250.

26. Z.P. Pach 1966, 'The development of feudal rent in Hungary in the fifteenth century' Economic History Review 19, 1-14.

27. W.G. East 1966, 299-322; 368-91 (quote p. 382); R.S. Lopez 1952, 'The trade of Medieval Europe: the South', M. Postan and H.K. Habakkuk eds. 257-354.

28. C.C. Giurescu 1976, 'Genoese on the lower Danube in the thirteenth and fourteenth centuries' Journal of European Economic History 5, 587-600.

29. T. Stoianovich 1953, 'Land tenure and related aspects of the Ottoman economy', Journal of Economic

History 13, 398-411. See also K. Karpat 1973, 'An enquiry into the social foundations of nationalism in the Ottoman Empire' (Princeton, N.J.: Princeton University, Woodrow Wilson School of Public & International Affairs, Centre of International Studies).

30. P.F. Sugar 1977, 219.

31. Ibid. 219.

32. T. Stoianovich 1953, op.cit. 398-411 (quote p. 401).

33. J.R. Lampe and M.R.Jackson 1982, 35.

34. F.W. Carter 1982, 'Polish-Balkan trade in the late sixteenth century: a Vichian interpretation' (Boston, Mass.: Third Joint N. American-Bulgarian Scholarly Meeting). See also L. Berov 1974, 'Changes in price conditions in trade between Turkey and Europe in the sixteenth-nineteenth centuries' Etudes Balkaniques 10, 169-78; A.H.L. Lybyer 1915, 'The rise of the Ottoman Turks upon the route of oriental trade' English Historical Review 30, 577-88.

35. S. Rokkan 1973, 'Cities states and nations: a dimensional model for the study of contrasts in development', S.N. Eisenstadt and S. Rokkan eds. 'Building states and nations' (Beverly Hills, Calif.: Sage Publications) I 73-97 (quote p. 77-8).

36. Ibid. I 79.

37. Z.P. Pach 1968, 'The shifting of international trade routes in the fifteenth-seventeenth centuries' Acta Historica Academiae Scientiarum Hungaricae 4, 287-321 (quote p. 306).

38. S. Rokkan 1973, op.cit. (note 35) I 81.

39. A. Kahan 1973, 'Notes on serfdom in Western and Eastern Europe' Journal of Economic History 33, 86-99 (quote p. 99).

Early Modern Eastern Europe

1648–1815

7

Political and Settlement Geography

This period is not particularly easy to define but it is necessary to consider a transition from the Medieval to the modern and convenient indicators may be the Peace of Westphalia (marking the conclusion of the Thirty Years War) and the Treaty of Vienna in 1815, at the end of the Napoleonic Wars. It was a period of considerable scientific advance, most evident of course in the west where the opportunities for colonial expansion overseas stimulated the consolidation of competing national economies with commensurate military and naval capacities. In Eastern Europe, where the later Medieval period had already seen a decline in the region's economic status, the challenge must have seemed a formidable one which few leaders were able to accept. But there was some solid commitment to modernisation based on a dispassionate assessment of opportunity and in several instances 'prejudice, tradition, prescription and the whole fabric of established order crumbled in the crucible of reason'.[1] There would no longer be any 'obedience to vague and mystic conceptions of international good but a clear calculation of individual interests'.[2] Eastern Europe therefore witnessed significant reorganisation in the economic and social structures of each state but also change in the political geography itself, with expansion by Prussia, Russia and the Habsburg Empire balanced by the destruction of Poland as an independent state and the demise of the Ottoman Empire as an active force in European affairs (Figure 7.1).

In spite of some ambivalence of attitude there can be little doubt about the fundamental change in outlook that took place and arguably the pace was set by Prussia whose ascendancy, on the basis on economic and military power, typified the age in the same way as the fading authority of

Figure 7.1: Political geography of Eastern Europe, c.1780

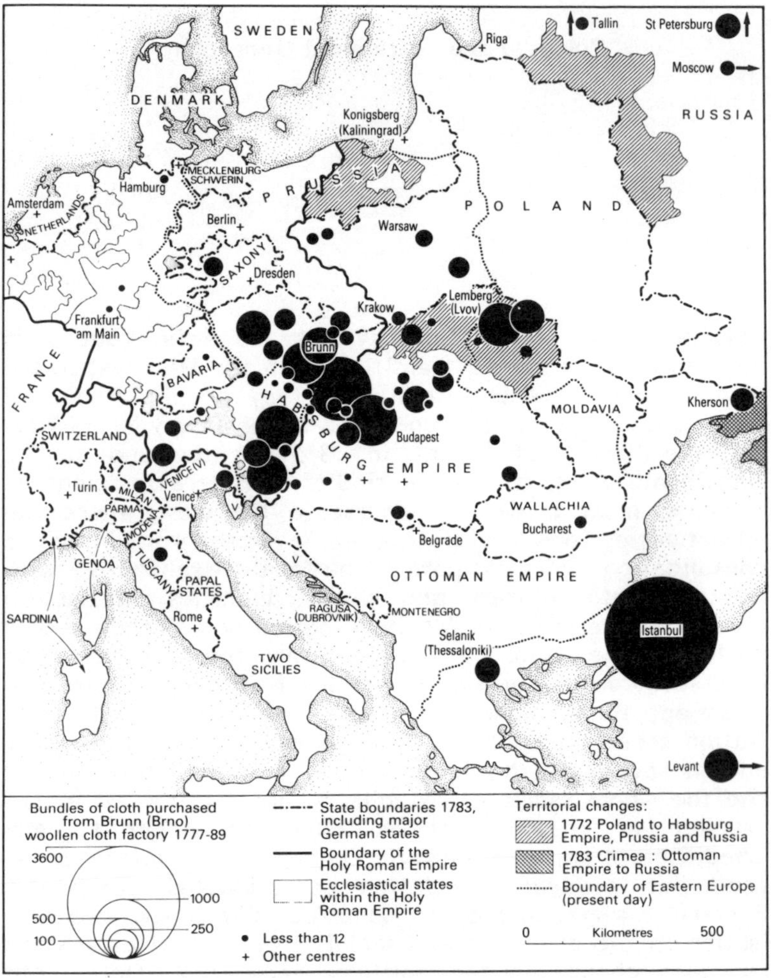

Note: 345 bundles of cloth were sold in the Levant and 260 in parts of the Russian Empire not shown on the map.

Source: Historical atlases; H. Freudenberger 1977.

the Holy Roman Emperor, resting on custom and tradition, expressed the spirit of the Middle Ages. In the aftermath of the Thirty Years War Germany was more divided politically that at any other time and there was little prospect of any form of union to replace the Landeshoheit (territorial supremacy) of the emperor whose authority could now be enjoyed only by prestige.[3] The existence of some 360 'states', with great differences in their internal consitutions, ensured that foreign pressures would be very influential in political and cultural life. France was in a powerful position at the beginning of the century but Russian influence steadily increased after the occupation of Mecklenburg in 1716. And the involvement of certain rulers with foreign thrones (like the Elector of Saxony who was chosen as King of Poland in 1697) strengthened the external dimension in German affairs. It was against this unpromising background that one of the three large eastern states (Brandenburg-Prussia) was able to eclipse her rivals (Mecklenburg-Schwerin and Saxony) and gain great power status.

The achievement cannot be related simply to position and resources, however significant these may have been. Rather it is necessary to consider the ideas behind the important actions that were taken. And this can perhaps be done most convincingly through the study of Frederick the Great. He made the most important contribution and despite the progress made by his predecessors Prussia would not have achieved greatness if Frederick had ruled in his father's image. Moreover as a scholar and writer Frederick the Great provides an ample testament. There is enthusiasm for the triumph of enlightenment following the work of French writers like Voltaire, chosen by Frederick 'not only as his stylistic model but also as his personal teacher and helper'.[4] But enlightenment is tied closely with furtherance of the German cause, by realism rather than emotion. Germany had been held back and it was now necessary to emulate the nations of Western Europe. Frederick saw clearly that success could only come through removal of the constraints that had limited a ruler's actions under the feudal system: French traditions of monarchical absolutism would have to be pushed to their logical conclusion. Hence the importance of a standing army and a disciplined bureaucracy to banish any lingering fear of a rebellious nobility.

But internal reorganisation had to be combined with territorial expansion and so the principle of aggrandisement had to be the fundamental law of every government. Operation of such a principle however meant that borrowings from the intellectual fashions of the day had to be blended by a pragmatism derived from personal experiences. If the monarchy was to retain authority in an intellectual climate it had to prove itself by way of supreme achievements in politics and war. Frederick was therefore driven to take great risks and moral laws were broken when he believed that such action was in the interest of the state. And thus a blend of philosophy and pragmatism, in the hands of a ruler with great ability and ambition, must be given recognition in considering the genesis of the modern nation state. Potential for growth could not be manufactured but it required recognition and a strategy to realise what seemed possible. Federick's contribution was all the more significant because it set a standard for Eastern Europe. Prussia inevitably aroused the lasting emnity of the Habsburgs through the seizure of Silesia in 1742 but this rival dynasty, holding the imperial title through the eighteenth century (apart from 1740-1745) and gaining further power from hereditary lands, was obliged to modernise in the spirit of the enlightenment and so prevent further humiliation. And Russia also took important initiatives under Peter the Great (1689-1725) and Catherine the Great (1762-1796) which had far-reaching implications for Eastern Europe.

Modernisation was not simply a matter of administrative reform. A powerful state required a strong and expanding economic base. So industrial development was inseparable from an effective military establishment. Economic development was necessary to prevent destitution during a period of substantial population increase (in the north especially) and not simply to generate taxable wealth. Governments had to stimulate the economy and those members of the community with wealth and influence had to give their support. Both parties had also to show some readiness (however cautious) to accept social change that would eventually lead to the abolition of serfdom. There seems to have been a significant mercantilist movement developing out of the Peace of Westphalia (1648). In 1653 for example a citizen of Brünn (Brno), P.R. Morgenthaler, sought the emperor's permission to bring in foreign artisans to reduce dependence on imported manufactures. The official response is not known, but interest in industrial development certainly escalated over subsequent decades. Growth was no longer restricted to the towns for the sharp decline in the ranks of urban artisans meant that the rural craftsmen now had a better chance of producing for the market. For a time the important areas of manufacturing remained tied to the long-established organising centres. The weavers in Bohemia produced mainly for Lusatian and Silesian merchants who sent goods to Western Europe. But encouraged by noble capital and enterprise the eighteenth century saw the rise of more independent textile industries covering cotton, lace, linen, silk and wool.

A larger scale of organisation was also evident in the iron industry. Various parts of Eastern Europe were involved, like the Elbingerode area of the Bode valley in the Harz Mountains, the upper Oder basin east of Oppeln (Opole) and Ratibor (Raciborz) and the Czatna, Kamienna and Radomka valleys in the Holy Cross Mountains (Gory Swietokrzyskie). But larger-scale developments occurred in Bohemia for in the 1690s a blast furnace was built in the Ore Mountains at Rothenhaus (Cerveny Hradek), by an entrepreneur named A. Mayer, apparently as a response to poor timber prices which suggested supply of wood to local industries instead.[5] The works quickly passed into the hands of the estate owner Count F.M.H. von Harras and, despite the disadvantage of a remote location, the complex of charcoal furnaces (Gabrielahütte, Kallich and Natschung) survived well into the nineteenth century. It stands comparison with other durable projects such as those west of Prague on Prince Furstenberg's Pürglitz (Krivoklat) estate and at Zbirow (Zbiroh), which were modernised by the German capitalist B.H. Strousberg in the 1870s. In Silesia on the other hand the state played a very important role in the growth of mining and metallurgy which not only bolstered the Prussian economy but provided a major industrial complex in a strategically-sensitive area.

The states and regions that did not develop were increasingly perceived as backward in the eyes of modernisers who were able to justify intervention against traditionally-minded governments as a latter-day crusade or civilising mission. In Poland the chaotic conditions, arising in no small measure from external pressures to undermine the state, led to a surprising level of European acquiescence in the partitions of the late eighteenth century.[6] But the supreme case of arrogant dismissal of the values of a materially-backward society concerns the Ottoman Empire in which western scholars have only recently begun to take a dispassionate interest. 'Throughout the eighteenth century

Moslem economies were everywhere shrinking under European pressure'.[7] There were attempts made to copy Western European achievements in the economic and military fields but without any powerful disposition to accept radical change. Foreign craftsmen and technicians were unable to accomplish the innovations for which the western, and especially British, environment was conducive. The Ottoman Empire was now seen as backward and her increasing dependence on the rest of Europe was accepted as a political fact by European statesmen. By the beginning of the nineteenth century the Ottoman government could defeat neither foreign armies nor rebellious Muslim notables and conditions were becoming increasingly favourable for Christian uprising.

The British traveller in the Balkans, moving from the most developed to the least developed part of the continent, 'met precisely the political conditions which he had learnt to abhor: irresponsible despotic government, economic anarchy and religious intolerance'.[8] His reports were to colour western perceptions of the Ottoman Empire during the eighteenth and nineteenth centuries as a backward, corrupt and even barbarous state. Against the beauties of Balkan scenery the settlements were squalid and subject to serious health hazards: bubonic plague menaced the Ottoman lands throughout the period and the situation was particularly bad for children. Although the distant prospect of trees and gardens was not unpleasant Ottoman cities were seen as dirty, congested and primitive in comparison with those of the west. For example Robert Stockdale, a wealthy young Englishman who decided to travel overland to the Ottoman Empire in 1793, described the thoroughly oriental atmosphere of Bucharest.[9] He was struck by 'those greasy cook shops that abound in every town in Turkey and remind you of the tales in the Arabian Knights entertainments'; also by the wretched condition of the buildings and streets, the latter laid with 'thick loose planks close to one another ... often out of place and certainly very dangerous for horses'.[10] Of course any assessment of the Ottoman Empire must take into account the highly peripheral position in relation to the West European market. As previously noted, there was a reorganisation of landholding (involving the replacement of the timar with the ciftlik) which may be related in part to participation in world trade during this period, with production from fertile areas like the Maritsa valley geared to meet foreign demand. But Ottoman agriculture was bound to be more extensive than in the west, for heavy inputs of labour and capital could not be justified economically if products were to be competitively priced in distant markets. Even so transport costs had to be kept to a minimum and hence Moldavian cattle were driven in herds to Vienna and Frankfurt.[11]

THEMES IN POLITICAL GEOGRAPHY: THE GROWTH OF BRANDENBURG-PRUSSIA

The outstanding development in eighteenth century Germany can hardly be other than 'the success of Brandenburg-Prussia in raising herself to the status of a great power'.[12] Despite initial territorial fragmentation Prussia was able to consolidate its position controlling the great rivers of the North European Plain.[13] Its position across the routeways south from the Baltic guaranteed devastation in the Thirty Years War but despite great losses of population and production territorial gains were made in eastern Pomerania, unfortunately not then including the estuary of the Oder and the port of Stettin (Szczecin), in the Elbe Valley where the lands of the Archbishop of Magdeburg and Bishop of Halberstadt were annexed and at Cammin overlooking Wollin (Wolin) island. The state possessed considerable areas of uncultivated land, giving scope for an increase in population through internal colonisation. The Habsburg territories might still comprise the greatest power in the Holy Roman Empire but Brandenburg-Prussia was certainly dominant in the northern part and in 1701 after the War of the Spanish Succession the elector assumed the title of king for those Prussian lands lying outside the empire. The building of a powerful army and an efficient administration really began under the 'Great Elector' Friedrich Wilhelm (Frederick William, 1640-1688).[14] But this work was particularly well consolidated by King Frederick William (1713-1740). He certainly appreciated the importance of an efficient army, though it was mainly by diplomacy that he made further gains; with the Oder ports particularly relevant in the East European context. The acquisition of Pomerania in 1719, through the dismemberment of the Swedish Empire, may seem a distinctly modest gain by an ambitious ruler who worked so hard to build up the power of the state on rather slender economic and demographic foundations, yet a policy of caution and consolidation seemed appropriate at a time when loyalty to the emperor still counted. However relations with the emperor were strained over the Pragmatic Sanction, an important element of European diplomacy in the early eighteenth century: the emperor wanted approval of his plan for the inheritance of his territories and in return for Prussian support the succession to Berg was agreed.

Subsequent resistance to this Hohenzollern inheritance contributed to Friedrich der Grosse's decision (Frederick the Great, 1740-1786) to invade Silesia soon after coming to power.[15] This amounted to a carefully calculated step to boost the power of the state by gaining a valuable province (completing control of the Oder basin) while simultaneously driving a Prussian wedge between the German lands of the Elector of Saxony and his Polish kingdom. He had a fine army and a full treasury behind him, thanks to his father, and his adversary was the as-yet inexperienced Empress Maria Theresa. The inevitable hostility of the Habsburgs meant that initial acceptance of Frederick's gain of Silesia in 1745 was followed up by the emergence of a defensive alliance against further Prussian encroachments in which he enjoyed only the support of Great Britain against France, the Habsburg Empire, Russia and Saxony. Rather than wait to be attacked Frederick took the initiative by invading Saxony in 1756. After desperate struggles and dramatic changes in fortune the Seven Year War brought a return to the status quo ante bellum.[16] But Frederick remained sufficiently aware of the delicacy of his position to ensure that any further annexations were made with the approval of his main rivals. Gains at the expense of Poland in 1772 helped in the process of linking up Silesia with East Prussia and Pomerania and on his death in 1786 Frederick left an inheritance fifty per cent larger in area and one hundred per cent larger in population: only in the west were there still detached lands. Moreover the bulk of the land was now sovereign Prussian territory, lying outside the empire.

On the other hand the centre of gravity shifted eastwards, a trend accentuated by the final partitions of Poland in 1793 and 1795 which involved the middle Vistula lands, along with the cities of Danzig (Gdansk) and Thorn (Torun), and the Germanic character of the country was weakened. The response to this was seen in the settlement of Germans in Polish territory. The problem was modified somewhat by the Napoleonic Wars when losses in 1807 (after the defeat at Jena) were compensated for in 1815 in such a way as to create a more ethnically homogenous state. A

Polish majority however remained in the province of Posen (Poznan) where persistent though largely abortive Germanising efforts were made during the rest of the nineteenth century. One reason for this failure was the great success in building an industrial establishment in the west and the consequent reassessment of the eastern provinces as a relatively backward area. Yet it was this industrial growth which was largely instrumental in promoting Prussia from the rather indifferent position of fifth power in Europe in 1815: one rendered even more challenging by the common frontier shared with three of the leaders (Austria, France and Russia) and exposure to the naval power of the other (UK).

Partition of Poland (Figure 7.2)

The most important territorial change of the period was the disappearance of the Polish-Lithuanian Commonwealth in a series of three partitions, with Prussia and the Habsburg and Russian empires as the beneficiaries.[17] This indicates a dramatic change in the country's fortunes over the century following J. Sobieski's spectacular expedition to save Vienna from Turkish siege in 1683. Yet that remarkable intervention gives a misleading impression of Poland as a cohesive and progressive state, for the Commonwealth's ascendency in Eastern Europe probably ended with the close of the Jagiellonian period. Trials of strength with neighbouring powers, including the Ottoman Empire, Sweden and Russia were not satisfactorily resolved in the seventeenth century because of feeble diplomacy and the failure of the nobility to give full support to the Polish kings. That Poland might suffer the fate of partition was evident in the aggressive plans of Brandenburg-Prussia in 1655-9 when a break-up of Poland was first seriously envisaged. Nevertheless when the throne fell to the Elector of Saxony on the death of Sobieski in 1696 it was by no means inevitable that Poland would founder. The Saxon connection offered a breathing space for recovery, but it was not used to advantage since the opposition of the nobility to any strengthening of royal power compounded the adverse effects of previous interference from the powers to undermine the Wettin dynasty. Political life tended to be dominated by struggles between noble families such as the pro-French Potockis and the (ultimately) pro-Russian Czartoryskis. Public revenue was pathetically small but the

Figure 7.2: The partitions of Poland. Inset: Usurpations by Prussia 1772-1774.

Sources: Historical atlases; J.K. Fedorowicz et al. 1982; J. Topolski 1969 (note 19).

impossibility of defending a vast territory was made more certain by stringent limitations on the size of the army. Allowed to maintain a standing army of no more than 24,000 men after 1717 the Commonwealth was condemned to military weakness. It was the Great Northern War against Sweden, which Poland entered in alliance with Denmark and Russia, that brought the most dramatic shift in relations as Poland failed to achieve gains and Russia emerged to dominate the commonwealth in succession to Sweden.[18] Russian power was seen again in the War of the Polish Succession (1733-5) when the Russian minister brought about the signature of the so-called Treaty of Warsaw between Augustus II and the Polish nobility to impose the Elector of Saxony, Augustus III, in preference to a more popular claimant. During the Seven Years War Poland was 'treated like a wayside inn ..., plagued by frequent requisitions of supplies, troop movements and direct Prusso-Russian hostilities'.[19] Of course Austria and Prussia could not tolerate such a shift in the balance of power in Russia's favour but at the same time they would not countenance territorial gains that would leave the Polish king with increased authority in a smaller estate.

A solution was envisaged through the principle of equivalent aggrandisement for the three powers, leaving Russia with a protectorate over the remainder (though with political arrangements guaranteed by three powers). But for some years the Russians seemed happy to retain Poland as a buffer state which would avoid direct contact betwen powerful rivals while allowing strong Russian influence to penetrate. But during the 1760s there were several hints from Russian statesmen that security considerations now called for territorial changes, with a pretext for intervention provided by allegations of intolerance by the Catholic population of Poland towards the Orthodox and Uniate people. The only formula attractive to the Russians which would respect Poland's territorial integrity was the idea of a northern alliance system, including Britain, Denmark-Norway and Sweden in addition to Poland and Prussia, but this grandiose plan could not succeed because the prospective allies were not prepared to support Russian ambitions in the Balkans. And of course it was the great Russian successes in the Balkans and the consequent danger of a Habsburg-Russian war (into which Prussia would be inevitably drawn) that sealed Poland's fate. Even before the partition process began Prussia's aggressive stance was demonstrated by the establishment of a cordon sanitaire (Pestcordon) between Pomerania and Great Poland, involving some Polish territory. A gentle push was also supplied by Austria through the seizure of Zips (an enclave within the Hungarian frontier) in 1769 and firm proposals emerged through diplomatic contacts between Prussia and Russia in 1770-1.[20] It is evident furthermore that Prussia used the period of uncertainty after the first partition (pending the demarcation of an agreed frontier line) to make encroachments which threatened Gdansk, Poznan and Torun. In the case of Gdansk the city was imperilled by Prussian occupation of the Hel Peninsula and Nowy Port as well as the southern suburbs of Ostrow and Siedlec which were organised into a separate town of Stolzenberg (Chełm). In Great Poland there were no less than six usurpations of the frontier between 1772 and 1776/7 when the Warsaw Conventions achieved a settlement. Despite some Russian support for Poland's case the Prussians were able to retain four-fifths of the additional territory seized south of the Notec, including the towns of Bromberg (Bydgoszcz) and Hohensalza (Inowrocław).[21] This was a prelude to the annexation of Great Poland, achieved through the partition of 1793.

The partitions attracted remarkably little protest, so chaotic had the situation in Poland become. The real tragedy arose when Poland's attempt to recover its independence coincided with hostilities in Europe against revolutionary France, and it was ironically because of the radical threat posed by the Kosciuszko insurrection (1794) that the final round of partition was implemented. The late eighteenth century revival was based on economic success, especially evident in Poznan/Gniezno which comprised the core of Great Poland (Wielkopolska). Local trade was also on the increase with a growth in the number of villages and in the amount of cultivated land, combined with a shift from feudal obligations to money rents. While agricultural surpluses in grain, livestock and wool were drawn into the international trading system they also stimulated local industry and many workshops arose in the Poznan/Gniezno area concerned with textiles and leather, soap and glass. And in turn the growing industrial sector stimulated further agricultural effort. Poznan was also an international trading centre with overland routes from Russia and Lithuania to the west intersecting with those from the Baltic coast leading south to Bohemia, Galicia and Hungary. Poznan was therefore in close touch with all neighbouring cities of comparable rank: sea-born export commodities were despatched to Gdansk and Stettin. An eastward flow of textiles moved through Warsaw and cattle were driven to Breslau (Wrocław) in exchange for Silesian cloth.[22] The first partition gravely affected trade however. It is recorded that the shipping manager of Princess Ludwika Lubormirska had to pay customs duties and tolls to all the occupying powers in 1773 although Gdansk itself remained Polish at that time. For the Prussians were particularly anxious to destroy the trade of Gdansk and used exorbitant customs tariffs to divert Polish trade to Elbing (Elblag), Königsberg (Kaliningrad), Riga and Stettin. Even the option of export via the Black Sea route created by the Treaty of Kuciuk Kainardji was quickly closed by renewed fighting between Russians and Turks. Hence the view of E. Cieslak that Poland's commerce remained 'at the mercy of the Prussians who used every means possible, from high customs duties, administrative hold-ups on the frontier and even open violence to crush Danzig's economy and force the town to yield 'voluntarily' to Prussian domination to exploit further the reduced Polish state'.[23] Nevertheless there was continuing trade with France, exchanging timber and wool for colonial products (indigo, sugar and wine), with the balance favourable to France however.[24]

OTTOMAN EMPIRE

The events in Poland deprived Russia of the option of subjecting the whole country to satellite status. But Russia did nevertheless gain considerable territory and made sure that the Turks would not have any effective outside help in a further war. Soon after the first partition Catherine was able to bring her efforts on the Black Sea to a successful conclusion with peace established in 1774 in the Bulgarian village of Kuciuk Kainardji (near Silistra).[25] However the offering of Poland as a sacrificial lamb to whet the appetities of the stronger powers contributed a force for stability in the Balkans, so that territorially speaking the Ottoman Empire remained remarkably stable during the eighteenth century considering its poor performance over economic growth and social reform. However the rivalries between the great powers forced the Habsburg and Russian empires to deal leniently with the Porte. By the end of the period the net losses in relation to the limits reached in

1574 comprised only Hungary and Transylvania, along with Bessarabia, Bucovina and the adjacent Black Sea coastlands.[26] The economic consequences were hardly devastating, especially considering the ecological crisis in Hungary, but there was a growing military weakness against powerful neighbours who now had forces marshalled on the Danube-Sava and Prut boundaries ready for further intervention. And in both cases migrations of Christians (notably Serbs moving into Pannonia) generated cultural movements which helped to encourage the growth of nationalism in the Balkans. Thus the territorial losses greatly underplay the real loss in Ottoman power and ability to rule. Turkish armies were now on the defensive and the sultan had to rely primarily on the skill of his diplomats.

When the Russians first reached the lower Danube in 1711 they suffered a heavy defeat at the Battle of Stanilesti, whereas the conflict which erupted in 1768 (after a series of Russian provocations) brought Russia sweeping military and naval success enabling the frontier to advance to the Dnieper by 1774, followed in 1783 by the incorporation of the nominally independent state of Crimea. Habsburg invasion of Ottoman territory as far south as Belgrade, Nis and Vidin in 1689 was repulsed by the Turks the following year but the treaty of Karlowitz (Sremski Karlovci) in 1699 brought Ottoman acceptance of the loss of Hungary and Transylvania to the Habsburgs as well as recognition of Venetian conquests in Dalmatia. However the stabilising effect of great power rivalry was evident in 1718 at the Treaty of Passarowitz (Pozarevac) when British intervention protected the Turks from further heavy losses to satisfy Habsburg and Venetian interests. In 1716-8 Prince Eugene had captured Belgrade, Peterwardein (Petrovaradin) and an extensive strip of land on both sides of the Danube as far as the Iron Gates, as well the westernmost part of Wallachia known as Oltenia. But the Ottomans were compensated for this loss by the acquisition of the Morea in 1718. They went on to regain Oltenia and the lands south of the Danube in 1739, thus restricting the Habsburg gains to the southern part of the Pannonian Plain, known as Banat. Only in 1775, with the Ottoman Empire embarrassed by overwhelming Russian pressure, were the Habsburgs able to take more territory as the northernmost part of Moldavia (Bucovina) was ceded by the Porte in recognition of Austrian neutrality.[27] However this transfer (like the annexation of Bessarabia by Russia in 1812) was a violation of the agreements governing Ottoman suzerainty over Moldavia and was a particularly grievous loss since the Suceava area was the core around which the state had first developed. But on the whole the Habsburg Empire was preoccupied during the eighteenth century with the creation and maintenance of stable buffer zones on its periphery and the conquest of new territories was not such a major concern. There was no clear plan of action by the emperor and his ministers to deal with the dangers to security in Bavaria and Italy as well as the Balkans and Silesia: 'rather like actors reading a new script for the first time they simply stumbled through their lines without benefitting from the perspective that comes from familiarity with the plot'.[28]

Nevertheless there was great suffering among the Balkan peoples and P.F. Sugar asserts that 'for all who lived under Ottoman domination the eighteenth was the worst century', as the empire was 'constantly on the defensive and always in search of additional human and material resources to maintain its very existence and to re-establish the authority of the central government in the provinces and dependencies'.[29] Seven wars, each of several years duration (twenty-two in all), between 1710 and 1792 were fought out on the Romanian and Slav lands of the empire. The people suffered loss of life and property and were further demoralised by higher taxes and compulsory food deliveries. With the failure of the Bosnians to respond to the Porte's demands the privileges of even the Muslim population were abrogated, thus fermenting Muslim opposition to Istanbul for the first time.[30] Even when there was no large-scale war the environment remained insecure and local armed conflicts reflected the Ottomans' near inability to maintain minimal law and order. Local powers emerged to fill the vacuum, some of them hereditary dignitaries, ruling princes or pashas appointed by the sultan (like Osman Pasvanoglu of Vidin who carved out a state within a state). Others were leaders of marauding bands who preyed on the peasants with such ruthlessness as to provoke armed popular resistance and so provide a training ground for the leaders of nineteenth century independence wars. Such spontaneous nationalism, not based on any conscious imitation of western values, demonstrated the importance of the eighteenth century for the historical development of the Balkan peoples, reacting to tribulations heaped upon them by a degenerate empire 'to generate meaningful and long-lasting changes on their own'.[31]

Why did the Ottoman growth process go into reverse during the seventeenth and eighteenth centuries? No doubt the end of the expansion phase had some negative effects in that the supply of booty dried up, but the economic future of the state was not based to any significant degree on income of this kind. Reference must be made to the inevitable consequences of having to adapt to fixed frontiers. Land was now distributed 'to serve the ambitions and greed of provincial governors who gave the timars to their friends and clients and frequently to men who could not fulfil the military obligations attached to them'.[32] Other Ottoman institutions deteriorated; even the sultanate which was plagued by personal deficiencies after the reign of Suleiman the Magnificent. There seemed to be a difference in basic concepts between the Ottoman Empire and the west: 'the Ottoman world was rigid while the west was constantly changing and adapting to the socio-economic and political requirements of a steadily expanding world whose centre it became!'[33] But in fact since the empire was economically peripheral participation in the European economy required special arrangements. Thus the ciftlik emerged in the Vidin area out of a locally-perceived scope for a Danube grain trade: local officials seem to have cooperated wishing to invest in property by providing deed-like transfer certificates to secure inheritable estates.

Similar developments occurred on the coastlands of Albania and, increasingly after the opening of the Straits, Bulgaria and Dobrogea, though not until 1858 did the law provide for landownership in the modern capitalist sense. Cultivators were not labourers working under terms dictated by the owner rather than dependents with legal rights under the old timar system. The economic transition was anything but smooth. T. Stoianovich emphasises the acute problem of inflation, associated initially with the impact of American silver on Mediterranean commodity prices. The wages of unskilled labour were gravely depressed while more entrepreneurial skill went into political manoeuvrings to stave off bankruptcy. The government response was a mixed one covering the close scrutiny of the business community and the ad hoc prohibition of certain exotic products, but including 'a relentless drive in the capital against the social group identified by contemporary French observers as the useless and unemployed people', with executions and deportations to subject European lands.[34] Provincial capitals reacted in similar fashion and the net result was increased lawlessness in the countryside. Thus 'the continued abundance of unskilled labour and resultant depression of wages were sufficient conditions to assure the continuance and intensification of many different forms of vagabondage for more than two centuries'.[35]

The rural adventurers it seems made periodic forays to seize land and buildings, offering protection to the peasantry in return for a certain portion of their crops. And so in the more fertile and accessible parts of the Balkans the peasants acquired a second lord who imposed labour services and controlled migration. Christian elements may also have participated in reaction either to the loss of ancient rights or to Muslim brigandage. Hence the society of hajduk bands: Christian brigands who could not find employment in the service of the Ottoman state. Thus the leading rural families had to take security into consideration when building their homes: for example the cula of Wallachia was an eighteenth century domestic citadel of two or three storeys in a style which may have originated in Dalmatia. One well-known example, Maldaresti, stands in hilly country close to the Carpathian edge at Horezu, but there can be no doubt about the vulnerability of another surviving example to Turkish attack, for Cerneti lies on the Topolnita plain close to Drobeta-Turnu Severin and the Turkish garrison on the island of Ada Kaleh. The cula here stands on a hill above the village and faces southwestwards towards the Danube. The entrance door of thick oakwood gave access to a windowless ground floor: a large cylindrical vault with reinforced brickwork and firing slits to meet the needs for ventilation and defence. Upstairs there was more comfortable accommodation although windows were still relatively few in number. Originally there would have been a battlemented look-out but it has been usual to convert this to the characteristic Romanian verandah with Brancovan arches. Interestingly a number of cula owners in Oltenia were prominent in the 1821 revolutionary movement including the leader T. Vladimirescu whose house (evidently used as an armoury in preparation for the rising) was restored in its original form in 1959.

Serbia

Unrest in the Ottoman territories was largely confined to Serbia and it arose in 1804 in the form of a protest against usurpations by the sipahis (estate holders) in the pashalik of

Belgrade. It was hardly a nationalist uprising at this stage: indeed it could be regarded as a loyalist manifestation because the sipahis were really in revolt against the sultan, having killed his appointee as pasha in 1801. The Serbs were successful militarily but failed to extract political concessions from the sultan: they requested the right to choose a chief (knez) to act as an intermediary between the Turkish representative in Belgrade and local leaders and to have this status guaranteed by a foreign power. Possibly inspired by Napoleon's 'Illyrian Idea', backed up by administration, education and public works on the French model, the Serbs maintained their activity. But a Serb national revolution in 1810 foundered on the rocks of conflict between pro-Habsburg and pro-Russian factions. It was not until 1830 that progress was made when, in the aftermath of the revolution in Greece and the Russo-Turkish War of 1827-8, M. Obrenovic was recognised as prince of an autonomous principality. Nevertheless the Serb performance was quite remarkable by general Balkan standards, for the success in expelling Moslem elements and simultaneously resisting Greek culture resulted in a high degree of ethnic-cultural unity. This applied not only in the rural areas but also in the towns, initially deurbanised but later repopulated to provide some of the few uninational towns in nineteenth century Eastern Europe. Thus the national movement could advance without the distraction of minority interests. Greater ethnic and cultural complexity in most other Balkan territories (Bosnia-Hercegovina, Kosovo and Macedonia), arising from the influence of Islam and the penetration of Greek commercial interests, arguably delayed the emergence of strong popular political movements. The Serb success was all the more significant because it established a pattern of national liberation outside the imperial framework. 'It appears possible, though by no means certain, that had Austria acquired Bosnia instead of fragments of more remote Serbian and Romanian territories in the eighteenth century there might have been an opportunity to solve the South Slav problem within the Habsburg boundaries, even to gain the Serbs' support for such a solution prior to their decisive early nineteenth-century risings against the Turks'.[36] But as it was national independence became par for the Balkan course even though some leaders were happy to keep on good terms with the Habsburgs rather than give top priority to the completion of unification. The belated Austro-Hungarian occupation of Bosnia in 1878, followed by annexation in 1908, merely inflamed tension among the South Slavs and placed the provinces in the centre of the World War crisis of 1914.

ROMANIAN PRINCIPALITIES

A prominent feature of eighteenth century government in the Romanian Principalities was the role of the Phanariots in the office of governor (hospodar) in Moldavia and Wallachia in place of native princes. It represents a more direct Ottoman control, although one exerted by Greeks rather than by Turks. This in turn reflects the tremendous influences of the more successful Greek merchants who were able to penetrate the Ottoman administration. During the seventeenth century their commercial role in the Principalities was greatly strengthened and through intermarriage with Romanian families Hellenisation began to permeate the ranks of the aristocracy, introducing them to a foreign life style which took them further from the peasantry. It is a reflection of Ottoman weakness that the Turks could only tighten their grip on the Principalities by using the Phanariots. The option of removing governors at frequent intervals gave the Porte some initiative but at the expense of the peasantry who suffered at the hands of greedy rulers anxious to make immediate personal gains. The situation was one that the Russians could readily exploit. Russian influence increased after 1774 when consuls in Bucharest and Iasi reflected the newly-won right to protect the sultan's Christian subjects. Insistence in 1802 on a seven year term for governors in the Principalities won some Phanariot support for the Russians but it was western culture and western trade that was to dominate during the nineteenth century. The national movement clearly arose through the contact of Romanian intellectuals with Western Europe. Uniate clerics returned from education in the west and began to lay the foundations to a cultural and political programme. The work was extended by laymen with a similar background thus reinforcing the liberal character of the movement. Accommodations with the Hungarians in Transylvania were initially sought and only when attempts at cooperation failed was the pacifist stance modified. Of course the input by western culture was not sufficient to create a movement that became an irresistible political force: considerable interaction with indigenous traditions was necessary to create the more radical movement of 1848 with its demand for the recognition of an autonomous Romanian nation.[37]

The economic importance of the Principalities was enhanced by the difficulties faced by the Porte in holding on to land in southern Russia. So increasing numbers of Greek merchants were sent to Bucharest to collect compulsory deliveries (zaharea) of wheat and livestock. Because shipping through the straits could be strictly controlled (in any case European ships had been banned since 1592) grain from the Principalities could not be syphoned off to deal with shortages in the western Mediterranean. However the lack of commercial outlets (once Ottoman requirements had been met) prompted a large-scale conversion of cereal lands from wheat to maize, a high-yielding crop which was exempt from zaharea: production was for both animal fodder and human food, while vegetables could be planted between the rows. However commercial forces in agriculture were rather slow to appear and it was only towards the end of the eighteenth century that the market economy and the circulation of money began to stimulate landlord demands for higher labour services and rents. Previously conditions for the rumâni in Wallachia and vecini in Moldavia were not unbearable and the agrarian economy was based on livestock rearing rather than cereals: services were moderate while the peasants enjoyed the usufruct of the land they cultivated. An interesting feature of the serf system in the Principalities (arising out of the Ottoman suzerainty) was that the state maintained direct control, both fiscally and judicially, and the serfs' dependence on landlords was only secondary. Nevertheless, this had only limited practical value as there was a strong community of interest between the central authorities and the great landowners. This was evident even in the Phanariot period by princely ownership of estates by marriage or purchase.

POPULATION AND SETTLEMENT

In Poland it has been established that further woodland clearances were made in Great Poland as dispersed settlement was forced on to the lighter soils of the morainic plateaux, while a parallel process was occurring on the marshy lands of the Torun-Eberswalde pradolina where street villages developed through reclamation in the Dutch manner.[38] In Sandomierz a case study highlights the forest as an area of spontaneous peasant settlement, facilitated by long-established grazing rights, the needs of the wood-distillation industry and opportunities for working ores or setting up water-powered mills (Figure 7.3). 'Chaotically scattered small fields and one family homesteads grew quickly' and the exploitative nature of some 'shifting cultivation' is brought out by evidence of abandoned fields.[39] However in many cases the individual homesteads coalesced to form hamlets and even villages, though necessarily with a high irregular morphology. However some planned settlements were established in the late eighteenth century as German migrants built regular street villages with three field systems. These seem to have been the result of development schemes initiated by the estates, as for example at Dzikow between Stalowa Wola and Tarnobrzeg where swamps were drained to make way for new villages. Similar efforts were probably made elsewhere on the North European Plain in response to a growth in population.

The situation was very different in the Balkans where a desire to escape from wars and from burdensome feudal obligations diverted interest from the low ground and prompted considerable peasant colonisation in remote mountainous areas. As well as large-scale war there was a significant increase in banditry which local Muslim rulers could not combat effectively. Some were able to oppose the armed bands of robbers but others fell victim to bribery - one aspect of the corruption which was undermining the whole fabric of the empire. Smal wonder therefore that some areas of the Balkans became virtually uninhabitable and substantial migrations occurred.

Considerable migration was triggered off in the 1790s by waves of banditry initiated by the Pasha of Vidin who seized a chain of settlements along the south bank of the Danube as far as the Ottoman naval base of Ruse. People now fled across the river, to escape violence and the threat of _ciftlik_ obligations, and settled in Bucharest where they provided a supply of labour to Bulgarian cloth merchants who had arrived at an earlier time. These Bulgarian enclaves in Bucharest (and also the Danube port of Giurgiu) were increased by subsequent migrations during the Russo-Turkish wars of 1806-12 and 1828-9. But many people fled to the Habsburg Empire: Romanians to Transylvania and Serbs to Hungary (especially Vojvodina and the town of Novi Sad in the years 1753-1763 especially). In both reception areas much land was already occupied but employment openings were available in commerce as well as agriculture. Serbs

Figure 7.3: Colonisation of Sandomierz Forest (Poland) since the fourteenth century

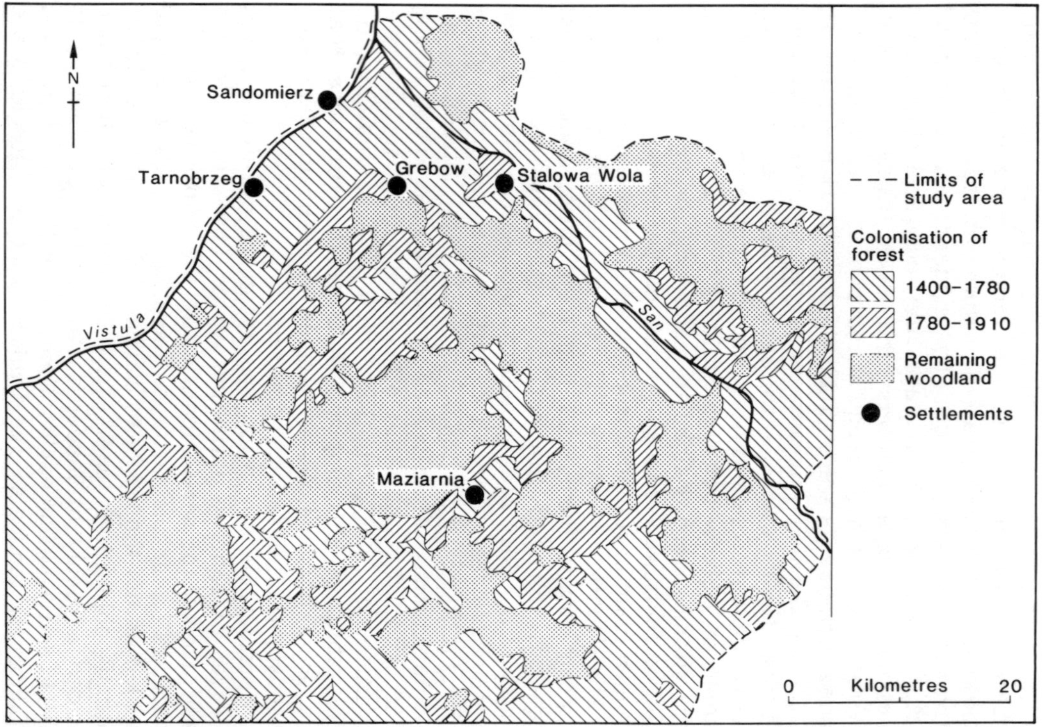

Source: M. Dobrowolska (note 39).

also moved into southern Russia, leaving much of old Serbia open to settlement by Albanian herdsmen and mercenaries, and migration to France for military purposes is thought to have involved about five thousand people (Serbs and others) in the seventeenth and eighteenth centuries.[40]

Movement was not all one way. Some 12,000 dissatisfied Grenzers in Transylvania are thought to have deserted to the Principalities by 1784. The scattered nature of their settlements and the diversionary effect of military duties discouraged crop cultivation and the objections by Hungarian landowners prevented the growth of a timber industry that might have been profitable for the peasantry. Thus it is virtually certain that population was falling in many parts of the Balkans, perhaps to less than a million in Serbia and the two Romanian Principalities. There may have been slightly more people in Bulgaria, where there seems to have been a somewhat higher urban population, but the population of the Ottoman Empire in Europe may have fallen as low as three million (compared with eight million two centuries earlier). Any decrease may be ascribed to 'the increasing disorder and actual warfare that accompanied the Porte's weakening control' but epidemics also took their toll.[41] Üsküb (Skopje) suffered a major collapse of population due to plague as well as war damage in the 1683-1690 period: from an estimated 50,000 the population was reduced to only 6,000 at the turn of the eighteenth century. Demographic upheavals in the towns were marked not only by numerical changes but by shifts in the ethnic balance, for generally speaking Albanians, Greeks, Slavs (both Christian and Muslim) and Vlachs became more prominent vis-à-vis Jews, Ragusans and Turks. Many Jews moved into Hungary in the eighteenth century, finding new commercial opportunities and an escape from Greek intolerance: from an estimated 12,000 in 1735 the Jewish population exploded to a quarter of a million by 1825, development far greater than the estimated 4.5 fold increase for the total population of Hungary and Croatia-Slavonia (from two to nine million).

The situation in the Romanian Principalities has been clarified through a surge of interest in historical demography, although relatively little research has so far been published in English. In Wallachia the population is thought to have risen from 1.08 million in 1740 to 1.92 million in 1831. This net growth of 0.84 million is believed to consist of a growth of 1.01 million (natural increase 0.90 and in-migration 0.11, of which half was from Transylvania and half from regions south of the Danube) against a decline of 0.17 million (premature deaths from epidemics 0.13 and out-migration 0.04). Evidently natural disasters were a serious hazard in view of the loss of life and the migrations that might result from them. Earthquakes occurred in Vrancea at approximately fifty year intervals and are documented from 1411 onwards, while sharp variations in temperature and rainfall have given rise to dismal scenarios involving flood and drought, famine and plague and invasions by locusts and rodents. Considerable evidence is available for the sixteenth century, but even in the present period it is clear that the Romanian lands were acutely embarrassed, with severe drought in 1660, floods in 1668 and 1699 and locust plagues in 1690-1. Under such conditions it is understandable that people might go to such lengths as selling themselves into bondage in order to avoid death. In 1660 people in Buzau sold themselves to Bradu monastery for this reason, with food restricted to tree bark and dried bulrush. For the eighteenth century P. Cernovodeanu has found evidence of drought in 1746-9, 1786 and 1794-5, floods in 1750-1, 1771 and 1783 and locust plagues in 1709, 1718, 1747-8 and 1795-8. These calamities complicated the task of supplying the armed forces and may well have influenced the timing of civil reforms. Thus the easement of feudal obligations by Prince C. Mavrocordat in 1746 (Wallachia) and 1749 (Moldavia) 'was partly due to the untold suffering experienced by the bondsmen mercilessly hit by the unprecedentedly wide and long-lasting natural disasters'.[42]

Resettlement in Pannonia

While potentially valuable grain lands were left empty in the Balkans until the nineteenth century a most important colonisation programme did go ahead on the Pannonian Plain from which the Turks were expelled in 1699 after an occupation of nearly two centuries. There are conflicting views on the circumstances that gave rise to colonisation. T. Stoianovich asserts that 'the wars of the sixteenth and seventeenth centuries had turned the Pannonian Basin into a desolate marshland and depopulated grassland in which lurked numerous robber bands. Malaria kept the remaining inhabitants of the area in ill health and epidemic diseases prevented them from multiplying'.[43] Certainly the plain supported a large population before the Turks arrived and much grain was produced; when the farmers were displaced by the advancing Turks the land rapidly deteriorated. Yet P.F. Sugar believes that it is wrong to blame the Turks for the degradation of the area.[44] The soil was already deteriorating through increasing population pressure, not to mention the struggles between the nobility and the peasantry in the years before the crucial battle of Mohacs in 1527. The farmers were doing their best to adjust to the environmental change as progressive deforestation threatened the steady water supply essential for crop production, but it cannot be assumed that without Turkish intervention a major ecological catastrophe would not have occurred.

Early efforts at colonisation were related to the military frontier (Militärgrenze) with small detachments of soldiers backed up by peasant settlers who were given land on favourable terms in return for military service.[45] The strategy was implemented during the seventeenth century and by the end of it there were frontier administrations based on Esseg (Osijek) for Slavonia and Peterwardein (Petrovaradin) for the Tisza. Forward from these bases were lines of frontier garrisons along the Sava and Maros/Mures respectively. The military border was eventually extended through Transylvania in 1762 and the entire frontier was bolstered by the Sanitätskordon eight years later. However the departure of the Turks also paved the way for colonisation related to economic development as a result of which the population became culturally and ethnically heterogenous. To begin with, tens of thousands of Serbs were settled on Hungary's new southern frontiers at the end of the seventeenth century to prevent further Turkish intrusions, to weaken the homogeneity of the allegedly unreliable Magyars and at the same time to restore the agricultural productivity of the ravaged Hungarian lands'.[46] But the Serbs adhered to the Orthodox Church while Magyars had embraced Protestantism during the Turkish occupation and so in order to counterbalance these influences the Catholic Habsburgs introduced additional settlers from Germany, including some viticultural specialists from the Rhineland areas devastated by the War of the Spanish Succession. This recalled colonisation before the Turkish onslaught when Saxon artisans and merchants had been invited to Hungary's towns and rapidly assumed the ascendancy in financial and commercial matters. 'It was hoped in Vienna that the new Swabian settlers would achieve the same type of leadership in the countryside as the Saxons had attained in the towns, while also maintaining a devoted attachment to their German ideals'.[47] There are also references to settlement by some Catholics from Bulgaria and Romanians appear to have moved down from the Banat Mountains in the later decades of the century. However these initial colonising efforts were not conspicuously successful. Some 25,000 Swabian settlers suffered from the climatic extremes and poor infrastructure (poor roads and inadequate medical facilities) and their efforts to supply the Habsburg army with grain and cultivate hops and tobacco were largely undermined by renewed fighting with the Turks in 1736-9.

The larger-scale colonisation between 1740 and 1770 was better organised. It involved some 43,000 Germans, along with Serbs and Romanians who now adopted the German arable farming system, and generated food for the army as well as surpluses for export to the Ottoman lands. Altogether some eight hundred new German settlements were established up to 1780, with generous support from the Habsburgs through charter privileges, subsidies and exemption from taxes and military service. Government also helped through the provision of building materials, seed and tools. All this may have helped the settlers to reconcile themselves to their new steppeland environment, although one where the black chernozem soils were sometimes interspersed (especially in Banat) by marshland and by sandy deposits. With strong political backing and superior agricultural skills the Swabians were able to compete very effectively for land against the Magyars and Serbs. Indeed two clear stages in the colonisation process may be noted in some individual villages with an initial Serb settlement, and its Orthodox Church, later enlarged by the arrival of Germans and the eventual construction of a Catholic Church which could split the settlement into distinct quarters with an ethnic basis. Generally speaking however the pastoralists (Serbs) gave way before the arable farmers, and rising prosperity was reflected in a growing number of village craftsmen and artisans, although basic services like a water supply and some professional services (for basic education and spiritual needs) were provided at the outset by the government.

The ten year reign of Joseph II (1780-90) witnessed another wave of migration by Protestant Germans, Hungarians and Slovaks. Jews were also encouraged to settle although they went to the towns like Novi Sad, Pancsova (Pancevo), Subotica and Semlin (Zemun). This pattern of migration continued past the turn of the century with strong direction from Budapest which sought to use Hungarians and (less sensibly) Slovaks to boost the Magyar interest in the borderlands. This was necessary because during the eighteenth century the Magyar share of the total population fell from two thirds to a half with particular weakness evident in the towns. The towns in Hungary remained generally small although the great increase in agricultural production did support a network of market centres and the long established administrative-military centres were backed up by local markets which developed in the best-placed villages. The emphasis on cropping extended the range of industries from tanning to milling, oil-pressing and distilling. The hierarchy was then underpinned by modern communications which included the Bega Canal (connecting Temesvar (Timisoara) with the Danube). The few centres with population exceeding 20,000 at the beginning of the nineteenth century had no significant native group amongst the merchants and other members of the middle classes, such as the commercial grip of the Jews and Serbs. However in the countryside it was the Swabian influence that predominated and the ascendancy was maintained by a deep concern for education, motivated partly by national pride and partly by support from Vienna culminating in Joseph II's attempts to use German rather than Latin as Hungary's official language. It was understandable however that such obvious discrimination would help fuel a nationalist reaction which eventually flowered into the Magyar renaissance of the nineteenth century.

And there were other social implications that were evident by the end of the eighteenth century. Once the repopulation was complete and virgin land had been fully occupied the peasants became vulnerable to exploitation by landowners. Official permission for the sale of land in Vojvodina by the end of the century opened the way for Hungarian estate owners and contributed to the growth of a landless Yugoslav peasantry. Even when feudal powers were compromised by the emancipation of the peasantry the lack of non-agricultural employment meant that continued dependence on the lord was inevitable. The lord's interest in maximising food production was increased by the market opportunities provided by the wars of the eighteenth century and increased the resources available for the construction of mansion houses and the enjoyment of more luxurious and sophisticated living. At the time the limited improvements in transport made it impossible to build up a major export business in peacetime and the lack of attention to industrialisation (in contrast to Bohemia and Prussia) greatly limited the employment opportunities which the towns could offer, though part of the blame for this must lie with the Habsburgs' preference for growth in the 'hereditary lands'. 'The worsening of the serfs' condition and the absence of any industrialisation in Hungary made the eighteenth century an era of great social tension and ferocious peasant revolts'.[48] Change was heralded by the return home of young noblemen after exposure to the enlightenment of Vienna, provoking an intellectual resurgence at the end of the century.

Abolition of serfdom

Very important changes began to emerge in agriculture through a modification of feudal relationships to encourage capitalist production in the northwestern parts of the region. The result was the replacement of feudal serfdom with a more effective system of exploitation and some significant moves were made during the eighteenth century. The literature on the Habsburg Empire throws up certain problems of terminology with the term 'hereditary subjection' (Erbuntertänigkeit) appearing rather than 'serfdom' (Leibeigenschaft) but it is clear that at the beginning of the period the peasant was burdened by his feudal obligations, with payments in cash, produce and work (the Robot) required in return for the privilege of using land. The nobility enjoyed ownership over all lands on their domains and could press their claims as local justices, often with the power of life and death, and through influences in provincial government involving the assembly of estates. Despite the presence of imperially-appointed officials in the provinces 'any vigorous centralizing activity seems to have been almost totally lacking' before the reign of Maria Theresa.[49] However the Prussian invasion of Silesia in 1740 created an awareness of the need for social change, for in order to defend the state 'it was necessary to raise the general level of the health and welfare of the population. This meant the improvement both of agricultural methods and of living conditions in rural areas'.[50] Yet despite her sympathy with peasants Maria Theresa could not contemplate the abolition of subjection because it would erode the distinction between lords and subjects, eventually rendering meaningless the status of nobility without which the succession could not be guaranteed. In abolishing labour services on her private estates she therefore acted as a manorial lord and not as sovereign. But the nobles lost their exemption from taxation, limits were placed on patrimonial justice and local governments were introduced to protect the peasantry. Joseph II maintained the momentum with a challenge to the nobility's right of ownership: 'it is not nonsense to believe that the landowners possessed land before subjects existed and that they then, under certain conditions, conferred what was their own upon the latter'.[51]

However it is plainly evident that 'emancipation occurred at a time when the landowning class was firmly in control and it was undertaken in a form which maximised the benefits to the large landowners, subject only to the need for sheer survival of the peasantry as a source of labour for the landlord and of taxation and army recruitment for the state'.[52] The role of the Junkers in the German Empire merits some discussion. In Prussia the Act of 1807, granting freedom of choice of occupation to everyone, followed up prohibition of the landlord practice of Bauernlegen (driving peasants off their lands). But this did not create a free peasantry on the Westphalian model. Peasants were to receive the freehold of their holdings less a proportion of up to one half which was forfeited to the landowner in lieu of payment. Modifications to this system were made in 1816 against the peasant interest which made it even more likely that peasants would finish up with holdings of derisory size and therefore be largely dependent on wage labour on the Junker estates. Removal of feudal obligations could also work against the peasant since the lord's responsibilities were curtailed and privileges such as the use of common land were phased out. Given this context emancipation led to Junker purchase of smallholdings from the more impoverished peasants and completed a massive transfer of land from peasant to landlord management. Such was the basis of the Gutswirtschaft or large estate economy which used cheap land and cheap labour to generate the vast amounts of food which flowed westwards along the canals, and later the railways with hardly a hiccup until the 1870s.

Poland

The position of the peasant serfs in Poland has been discussed by W. Kula who emphasises the very small surpluses which the peasant was able to place on the market as a result of labour obligations to the lord and the need to provide food for his own family.[53] However there was still some modest contact with the towns. The feudal system itself required this because there were still cash rents that had to be paid, even though the amount was fairly nominal. Moreover the prohibition on home distillation meant that peasants would have to find the cash to buy vodka from the lord. There were also occasional taxes or church fees to be met while the purchase of salt (from noblemen who were privileged to receive it gratuitously) was a further call on the peasants' limited cash resources which could only be generated by sale of produce on the market. Then there were certain manufactured goods which could only be bought in the towns like nails and panes of glass: every nail and piece of glass was handled with great care and such goods would comprise an important part of the family inheritance. It seems that the lords tried to intercept the modest amounts of money occasionally spent in the towns by establishing factories on the estates, but they were not usually successful despite access to free labour, raw materials and water power. Rather larger sums of money could be earned by peasants when estates could not use all the serf labour to which they were entitled. There was now greater opportunity to produce crops for the market and use the money in part to meet the demand for labour services now commuted to cash payments. Commutation might also encourage peasants to take up work in the forests and towns to an increasing extent.

The late eighteenth century brought some attempts at a modification of the serf system in Poland. The accession of Stanislaw A. Poniatowski in 1764 marked a revival in political life after a long period of decline brought about by wars and epidemics.[54] It was unfortunate that within a few years the first partition reduced Poland to a relatively small country with few industrial centres. Loss of access to Gdansk led to a decrease in river traffic and brought a change in emphasis from cereal export to the production of alcohol. This may not have been evident everywhere, for there is some evidence to suggest that the high cereal prices at the beginning of the nineteenth century may have been in force over the previous decades as well, but nevertheless there was some moderation of serfdom in the eighteenth century as folwark lands were transferred to peasants against money payments: the peasant gained greater economic independence while the landowner was relieved of many of the hazards of agricultural production. At the same time it is evident that certain estates tried to increase their efficiency through tighter organisation and rationalisation of peasant obligations (as on the Potocki family's Wilanow estates and the Puławy estates of the Czartoryski family). All this could imply a reduced profitability for landlord farming: hence the emphasis on efficient management and transfer of more responsibility for production to the peasants. Some of the leasing may however relate to the colonisation of empty lands. With the further partitioning of Poland responsibility for state legislation over the serf system rested with the occupying powers who did try and defend the peasant population against exploitation by the landlords. Laws were passed in order to allocate land to the peasants, beginning with the Prussian edict of 1811. There is little doubt that the intention of the legislation was to abolish feudal privileges but is not clear just what the effect was on peasant agriculture: how much land did the peasants obtain, how were the landlords indemnified and what differentiation emerged within the peasant class? Until the legislation on this issue was rounded off in 1864 the estates in Russia tended to pursue a policy of replacing serfs with wage-earning farm workers on the landlord farms while remaining land was leased to peasants in units large enough to yield an acceptable rent. Such changes, implemented for example on the Zamoyski estates between 1833 and 1864, were enlightened in some respects but heavily conditioned by self-interest on the part of the landowners in overhauling social relations without affecting the integrity of the estates. In contrast the ukase of 1864 finally recognised the peasants' right to own the land they farmed.

CONCLUSION

The transition examined in this chapter involved change at a remarkably uneven rate in different parts of Europe and even in different parts of Eastern Europe. 'Even by 1648 Europe was more varied in its economy, its political organization and in its ideas than it had been a century earlier. A bourgeois republic and free exchange economy had won their place. The exact sciences were recognisable; and if toleration was still alien to most minds it was at least becoming plain that the new aspects of society had to be lived with'.[55] Yet the generation 1685-1715 has been assessed by another historian as being 'more in tune with seventeenth or even sixteenth century apologists for divine right than with the critical and utilitarian attitudes which were to mark eighteenth century thinking'.[56] But there was bound to be an element of ambivalence in government circles especially in Eastern Europe where economic development had previously rested on an extension rather than a softening of the feudal system. Prussia was the outstanding example of a country growing in strength through an efficient bureaucracy, a powerful army and a more independent judiciary. Economy in expenditure was matched by efforts to exploit every possible source of income: excise duties and government monopolies as well as the development of royal domains, where opportunities for the reclamation of waste land resulted in further rural settlement in Brandenburg and Pomerania.[57] But at the same time it has to be recognised that territorial development through imperialism rather than nationalism made efficient administration absolutely crucial and already the Habsburg Empire (even more so the Ottoman Empire) can be seen struggling to retain control of peripheral territories, with the irony of better administration tending to strengthen national awareness as much as loyalty to the empire. It is interesting to speculate whether or not the nationalist revolt against Habsburg rule in Hungary in 1703, ended by the Peace of Szatmar (Satu Mare) in 1711, had any bearing on subsequent decisions to maintain the social fabric and the agricultural economy while introducing substantial reforms and economic initiatives in the hereditary territories.

Statesmen were not always conditioned to take a dynamic view of society, accepting continual reshaping an inevitable consequence of the search for greater efficiency and justice. While Joseph II of Austria showed extraordinary touches of enlightenment Frederick II of Prussia saw 'society as something given, the work of time and nature, buttressed by a vast structure of rights and privileges and rooted in the essentially conservative idea of natural law'.[58] Manufacturing could not succeed as well as agriculture on a basis of servile labour and the contradictions between economic advance through industrialisation and social development on the basis of aristocratic privilege (which in Hungary amounted to exemption from all taxes in 1731) may be advanced as one of the factors responsible for the increasing backwardness of the region in comparison with Western Europe. Respect for the individual was hardly unlimited in Western Europe but in the east conventions were even less effective in inhibiting excessive cruelty and exploitation, as can be seen in the brutal treatment of feudal dependents in peacetime and savage treatment of enemy troops in war (witnessed by the Russian descent on East Prussia in 1758). However it may be significant that whereas wars in the west were quite localised those in Eastern Europe were much greater in scope: centralisation and the development of diplomatic contacts contributed to a larger scale of warfare with confrontations between rival alliance systems, but there was also a considerable ideological content, continuing the inherited pattern of conflict between alien cultures. Even when the great powers were at peace there was an undercurrent of protracted violent war between people belonging to different civilisations. Wars in Eastern Europe thus mobilised and motivated a higher proportion of the population than in the west, like the Hungarian War for Independence (1703-11, the insurrection of Ferenc II Rakoczi) at the beginning of the century and the Polish War for Independence (1794, the Kosciuszko insurrection) which comes right at the end.[59]

NOTES

1. H. Temperley 1968, 'Frederick the Great and Kaiser Joseph: an episode of war and diplomacy in the eighteenth century' (London: Frank Cass).
2. Ibid. 8.
3. G. Benecke 1978, 'Germany in the Thirty Years War' (London: Arnold); S.H. Steinberg 1966, 'The Thirty Years' War and the conflict for European hegemony 1600-1660' (London: Arnold).
4. G. Ritter 1968, 'Frederick the Great: an historical profile' (London: Eyre & Spottiswoode) 44. See also W. Hubatsch 1973, 'Frederick the Great and Prussian absolutism' (London: Thames & Hudson); H.C. Johnson 1975, 'Frederick the Great and his officials' (New Haven, Conn.: Yale University Press).
5. H. Freudenberger 1969, 'Records of the Bohemian iron industry 1694-1875' Business History Review 43, 381-4. See also R.J. Kerner 1969, 'Bohemia in the eighteenth century' (New York: A.M.S. Press); A. Klima 1957, 'Industrial development in Bohemia 1648-1781' Past and Present 12, 87-99.
6. P.S. Wandycz 1975, 'The lands of partitioned

Poland' (Seattle: University of Washington Press).

7. P. Coles, 1968, *'The Ottoman impact on Europe'* (London: Thames & Hudson) 195.

8. B. Jelavich 1955, 'The British traveller in the Balkans: the abuses of Ottoman administration in the Slavonic provinces' *Slavonic & East European Review* *33*, 396-413 (quote p. 396).

9. E.D. Tappe and T.J. Hope 1980, 'A Cambridge don and his companions in the Balkans 1794' *Revue des Etudes Sudosteuropeennes* *18*, 591-615.

10. Ibid. 598-9.

11. B. McGowan 1981, *'Economic life in the Ottoman Empire: taxation trade and the struggle for land'* (Cambridge: Cambridge University Press).

12. M.S. Anderson 1961, 248. See also T.C.W. Banning 1974, 'The 'German Problem' in the eighteenth century', T.C.W. Banning *'Reform and revolution in Mainz 1743-1803'* (Cambridge: Cambridge University Press); W.G. East 1966, 261-76; C.A. Macartney ed. 1970, *'The Habsburg and Hohenzollern dynasties in the seventeenth and eighteenth centuries'* (London: Macmillan); C.M. Rose 1974, 'Empire and territories at the end of the Old Reich', J.A. Vann and S.W. Brown eds. *'The Old Reich: essays on German political institutions 1495-1806'* (Brussels: Editions de la Librairie Encyclopédique).

13. F.L. Carsten 1954, *'The origins of Prussia'* (Oxford: Clarendon Press); H.W. Koch 1978, *'A history of Prussia'* (London: Longman); J.A.R. Marriott and C. G. Robertson 1915, *'The evolution of Prussia: the making of an empire'* (Oxford: Clarendon Press).

14. F. Schevill 1947, *'The Great Elector'* (Chicago: University of Chicago Press).

15. W. Hubatsch 1975, *'Frederick the Great of Prussia: absolutism and administration'* (London: Thames & Hudson); G. Ritter 1968, *'Frederick the Great: a profile'* (London: Eyre & Spottiswoode); H. Temperley 1968, *'Frederick the Great and Kaiser Joseph: an episode of war and diplomacy in the eighteenth century'* (London: F. Cass).

16. C. Duffy 1982, 'The Seven Years War as a limited war', G.E. Rothenburg *et al.* eds. 67-74.

17. O. Helecki 1978, *'A History of Poland'* (London: Routledge & Kegan Paul); L.R. Lewitter 1958-9, 'The partitions of Poland' *History Today* *8*, 813-20; *9*, 30-9; W.F. Reddaway *et al.* eds. 1941, *'The Cambridge history of Poland 1697-1935'* (Cambridge: Cambridge University Press); J.

Topolski 1972, 'The partitions of Poland in German and Polish historiography' Polish Western Affairs 13, 3-42.

18. L.R. Lewitter 1968, 'Russia Poland and the Baltic 1697-1721' Historical Journal 11, 3-34.

19. J. Topolski 1969, 'The Polish-Prussian frontier during the period of the partition 1772-7' Polish Western Affairs 10, 81-110 (quote p. 83).

20. H.H. Kaplan 1962, 'The first partition of Poland' (New York: Columbia University Press); S.K. Padover 1934-5, 'Prince Kaunitz and the first partition of Poland' Slavonic & East European Review 13, 384-98.

21. J. Topolski 1969 op.cit. (note 19).

22. E. Cieslak 1977, 'Seaborne trade between France and Poland in the eighteenth century' Journal of European Economic History 6, 49-62; K. Kuklinska 1977, 'Commercial expansion in eighteenth century Poland: the case of Poznan' Journal of European Economic History 6, 443-60.

23. E. Cieslak 1977, op.cit. p. 62.

24. Ibid.

25. J.A. Gierowski 1982, 'The international position of Poland in the seventeenth and eighteenth centuries', J.K. Fedorowicz et al. eds. 218-38; L.R. Lewitter 1948-9, 'Poland the Ukraine and Russia in the seventeenth century' Slavonic & East European Review 27, 157-71; 414-29; R.H. Lord 1969, 'The second partition of Poland: a study in diplomatic history' (New York: Ams Press); D. Stone 1976, 'Polish politics and national reform 1775-1788' (Boulder, Col.: East European Monographs).

26. M.S. Anderson 1966, 'The Eastern Question 1774-1923' (London: Macmillan); L. Cassels 1966, 'The struggle for the Ottoman Empire 1717-1740' (London: John Murray); S.J. Shaw 1971, 'Between old and new: the Ottoman Empire under Sultan Selim III 1789-1807' (Cambridge, Mass.: Harvard University Press); A. Sorel 1898, 'The Eastern Question in the eighteenth century' (London: Methuen).

27. G.F. Jewsbury 1976, 'The Russian annexation of Bessarabia 1774-1828' (Boulder, Col.: East European Monographs); A. Lobanov-Rostovsky 1947, 'Russia and Europe 1789-1825' (Durham, N.C.: Duke University). W.H. McNeill 1964, 'Europe's steppe frontier 1500-1800' (Chicago: University of Chicago Press); B.H. Sumner 1949, 'Peter the Great and the Ottoman Empire' (Oxford: Blackwell).

28. C.W. Ingrao 1982, 'Habsburg strategy and geopolitics during the eighteenth century', G.F. Rothenburg et al. eds. 49-66 (quote p. 63). See also R.J.W. Evans 1979, 'The

making of the Habsburg monarchy 1550-1700: an interpretation' (Oxford: Clarendon Press); C.W. Ingrao 1979, 'In quest and crisis: Emperor Joseph I and the Habsburg monarchy' (West Lafayette, Ind.: Purdue); R.A. Kann 1974, 'A history of the Habsburg Empire 1526-1918' (Berkeley: University of California Press); K.A. Roider 1972, 'The reluctant ally: Austria's policy in the Austro-Turkish War 1737-1739' (Baton Rouge: Louisiana State University Press); K.A. Roider 1982, 'Austria's Eastern Question 1700-1900' (Princeton, N.J.: Princeton University Press).

29. P.F. Sugar 1982, 'Unity and diversity in the lands of southeastern Europe in the eighteenth century', G.E. Rothenburg et al. eds. 255-70 (quote p. 255).

30. A. Suceska 1982, 'The eighteenth century Austro-Ottoman wars' economic impact on the population of Bosnia', G.E. Rothenburg et al. eds. 339-50.

31. P.F. Sugar 1982, op.cit. (note 29) 262. See also B. Cvetkova 1982, 'The Bulgarian haiduk movement in the fifteenth-eighteenth centuries', G.E. Rothenburg et al. eds. 310-38.

32. H.G. Koenigsberger and G.L. Mosse 1968, 'Europe in the sixteenth century' (London: Longman) 195. See also T. Stoianovich 1962, 'Factors in the decline of Ottoman society in the Balkans' Slavic Review 21, 623-32.

33. P.F. Sugar 1977, 193.

34. T. Stoianovich 1962, op.cit. 628.

35. Ibid. 629.

36. R.A. Kann 1982, 'Reflections on the causes of eighteenth century warfare in Europe', G.E. Rothenburg et al. eds. 29-45 (quote p. 41).

37. K. Hitchins 1969, 'The Rumanian national movement in Transylvania 1780-1849' (Cambridge, Mass: Harvard University Press). See also I. Ceausescu 1982, 'Military aspects of the national struggle of the Rumanian Principalities in the eighteenth century', G.E. Rothenburg et al. eds. 371-99; P.F. Sugar 1975, 'The enlightenment in the Balkans: some basic considerations' East European Quarterly 4, 499-507.

38. S. Zajchowska 1978, 'Change in the forest area and the development of settlement in Great Poland' Geographia Polonica 38, 289-93.

39. M. Dobrowolska 1978, 'Changes in the agrarian structure and the villages of southern Poland' Geographia Polonica 38, 41-8 (quote p. 43).

40. A. Corvisier 1982, 'Military emigration from

Central and Eastern Europe to France in the seventeenth and eighteenth century' G.E. Rothenburg et al. eds. 513-45.

41. T. Stoianovich 1960, 248-54. See also J.R. Lampe 1975, 'Varieties of unsuccessful industrialisation: the Balkan states before 1914' Journal of Economic History 35, 56-85.

42. P. Cernavodeanu 1980, 'Environment and history: some considerations on the impact of natural disasters on the socio-economic and demographic situation of the Romanian countries' Nouvelles etudes d'histoire 6, 297-307. See also M. Flinn 1983, 'The European demographic system' (Brighton: Harvester Press); E.L. Jones 1981, 'The European miracle' (Cambridge: Cambridge University Press).

43. T. Stoianovich 1960, 264.

44. P.F. Sugar 1977, 88.

45. G.E. Rothenburg 1960, 'The Austria military border in Croatia 1522-1747' (Urbana: University of Illinois Press); G.E. Rothenburg 1966, 'The military border in Croatia 1740-1881' (Chicago: University of Chicago Press).

46. T. Spira 1977, 1-2.

47. Ibid. 2.

48. B.K. Kiraly 1969, 'Hungary in the late eighteenth century: the decline of enlightened despotism' (New York: Columbia University Press) 10.

49. E.M. Link 1949, 'The emancipation of the Austrian peasant 1740-1798' (New York: Columbia University Press) 19.

50. Ibid. 31.

51. Ibid. 16.

52. S. Pollard 1981, 193.

53. W. Kula 1980, 'Money and serfs in eighteenth century Poland', E.J. Hobsbawm et al. 'Peasants in history' (Calcutta: Oxford University Press) 30-41.

54. J. Leskiewicz 1972, 'Land reforms in Poland 1764-1870' Journal of European History 1, 435-48.

55. C. Wilson 1976, 'The transformation of Europe' (London: Weidenfeld & Nicholson) xi.

56. M.S. Anderson 1961, 2-3. See also S. Andrews 1965, 'Eighteenth century Europe: the 1680s to 1815' (London: Longman); H. Braunschweig 1974, 'Enlightenment and romanticism in eighteenth century Prussia' (Chicago: University of Chicago Press); W. Doyle 1978, 'The old European order 1660-1800' (Oxford: Oxford University Press); D. Gerhard 1981, 'Old Europe: a study in continuity 1000-1800' (London: Academic Press); G. Rudé 1972, 'Europe in the eighteenth century: aristocracy and the bourgeois

challenge' (London: Weidenfeld & Nicholson).

57. R.A. Dorwart 1953, 'The administrative reforms of Frederick William I of Prussia' (Cambridge, Mass.: Harvard University Press); R.A. Dorwart 1971, 'The Prussian welfare state before 1740' (Cambridge, Mass.: Harvard University Press).

58. M.S. Anderson 1961, 32.

59. B.K. Kiraly 1982, 'War and society in Western and East-Central Europe in the pre-revolutionary eighteenth century', G.E. Rothenburg et al. eds. 1-25.

8

Industrial Geography and Trade

Complementing the divergent trends over the reform of government and social relations was the varied East European experience with industrialisation. Industry may have been encouraged by some governments as a means to an end but it developed a momentum of its own, supporting a significant capitalist class and contributing to the momentum for further social reform in the nineteenth century. This served to widen the gap between the northern lands of Eastern Europe and the Ottoman provinces where the prevailing Muslim values inhibited economic growth. In this review the close relations between governments and capitalists are brought out through case studies which throw considerable light on the outlook of the progressively-minded elite.

INDUSTRIALISATION IN A CHANGING ENVIRONMENT

The first initiatives were taken with the feudal system still in force but industrial growth was by no means irreconcilable with serfdom and 'estates worked by unfree labour were quite capable of switching from static self-supply to an expanding external market'.[1] But it is no coincidence that landlord encouragement of industry was most common in relatively infertile agricultural regions. A self-reinforcing growth process set in as cheap yet competent labour attracted more orders and in turn stimulated a growth in population through earlier marriages. The growth in labour supply kept costs low, especially in view of the low opportunity cost for labour available only during periods when agriculture made few demands. But family income rose sufficiently to justify higher rents and ensure the landowners' interest in encouraging industry further. It has also been argued that the system was socially satisfying through closer family life: 'where some agriculture still survived the agrarian rhythm combined with an indoor occupation seemed in a European climate to satisfy a deep human need better than full specialisation'.[2] There could however be heavier burdens if labour services had to be performed in industry as well as agriculture. Work with the peasants' own draught animals, in transport of raw materials or in wood cutting, was a common imposition. And it was much resented where there was a tradition of free peasant mineral working over which the landlords had gradually been able to impose control. Further difficulty might arise where access to firewood was restricted by a larger scale of charcoal smelting or where crop land was reduced through land endowments to key workers from outside. On the other hand where feudal dues were commuted to cash payments, as was often the case in the textile industry, a worker might start 'putting out' and thereby graduate to an entrepreneurial level of activity. Some putting out-systems became quite vast and must have involved a complex network of agencies. Altogether it is calculated that there were 0.23 million textile workers in Bohemia in 1780 rising to 0.53 million in 1799 (with another 0.15 million in Moravia and Czech Silesia).[3]

There could be no guarantee that this proto-industrialisation would progress through to modern factory industry without any relapse back to an agricultural system, with rural crafts geared only to the immediate needs of the community and family. But in Prussia and parts of the Habsburg Empire effective organisation through a well-developed market system, inter-connected by relatively efficient communications, underpinned a gradual shift towards the factory system as mechanisation made it feasible for the organisers to bring their workers together at central points and further weaken the ties with the land. And the tempo of industrial development undoubtedly helped to bring out further social change and allow individuals to move around freely rather than remain obliged to work for one of the major putting-out organisations. But it was not inevitable that these changes would occur and it seems important to recognise the role of government in stimulating industrial growth and related social reform. For contractual relations between entrepreneurs and workers were in fact demanded by the Habsburg authorities in 1775 in order to increase efficiency and break down the huge putting-out organisations which were bolstered by servile labour.

It is probable that the eighteenth century saw, for the first time, the establishment of a government body to carry out an exercise of central planning for industrial development. A Commercial Board (Kommerzien Direktorium) functioned in Vienna from 1746 until 1772, in conjunction with various regional equivalents, to bring about a rapid growth in manufacturing.[4] Despite some political weakness in relation to other branches of government it was able to overcome bureaucratic tendencies and treasury scepticism and preside over a short-lived industrial spurt which created momentum for further progress under a less protective regime. But it is important to stress that this was not an exercise in industrialisation for its own sake. The loss of Silesia led Maria Theresa to deplore the parochial attitudes of the aristocracy and to overcome the lack of coherence through a more centralised political system that would provide policies and financial resources appropriate to great power status. Industrialisation played a part in the new order through the expectation of taxable wealth that would help to sustain the armed forces and government machine. The middle class was not seen as a threat and the nobility did not apparently see any risk of loss of status through involvement in commerce and industry. However the prospect of a proletariat bearing revolutionary ideas was viewed with some dismay and this may have contributed to the Board's demise in 1772, although development continued on a laissez-faire basis. There appears to have been an underlying assumption that the Board would concentrate on the hereditary lands of the empire: Austria, Bohemia and Moravia. Hungary was regarded as a source of raw materials and a market for the manufacturers in adjacent provinces.

The overall achievement was considerable with the development measures followed up by creation of a free trade area within the empire covering Austria in 1775 and then extending to Galicia in 1784, Hungary in 1851 (though internally unified in 1784) and Dalmatia in 1880. This record compares favourably with Prussia where the removal of internal barriers began only in 1818. Under the enlightened despotism of Joseph II serfdom was harmonised with labour mobility and protection was given to both native and foreign entrepreneurs who would establish manufactures. A start was made on technical education (note the technical school in Prague founded in 1806) and the protection afforded under the continental system (which gave rise to the first mechanised spinning mill in Bohemia in 1797) picked up again after 1815 to allow further factory development when British competition would otherwise have been overwhelming. Unfortunately the value of the early start was lost in the nineteenth century partly through the centrifugal tendencies introduced by nationalist disputes and partly by the superior potential of Germany unlocked by the process of unification there. The result was that while the rise of Germany became closely linked with industrial growth the preservation of the Habsburg Monarchy could not be reconciled with a centralised programme.

Bohemia and Moravia

A. Klima has stressed the generally low levels of soil fertility revealed by the Theresian land survey of the mid-eighteenth century. In the least promising areas there were relatively large numbers of smallholders and landless peasants: cottage owners who, the survey declared, 'have nothing except an isolated dwelling and earn a miserable living for themselves and their children by weaving, spinning and handicrafts'.[5] This seems to bear out the contention that rural domestic industry was quite likely to emerge in areas with poor soils. But in these mountainous parts of Bohemia there was a further stimulus arising from the cultivation of a suitable strain of flax. So, where tradition demanded that there be only a single heir to each agricultural holding, work in the textile industry meant that a growing landless population could support itself. Indeed the population density in the mountains became greater than that in the more fertile agricultural areas: in 1789 there were 82 people per square kilometre in the linen district of northern Bohemia but only 56 in the most fertile parts of the province. The feudal lords controlled the industry because of the key role played by the yarn collectors who were serfs paying substantial fees for licences to engage in the trade: 'taking the spinners' yarn, sorting it according to quality and carrying it to the weekly markets of nearby towns for sale to weavers'.[6] Such people had a curious status, employing poorer villagers to work for them and even perform their labour services, yet unable to take decisions affecting their own children. One civil servant in 1766 saw the likely contradiction between feudalism and industrial development and suggested that traders should be able to purchase their freedom because 'as free men they might have more encouragement to expand their trade'.[7] The spinners werer completely dependent on the collectors because the latter alone remained in touch with the market: not only would the journey to market involve an excessive amount of time in relation to the value of their production but weavers might be compelled by decree to buy yarn only from authorised yarn collectors. But of course the ultimate control lay in the hands of the great merchant houses, like those in Nürnberg, whose representatives travelled around on horseback checking finished linens and also examining cloth on the loom.

The external influence is also seen in the activities of merchants from Greiffenberg (Gryfow) in Silesia who purchased both linen and yarn in northern Bohemia and (in the case of the woollen industry) in the state-owned company based in Linz in Upper Austria with which nearly 17,000 Bohemians were associated in 1786. Clearly not all the yarn produced was worked up into cloth in Bohemia: further evidence is supplied by the spinning business at Neuhaus (Jindrichuv Hradec), established in 1765, which sold its woollen yarn to a stocking factory in Austria. A more advanced form of organisation can be seen in a combination of factory and domestic work. An Englishman, R. Allason, established a factory for dressing, dyeing and finishing at Rumburg (Rumburk) to 1713 in connection with home-based linen spinners and weavers. This seems to have been an important development for it reduced the earlier emphasis on supplying yarn and unfinished cloth to weavers or finishers outside the province and gave rise to an autonomous industry. Similar establishments have been noted for linen at Böhmisch Leipa (Ceska Lipa) and woollen at Ossegg (Osek), the latter belonging to a Cistercian monastery, but the linen mill at Oberleutensdorf (Horni Litvinov), opened in 1715, had spinners working within the factory as well as others busy at home. It seems that the idea was to improve standards through close supervision of spinners in the mill who would then resume work at home, for we find Count E.J. Kinsky adopting the same approach as his Sloup (Chribska) estate through spinning schools established in each village within his domain in 1756. 'His organisation in textile and glass production meant that almost every house in his domain formed an extension of his manufacturing establishment'.[8] Cloth was taken to Kinsky's linen and cotton print works set up in 1759. Still larger businesses were built up later in the century by J.J. Leitenberger and J.M. Schmidt, both of whom employed more than 5,000 outworkers. The evolution process can be seen working through Kinsky's influence over a fellow aristocrat Count Bolza whose mill was established around 1760 and eventually became part of the Leitenberger empire.

Count J.J. Waldstein's Oberleutensdorf venture has been placed carefully in perspective by H. Freudenberger who argues that the Count was not motivated primarily by financial gain (for he was already wealthy) but by a sense of obligation to better the lot of his dependents: 'Christianity and nobility demanded that Waldstein feel a sense of responsibility towards his subjects'.[9] Nevertheless the venture involved so many problems that the noble entrepreneur must almost certainly have become personally interested in industrial development for its own sake. The many plates which have survived (and are used as illustrations in Freudenberger's monograph) demonstrate the founder's determination to build a model enterprise and thereby to transform the economic fortunes of a small poverty-stricken village which had no significant locational attributes other than association with noble ambition. He had to find capable managers, purchase machinery, ensure that labour was adequately skilled and seek out markets, all of which involved great difficulty. Equipment for the Dutch or Flemish method of wool production was secured and skilled workers were brought in. Some guild masters from Böhmisch Leipa were also recruited, although the training of local people should have been eased by the industrial traditions of the area: since the late seventeenth century the nearby Cistercian monastery of Ossegg had given work to some of Waldstein's peasants through domestic manufacture of stockings and the spinning of yarn for Silesian merchants was a commonplace. Marketing was complicated by initial prejudice in the empire against home production, but while Oberleutensdorf cloth could equal the English or Flemish product it gradually built up a reputation. Agents went to the principal fairs and goods were consigned regularly to merchants in large cities like Prague (where a warehouse was acquired) and Vienna. However Waldstein's cloth was quite costly and after working up to thirty looms by 1730 production hardly increased for the rest of the century and remained fairly constant at 1,000 pieces per annum.

Another problem related to the imposition of an industrial system within a traditional feudal environment with little non-agricultural activity apart from charcoal-burning and textile production which fitted in well with the basic work of the manor. The factory required a full-time labour force that could not be subjected to the agricultural Robot and evidence suggests that, while there may have been some element of coercion, the workers at the factory were paid in cash rather than kind. There must inevitably have been difficulties for the manorial bureaucracy in coming to terms with the new situation as the factory took away part of the servile labour it had previously controlled while simultaneously creating demand for food, timber and firewood. This is to say nothing of the disturbance created by the appearance of foreign workers and other strangers who were outside the jurisdiction of the manorial officials. It is hardly surprising therefore that the Oberleutensdorf experiment was not copied on any significant scale: its profitability can hardly have been great enough to justify the financial risks and the social upheavals. But although there was some assistance from the government under the prevailing mercantilist policy (for example an interest-free loan of 4000 fl. in 1754 to finance production of a new type of cloth in demand in the Ottoman Empire) the mill did survive for many years. The founder died in 1730 but the family actively participated in the enterprise until 1819 when the Waldsteins became silent partners and active management passed into the hands of commoners. In 1859 an order of Catholic nuns purchased the works outright but, for reasons not yet known, working ceased by 1867. So despite lack of immediate imitation the factory did demonstrate that a large centrally-administered industrial enterprise was feasible in the empire.

The fine cloth factory of Brünn

A further remarkable example, and one which provides the additional perspective of contrast between rural and urban location, is the fine cloth factory established in Brünn (Brno) in 1764. Although there was no particularly strong textile tradition in the town, Iglau (Jihlava) being more significant in this respect, there does seem to have been a receptive attitude to industry which may relate back to the favourable treatment of the town by the Habsburg government in recognition of the resistance offered to the Swedish invasion in 1645. Whereas most towns in the empire suffered greatly through the Counter-Reformation Brünn was allowed to exploit its advantages of proximity to Vienna and accessible situation on the route from the Danube through the Moravian Gate to Silesia. H. Freudenberger reports that 'the number of government officials, of resident noblemen with their retinues and of persons coming to transact business with state agencies thus became greater during the remainder of the seventeenth and eighteenth centuries'.[10] A precedent may have been provided by the woollen cloth and stocking factory opened in 1701 on the nearby estate of Austerlitz (Slavkov) by Count A.D. Kaunitz; although not very successful it did nevertheless continue for twelve years and developed some links with Brünn as the nearest market centre, providing thereby some experience in cloth manufacture for an area which was well-farmed and could generate considerable amounts of raw material. Thus in the context of Habsburg mercantilism, with industrial development required to promote general welfare, it is reasonable to expect that the Commercial Council (Commerzien-Concesse) for Moravia, based in Brünn would have cooperated fully with the central Court Commercial Council (Hofkommerzienrat) to get a woollen industry established.

Yet the enterprise that was successfully established in Brünn had previously tried two other locations. The story begins in 1749 when craftsmen were brought from Verviers to Iglau to teach the local master-weavers how to manufacture fine cloth. However guildsmen opposed the Flemish innovations and the conflict provoked by successful competitors in an area of high unemployment was increased by the arrogance of the Flemish director. But rather than abandon the experiment Maria Theresa decided to resettle the Flemings in less antagonistic surroundings, since they had managed to produce good cloth from native wool. A survey of imperial estates was undertaken on the presumption that 'in a perverse way the introduction of a new technology might be easier with the untutored peasants of the Bohemian manor'.[11] The selection of the village of Kladrau (Kladruby) on the Pardubitz (Pardubice) estate in preference to other settlements on the Brandeis (Brandys), Kolin (Kolin), Pardubitz and Podiebrad (Podebrady) properties seemed to have been determined largely by the water supply and the ease of laying out a small industrial complex. There was some coarse spinning in the area by people working on their own account, wool could be obtained from the surrounding area (including the imperial estates) and there was empty accommodation where the foreigners could be housed. However the water proved unsuitable for rinsing and dyeing and the local labour was found unsatisfactory for fine woollens: the peasant women worked in the fields in the summer and the cracking of the skin on their hands caused serious initial problems when spinning began in the autumn. Marketing also seems to have been insufficiently considered. Another crisis point was reached in 1761 on account of bad management and the frustrations of a suboptimal rural location: 'after more than a decade the fine-woollen mill in Kladrau had succeeded only in swallowing large sums of money, amassing great quantities of goods so poor in quality that they proved to be difficult to sell even under duress, and creating irritations from the lowest manorial official in Pardubitz to the highest ministers and councillors in Vienna whose combined bitterness washed like angry waves at the feet of the empress'.[12] It was at this juncture that the second radical decision was taken to relocate in Brünn, thanks to the interest of a local banker J.A. Kehrnhofer, who was personally interested in establishing a fine woollen industry and was one of several people appointed to investigate the Kladrau factory. The industry experienced further vicissitudes arising from the death of Kehrnhofer in 1765 but new drive was found in J.L. Koffiller, who eventually became the sole proprietor while government support continued with provision of substantial loans, recruitment of skilled labour and changes in tariffs to reduce competition from foreign cloth on the home market. Towards the end of the 1780s the factory was forced to close but the quarter century of activity was long enough to generate momentum. Koffiller did not make profits but within a decade of his demise there were six substantial woollen mills in the town, all of them owned by men who had been trained in the original factory. And there were also further mills which sprang up on the estates in the area, like Krzizanau (Krizanov) in 1794 and Namiest (Namest) in 1795. The example is instructive in many ways. Clearly the importance of government support is underlined as is the need for good management and a local environment conducive to manufacturing. Both rural and urban locations could be successful but the potential of the town was far greater than that of the village and the Brünn case demonstrates the large-scale production and the development of linkages which eventually generated not only a complex of textile industries but an important engineering industry as well. However statistics presented by H. Freudenberger show remarkable progress in the woollen industry throughout Bohemia in the late eighteenth century. This applied to both masters and employees in all the major sectors of production: cloth, stuffs and stockings. Masters were taking on more employees and the total number of participants went up from 6.0 per thousand of the total population in Bohemia and 5.1 in Moravia in 1775 to 9.2 and 9.9 respectively in 1788. The industry was widely distributed but there were strong concentrations in the Iglau and Prerau (Prerov) districts as well as Brünn.[13]

Stimulus to engineering

With a strong textile industry and considerable iron production (for there were 59 furnaces and 179 hammer mills in the Czech Lands in 1798) there was a good basis for machine building. The use of machinery seems to have come first in the cotton trade although it was the last branch of the textile industry to develop, being banned by mercantilist policies supporting industries using domestic raw materials until 1763. In Count Kinsky's time we hear of equipment for textile mills being supplied by Count J.J. Waldstein's iron works at Nizbor. But according to A. Klima the story really began in 1796 when E.E. Leitenberger was able to get hold of skilled workers who had helped with the installation of cotton spinning machines at a factory in Copenhagen. Similar machines were built for a factory at Wernstadt (Vernerice) in Bohemia, the site of one of Leitenberger's manufactories under the putting-out system. Later factories were built by Leitenberger as well as by other entrepreneurs like Hanke at Leibitschgrund (Lochovice) and Tretzer at Rothenhaus, both in the Reichenberg (Liberec) area. In the woollen industry spinning and carding machinery was imported from the Netherlands to the Berger factory in Reichenberg in 1803 but at the same time a machine was built in Brünn (Count Salin's ironworks at Blansko) with the assistance of Irish mechanics who happened to be working in Vienna. The woollen mill of Count Haugwitz at Namiest spawned an engineering business which was among the earliest builders of woollen spinning machinery. Flax spinning machinery was installed at the Klamm mill in 1811, but this initiative did not survive as the firm went out of business in 1815. With the introduction of machinery the interest in steam engines followed: the atmospheric principle was used by Prof. Gerstner of Prague Polytechnic in 1806 but the first steam engine on the Watt principle did not emerge until 1814, built by J. Baildon at the Stiepanau (Stepanov) ironworks (leased by Baildon) for the Wünsch factory in Brünn, Baildon had experience at Carron Ironworks in Scotland and had previously worked on a Silesian coke-smelting project. Then in 1817 a steam engine was built by a London firm at the Offermann factory at Brünn. These were modest beginnings involving a mixture of conventional trade contacts and opportunism over recruitment of skilled technicians. But the first steps in mechanisation gave rise to maintenance workshops in the larger factories and some of these became nurseries for specialist engineering companies that became prominent in the nineteenth century.

Prussia

A considerable range of royal manufactures can be identified in Prussia, notably the complex industries in Berlin including armaments (at Spandau), china and textiles (silk and wool).[14] But a wide range of both heavy and light industries were assisted in the transition from the 'manufactory' to the factory stage by the Seehandlung organisation which was in effect an investment bank. The influence of Prussian mercantilism is particularly clear in the growth of engineering, notably in connection with the construction of atmospheric engines. It seems that the inadequacy of horse-driven pumps (Rosskünste) at the Mansfeld copper mines near Hettstedt led to a successful attempt by one C.F. Bückling to pirate the Boulton & Watt engine at Soho in Birmingham.[15] A model was built in Berlin and put to work at Mansfeld in 1783, while another engine was assembled at Hettstedt from parts manufactured at various works in Berlin, Brandenburg and Silesia. But when the latter was put to work in 1785 at König Friedrich Schacht it was a failure. However with the help of an English mechanic working abroad, W. Richard, a successful enterprise was established at Rothenburg a.d. Saale: one engine was installed at Westschacht near Eisleben and another (built under Richard's management) at the Schönebeck salt works near Magdeburg. These various initiatives laid the foundation of a heavy engineering industry in Magdeburg which prospered in the nineteenth century.[16] But the greatest development took place in Berlin where the Royal Iron Foundry (Königliche Eisengiesserei) was established in the suburb of Pankow in 1803, partly for the purpose of supplying steam engines free of charge to stimulate technological advance in private industry. Capacity was enlarged by the private firms of G.C. Freund and E.A.J. Egells in 1816 and 1821 respectively.

However an important part of the story of industrial success relates to Silesia where the installation of an English-made atmospheric engine at Königliche Friedrichsgrube near Tarnowitz (Tarnowskie Gory) led to the manufacture of engines at that site using Buckling's designs. Parts were manufactured locally, but English cylinders were needed. The works was transferred to Gleiwitz (Gliwice) in the coalfield in 1794 and its first engine was supplied to the Royal China Works (Königliche Porzellan Manufaktur) in Berlin in 1799, indicating the close inter-relationships between the various elements of the mercantilist establishment. A fully-fledged machine shop (even capable of boring cylinders) was established by 1810 and under the capable management of W. Holtzhausen production progressed from atmospheric engines to steam engines, at which point the technology was evidently transmitted westwards as Holtzhausen engines were later built at Pankow. Engineering however depended on an iron industry which began very soon after Frederick the Great wrested control of the province from the Habsburgs in 1742 through the establishment of royal ironworks at Kreuzberg (Kluczbork) and Malapane (Małapane) as strategic industries. Modification of the previous industrial character of the area as a textile region was carried a stage further when the beginning of coalmining emphasised the enormous potential for heavy industry: mines like Königsgrube (1790) and Hindenburg (Zabrze) in 1791 supplied steam-powered pumps now introduced into the lead and silver mines as well as the new generation of blast furnaces. Ironworks appeared at Gleiwitz and Königshütte (Chorzow): skilled workers were attracted from Saxony and even further afield in the case of John Baildon who supervised the construction of the Gleiwitz furnace in 1796.

There was also a growth of non-ferrous metallurgy in Silesia. This dates back to 1704 when the Breslau (Wrocław) merchant G. von Giessche was granted a lease from the Count Henckel and other landowners to extract calamine. The lease was extended in 1782 when Georg von Giesches

Erben became well-known in the trade: some of the calamine was used in the brass industries of Breslau, Gleiwitz and Tarnowitz and the rest exported. A new process for the reduction of ore to metallic zinc was introduced at the Scharley, Schoris and Trockenburg mines by 1802: this was a British method observed by another Silesian entrepreneur, J.C. Ruberg, from Pless (Pszczyna) used at Glashütte in Wessola in 1799 (later at Friedrichshütte and Konigshütte). Lead smelting, with coke, was another development in the late eighteenth century with a plant opened at Friedrichshütte in 1789. Silesia now played an important role in non-ferrous metal production in Germany. Elsewhere the Mansfeld copper mines remained prominent (producing 400-500 tonnes per annum of fine copper in the mid-eighteenth century but weakening by the 1780s), but the Ore Mountains, with complex ores around Altenburg, Freiberg and Zwickau yielding copper, lead, silver and tin, had passed its late sixteenth century peak and a French visitor noted in 1803 that the mines were only kept going by royal subsidies.

However Silesia lay in a remote part of Prussia, disadvantaged by transport costs as well as by government preference for industrial growth in Berlin, so rapid expansion was hardly likely. A further drawback was the position of the region on the borders of the Habsburg and Russian empires which made it appropriate to locate downstream activities in less vulnerable places. Water transport helped to move minerals since the Oder was linked to the coalfield by the Klodnitz (Kłodnice) Canal of 1806 and Berlin was accessible by both the Oder-Spree Canal of 1669 and the Plauen/Finow Canals of 1755. The Oder itself was improved for navigation as part of a major programme of waterway development (affecting some 800 km. of rivers and canals) by the Prussian state between 1796 and 1836, although one effect of this was to improve Berlin's access to British coal which was usually cheaper than the Silesian product. It is also worth noting that the emphasis on heavy industry was strengthened by the failure of the textile industry to introduce machinery on a large scale. The linen industry experienced fluctuating fortunes.[17] The Prussian takeover initially produced a surge of growth as the prevailing mercantilist outlook in government brought an influx of settlers: some 13,000 people were settled in two hundred or so new villages and a network of spinning schools taught the basic skills. There appears to have been some shift in the main area of production however as deforestation of the lowlands, accentuated by the fuel demands of the bleaching process, gave greater advantages to the foothills of the Giant Mountains (Riesengebirge). Feudal landowners were only too happy to countenance an expanding population making cash payments in lieu of feudal obligations. However the demands on the peasantry (all the greater because the aristocracy were also totally exempt from taxation) became quite unacceptable in the 1780s and 1790s when competition from the industries of Ireland and Scotland caught the now-riotous peasants in a price scissors with falling prices for their production and increases in the cost of living. The century ended on a note of grave uncertainty with the industry conspicuously failing to diversify. In the nineteenth century further problems arose because of the remoteness of the area in the context of both the Prussian and the wider German economy.

Saxony

Until the rise of the Ruhr Saxony was the most densely-populated and highly-industrialised part of Germany, with a wide range of raw materials and power supplies combined with a dynamic trading city (Leipzig) and a positive attitude in government towards guild restrictions and peasant emancipation. 'She also had an unfavourable agricultural soil and a long mountainous frontier with Austrian Bohemia whence came skilled refugees as well as plain linens to be finished'.[18] The eighteenth century industrial growth of Saxony has been well summarised in R. Forberger's monograph on Die Manufaktur in Sachsen. A late seventeenth century recovery from the Thirty Years War was assisted by capital and expertise of Dutch and Huguenot origin which generated a range of industries to employ an increasing rural population. Subsidies and privileges from the government were important but, as one of the larger and more prosperous German states, Saxony could offer her industrialists the stimulus of an ample home market. There was a tradition in industry and trade inherited from the Medieval period and a useful range of resources which could be exploited by a larger scale of manufacturing, notably the minerals, raw wool, charcoal fuel and water power of the Ore Mountains. There was a great variety of industries concerned with metals and metal manufacture, along with glass, paper and porcelain, and most of the activity was concentrated in the upland districts within the Leipzig-Dresden-Plauen triangle along the Elbe and Mulde valleys. The domestic woollen industry was supplemented by silk manufacture introduced to Dresden and Leipzig by Huguenots while Dutch and Swiss immigrants brought the cotton industry to the Chemnitz (Karl Marx Stadt) and Plauen areas. Weaving mills were using British yarn at the end of the eighteenth century but spinning mills were built during the Napoleonic Wars and the transition to steam power began in 1831, with the demand for machinery stimulating an important engineering industry in Chemnitz. In the early stages the encouragement of the textile industry by the authorities was very important. Services for rural manufacturers were provided at Plauen where the local authority set up a calico printing works to obviate the need for local weavers to send their cloth further afield to places like Augsburg and Hamburg. Evidence from Chemnitz shows a trend towards integration as calico printers linked back to cloth production and organised a putting-out system which could help ensure a steady flow of material into the factory. The progressive business environment encouraged diversification in other places too: Zittau in Lusatia successfully completed the transition from linen to cotton in the eighteenth and nineteenth centuries while Vogtland not only turned from worsted to the finest cottons (cambric at Falkenstein) but diversified into embroidery and lace. Thus Saxony's industrial growth was not inevitable but arose out of circumstances which could have acted to constrain rather than encourage. A behavioural environment favourable to industry could not be taken for granted and the enlightenment evident in Saxony (and certain other places in Eastern Europe) may well have had a significance that was not appreciated at the time.

The Lauchammer enterprise

A particularly interesting example of industrial enterprise in Saxony concerns the Lauchammer iron works, studied by F. Redlich who has drawn heavily on a *Festschrift* written in 1825.[19] The project arose out of a desire by the owner of the Mückenburg estate to increase employment and income in the aftermath of the Thirty Years War. A sawmill was planned to generate work in lumbering, transport and processing but the discovery of iron ore (when the foundations of the mill were being laid) prompted a change of plan: the forests now supplied charcoal to the iron works that opened in 1725. Both blast furnaces and forges were installed at water power sites on the Schwarze Elster River and it is recorded that the construction of canals helped to drain swampland and improve the agricultural potential of the estate (Figure 8.1). Four forges were built in the space of a few years: Oberhammer (1725), Mittelhammer (1726), Unterhammer (1728) and Grünewalder Hammer (1729), all supplied by a single blast furnace. Valuable consolidation work followed to extend mineral and water rights in the area. In 1776 however the estate passed to the famous Saxon entrepreneur Count Detlev von Einsiedel, well-known for his efforts to improve the woollen industry through the import of Spanish merino sheep and the perfection of production techniques. He was also prominent in the chemical and engineering industries and was interested in road building as well as rural education. The Mückenburg estate prospered under his management and the iron works was substantially improved. A smithy for nails and tools in 1777 was followed by facilities for the production of bar iron (at Mittelhammer) in 1781. A new location at Gröditz was used for a forge (1780) and a stamp mill to crush limestone (1789). A further works was acquired in 1790, on the Klein Spree near Hoyerswerda, and two new forges were opened there in 1790 to add to the Burghammer furnace and Spreewitz forge already in existence. By the end of the century the range of products was considerable. Initially there were some cast iron goods for sale like pipes, pots and stoves while crude iron for the forges was worked up into axles, plough shares and rails, but in Count Einsiedel's time we hear not only of bar and rod iron (supplied by craftsmen) but additional finished products, like armaments (guns and ammunition) and wire.

There was little local competition because most other Saxon furnaces and forges were located in the Ore Mountains, a traditional ironworking area which supplied key workers to Mückenburg when the venture first started. However even after methods had been evolved to produce a satisfactory wrought iron from the local bog ores, probably containing more phosphorous than the metallurgists from the Ore Mountains were accustomed to, the costs of production were high. Lack of navigable waterways in the immediate vicinity meant that the limestone from Meissen and Pirna had to be brought by wagon from either Dresden or Grödel (both on the Elbe). Local roads were poor since

Figure 8.1: Lauchammer and related industrial projects in the context of modern settlement and communications

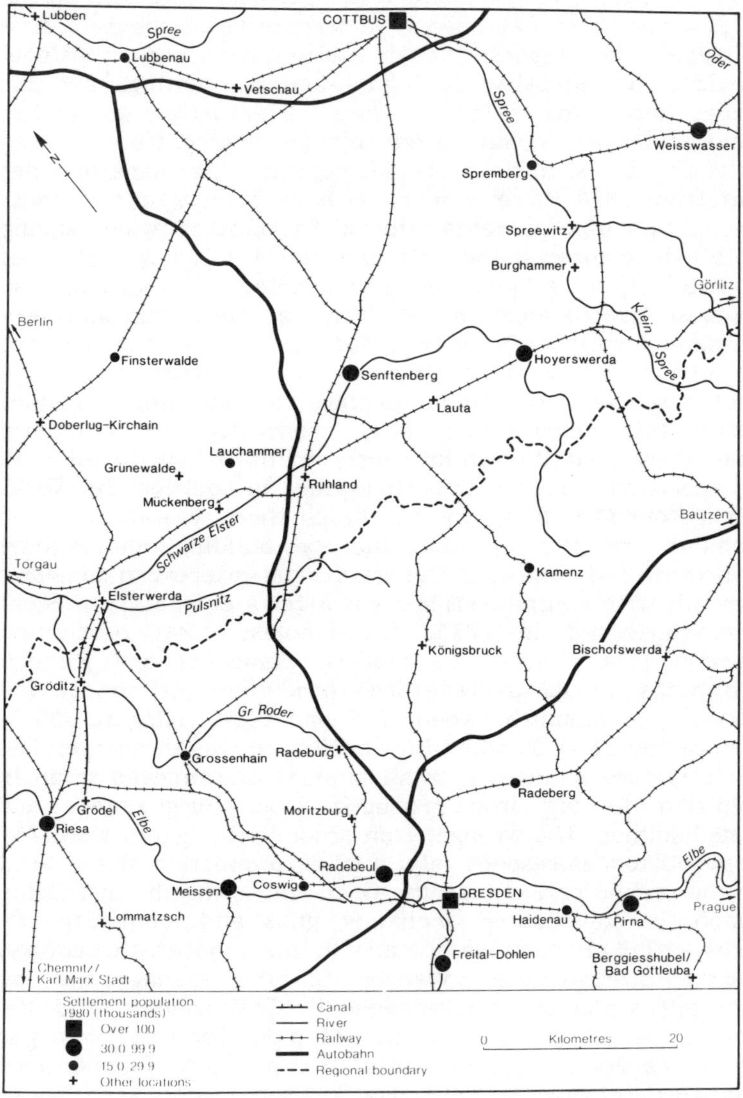

Sources: F. Redlich 1953 and modern topographical maps.

the estate lay away from both the Berlin-Dresden and Breslau-Torgau highways, but transport was eased by construction of a branch canal from Grödel to Gröditz in the 1780s, and later extended to Elsterwerda on the Schwarze Elster.[20] In response to this situation Count Einsiedel decided to specialise in highly artistic castings and his experiments of 1781-4 were eventually successful, embracing very complicated objects ranging from candlesticks to busts. Initially special objects were made to order but from 1816 there appears to have been a sort of mass production of ornamental items. The Count's wide ranging interests embraced the arts and hence this new policy of specialisation is quite understandable, all the more so because Lauchammer molten iron was quite thin and very suitable for intricate casting. But there was also an attempt to produce a range of castings for the engineering industry, including parts for steam engines and spinning machines (ultimately diversifying into production of complete machines), and the works seems to have coped well with competition from the Ore Mountains. In addition the works turned out structural iron for which there was also a rising demand, related to new factory building and mining ventures, and continued the traditional interest in domestic utensils with conspicuous success after a enamelling process was perfected in 1785. Nevertheless total production remained very small by modern standards and Redlich estimates annual average iron production of almost 500 tonnes per annum between 1776 and 1804, rising to 900 in the period 1805-24 when Einsiedel's son was in charge. The latter figure includes a small amount of remelted scrap in addition to pig iron produced from Burghammer and Lauchammer. The wrought iron production figures were 245 and 400 tonnes respectively, a lower proportion of the total in the second period than the first, reflecting the increasing emphasis on castings including guns and ammunition.[21] Substantial changes were made in the nineteenth century, partly through the takeover of the management by Einsiedel's son and his manager F. Trautscholdt, and the works specialised in production of pipes for water and gas works, as well as associated cast iron products. Furthermore territorial changes in 1815 attached some Saxon territory to Prussia and separated most of the Lauchammer installations from Gröditz which remained in Saxony. Tariff barriers necessitated separate development for Gröditz which was equipped with its own foundry (1819) and blast furnace

(1825). But it had to depend on local scrap for its raw material until the receipt of gangue ore, from Grossenhain and Moritzburg, north of Dresden, as well as from Berggiesshübel near Pirna, solved the problem of dwindling local bog ore supply. The whole enterprise however retained its technical lead up to 1825 and high quality production arose from care in manufacturing as well as in the selection and storage of raw materials. Redlich stresses the high standards set by the Lauchammer works. Under the leadership of Count Detlev von Einsiedel 'a spirit of scientific enlightenment, of restless improvement and of innovation came to permeate the Lauchammer works so that it became one of the leading German iron works'.[22]

Probably the greatest single innovation was the decision to install a steam engine to drive the blower of the furnace, using the fuel derived from the local lignite outcrops. The engine was installed in 1803 and worked successfully, although the fuel consumption was twice the anticipated level and the equipment was therefore sold in 1812. Shortcomings over water power however called for a further steam engine in 1821. The progressive nature of this East European enterprise arose in part out of Einsiedel's own expertise and his substantial library of technical books. But he was also fortunate in his selection of advisers like the engineer C.F. Bückling and the geologist A.G. Werner, and he was also prepared to arrange for visits to other works. One of his leading managers J.F. Lohrisch was sent to Austria, Bohemia and Franconia in 1788, and to Silesia in 1792; while it was the contact made by another employee with Bückling at Mansfeld in the Harz Mountains that led to the decision to install a steam engine. In 1821 we hear of another manager F. Trautscholdt visiting Count Wrbna's Horowitz ironworks near Teplitz (Teplice) in Bohemia to observe the low levels of fuel consumption. It would appear that, in contrast to craftsmen and merchants, noblemen did not behave in a secretive manner towards their colleagues. Rather Redlich argues there was a spirit of improvement which made for cooperation despite some degree of competition on the market: 'thus before the transmittal of technical and scientific knowledge had become institutionalised, noblemen had in certain fields the best opportunities for studying technical and scientific progress wherever achieved because they could obtain admission everywhere in government and nobility-owned enterprises'.[23]

Although the subsequent history of the enterprise

extends well beyond 1815 it is worth noting that technical innovation continued although the challenge of coke-smelting was not forcefully met. Puddling was taken up by 1830 and furnace gases were used for heating while additional energy was derived from gas manufactured from local peats. Locational difficulties arising from increased dependence on outside raw materials were partially overcome by acquisition of a plant on the Elbe at Riesa at which production of wrought iron was concentrated, leaving the older works to turn out foundry iron and diversify further into machine building, especially at Oberhammer. New mines were opened in the early 1830s and it was found more profitable to smelt the ores at source rather than transport them to Lauchaummer: hence the new furnace and forge at Gottleubal which eventually produced some steel after 1850. However a proposal to increase steel output was not accepted by a now ageing Count Einsiedel and his manager (Trautscholdt) therefore developed the idea independently in a separate enterprise at Döhlen which eventually took over Lauchammer's Gottleubal operations as the company degenerated following the Count's death in 1861. The rest of the assets comprised a new company based at Riesa in 1872 but there were further setbacks (necessitating the sale of land at Lauchammer later found to contain lignite deposits) and it was only with the support of Saxon banks and the engineering firm of Richard Hartmann in Chemnitz that the Lauchammer works were thoroughly overhauled in the 1880s, culminating in the installation of a new rolling mill and Siemens-Martin open hearth steel furnaces at Riesa. The link with engineering was strengthened after the First World War by a takeover by a Breslau locomotive firm to form Linke-Hoffman-Lauchammer A.G. The Silesian connection was severed after the Second World War but nevertheless according to N.J.G. Pounds, steelworks remain at Gröditz and Riesa (as well as Döhlen) while attempts have been made at Lauchammer to produce metallurgical coke from the local lignite.[24] So there is a thread of continuity from the eighteenth century to the present. The search for locational efficiency has of course required a shift from the ore deposits of a land-locked estate to the trading artery of the Elbe which retained its advantages through the nineteenth century thanks to supplementary railway links.

TRADE

Although all parts of Eastern Europe had commercial ties with the west there are signs of strong trading contacts between the northern and southern countries of Eastern Europe in recognition of the industrial growth in the north and the superior agricultural potential of the south, where the widespread cultivation of new crops like cotton and maize was taking place. Maize is mentioned as a significant export commodity at Durrës in 1716 and as a main cereal crop in Montenegro in 1780. This was stimulated by the external trade contacts which were particularly important in the peripheral territories of the Ottoman Empire in view of the chaos of the domestic market and the hazards of travel through a bandit-ridden countryside. Handicrafts did well in the Balkans and important manufacturing centres appeared in isolated mountain areas where artisans could practise their crafts with a minimum of Turkish interference. But the industrial growth should not be exaggerated. There seems to have been an acceptance of superior capacities elsewhere, for Turkish efforts to promote a textile industry in 1703 were not sustained and goods did not advance far into Eastern Europe from Edirne, Istanbul and Selanik (Thessaloniki): rather than persevere with domestic industry under a protective regime government appears to have preferred to gain advantage through trade in raw materials, particularly cotton and wool. There were advantages to the merchants, and to the elite who supported them, while the peasantry had the opportunity to produce a wider range of cash crops, even though their income was undermined by payments of rent and protection money. Balkan merchants took the raw materials to the ports for shipment to the west and chains of fairs developed along the Black Sea-Danube-Adriatic axis. They also sold western manufactures carted in from the coast. An overland trade with Leipzig exchanged cotton and wool for finished cloth made either in Germany or the Low Countries. It was not unusual for the Leipzig traders (Lipsicanes) to develop their travels between the Balkans and Germany into a triangular itinerary taking in Russian towns: since Russian traders did not enter the Ottoman Empire the Lipsicanes were able to bring Russian goods to Istanbul and could also take German goods into Russia. Previously the unsettled nature of the Cossack lands impeded links between the Ottoman Empire and Poland and Russia except by way of Transylvania.

'Greek' Traders of the Ottoman Empire

Who were the traders who kept the Ottoman Empire in touch with the wider world? First of all they were Turkish subjects for the most part. For after the Treaty of Passarowitz/Pozarevac (1718) there were only very modest customs charges (about three percent) involved when Ottoman traders entered Habsburg lands whereas Habsburg merchants had to pay heavy duties of up to forty percent. Despite the irritations arising from quarantine regulations which established the Sanitatskordon in 1770 there seems to have been a deliberate Habsburg policy, backed by military and political rather than economic motives, to encourage intercourse in the border areas. J.R. Lampe and M.R. Jackson therefore consider that this 'allowed Balkan traders to join German farmers and Italian bankers in carving out modernising enclaves in the economy of the imperial borderlands' and these enclaves were later to prove quite important in the development of national economies, not only in Romania but in Yugoslavia as well.[25] However T. Stoianovich has demonstrated that there were few Turks among the trading community.[26] It was overwhelmingly 'Greek', a label that covers not only ethnic Greeks but Hellenised Orthodox people such as Armenians, Bulgarians, Macedonians and Vlachs as well. Even Serbs who initially resisted any identification with Greek culture were being converted at the turn of the century: they had effectively established a uninational state within the empire, as a result of vigorous reaction to a growth of banditry which eliminated Moslem elements both Turkish and Albanian. But as Greek was the language of commerce throughout the Balkans some Serbs began to adjust, at least until a cultural reaction set in during the 1820s. Thus many of the 'Greeks' who carted textile raw materials to the coast were Slavs and Vlachs and in addition there were many Armenians taking the road to Germany and Russia.

There was also a significant Jewish contribution, which was tending to grow by the end of the eighteenth century. But perhaps the most interesting feature of the trading community of the Balkans was the gradual increase of interest among the free peasants in the mountain districts through the perception of growing opportunity in the eighteenth century. The Vlachs in Macedonia traditionally combined a number of occupations: the men were herdsmen as well as brigands, mercenaries and muleteers while the women were skilled weavers. The growth of the towns from the sixteenth century had allowed the Vlachs to become labourers on a seasonal basis but the eighteenth century brought a great increase in commerce. 'The availability of raw material surpluses - wool, cheese and skins - and craft products, the migratory habits of the men and their intimate knowledge of the difficult routes, the special privileges which allowed them to bear arms and their reluctance to allow the spread to the mountains of seigneurial reaction which enveloped ever larger areas of the coast, plains and valleys after 1600, finally persuaded a portion of the pasture folk to become carriers and traders of goods'.[27] Thanks to their travels as far afield as the Habsburg and Russian empires they achieved a significant improvement in living standards. Houses built in wood and stone replaced huts and tents, churches were embellished with carvings and frescoes and schools were founded. By the end of the century the most wretched villages in Macedonia were to be found not in the mountains but in the lowlands where the communities remained servile.

However two related themes may be mentioned. First the vulnerability of the trading centres to attack by brigands. One particular Vlach town attained a population of 40,000 by the middle of the eighteenth century thanks to its successful transition from pastoral farming to commerce. But Albanian mercenaries attacked the town in 1769 and 1788 and it reverted to a pastoral settlement as the merchants removed themselves to other Macedonian towns like Monastir (Bitola), Krusevo and Veles (Titov Veles). Others however moved north to Belgrade and to the Habsburg border settlement of Semlin across the river where they enjoyed the special privileges previously granted to the first of these Tsintsar merchants and came to dominate trade and money exchange in the town. Secondly of course it was inevitable that as one group gained expertise in commerce and established themselves it became difficult for others to win a share of the business. In Bulgaria the established position of Armenians, Greeks and Jews gave little scope to the natives, especially as much of the territory fell under the influence of the towns of Edirne, Filibe (Plovdiv) and Istanbul to the south. A few Bulgarians from the Rhodope and Stara Planina ventured as far afield as Hungary and Russia by 1750 but generally speaking the mountain folk remained at home until the end of the century when they began to move down to repopulate the empty lowlands. Even so commercial opportunities remained limited until the Treaty of Adrianople undermined the favoured position of the Greeks in trade with the Romanian Principalities and Bulgarians were able to cross the Danube and develop a carting and peddling trade to match the progress already made in Macedonia.

Surprisingly the Orthodox merchants were again involved in the transport of cereals from Hungary to the Adriatic as the colonisation movement gained momentum. The long overland route (opened to commerce in 1717) could be accomplished mainly by water, along the Tisza, Danube, Sava and Kupa to Karlstadt (Karlovac). But this was only possible after some improvements to the Sava-Kupa route had been put into effect (1756) and hazards still remained in the form of water mills, sunken tree trunks and an element of banditry. From Karlstadt roads were available to Fiume (Rijeka) (made a free port along with Trieste in 1719) and Senj: these were respectively the Caroline (1726) and Josephine (1776) routes. The Hungarian trade was monopolised by a privileged company at first but this was wound up in 1773 and the whole Adriatic cereal trade was then open to a newly-emergent 'Illyrian' trading company consisting of Greeks (many from Crete, the Ionian Islands and the Morea) along with Albanians and Slavs weaned away from a life of freebooting and piracy. There were also some from Hercegovina who had commercial experience as assistants to merchants in Dubrovnik. The traders were usually based at the Adriatic ports, shipping cereals to Italy in exchange for manufactures bound for the Habsburg and Ottoman empires. But they also worked inland from bases at Belgrade, Karlstadt or Sissek (Sisak) following the river routes into the interior to exchange cereals for olive oil, salt and sugar. Some cereals were of course supplied to deficit areas within the Balkans: Bosnia, Carinthia and the Military Frontier. In the case of Bosnia the journey back to the Adriatic could then be completed profitably by handling livestock or commodities such as fur, honey or timber. But by the end of the century perhaps the most remarkable trade in livestock consisted of the transfer of pigs (and some cattle and sheep) from Serbia to the Habsburg Empire. As the newly-colonised lands of Pannonia were used increasingly for cereal growing there was opportunity for peasants in upland country to sell more animals and the Serbs of Sumadija increased their herds of pigs using the acorn fodder from their oak woods. The trade was facilitated by the Austro-Ottoman commercial treaty of 1784 which liberalised trade while a further treaty in 1792 specifically granted the Serbs in the Pashalik of Belgrade the right to trade where they liked. The pig trade was very profitable to the Serbs and also to Greek, Macedonian and Vlach merchants based in the area: Belgrade, Pancsova (Pancevo) and Semlin (Zemun).

Evidently the Danube was little used by Balkan commerce. A commercial agreement in 1718 first allowed Habsburg vessels to trade down the Danube (only as far as Ruse) but the markets were small and Ottoman subjects (mainly Greeks) trading in Austria and Hungary had far superior Levantine connections. By 1739 the Turks had been driven from Pannonia and could not interfere with shipping north of Belgrade where a fortified outpost was retained. Yet despite unified control of the upstream section under Austria and Bavaria regular traffic seems to have been restricted to a passenger service operating in the downstream direction only from Ulm to Vienna and Pressburg (Bratislava). Navigation into Hungary was minimised by official disinterest in the development of the dependent kingdom while the Hungarian nobility's desire for isolation (to maintain the feudal regime) ensured non-compliance with government orders for the improvement of the channel and tow-paths of the Hungarian Danube and its tributaries in 1782-3. Local authorities are said to have destroyed tree trunks supplied for the improvement of the tow-paths. As already noted however much of Hungary's limited trade was being taken overland to Fiume while use of the Danube would in any case have been impeded by the several hundreds of water mills operating along the river between Pressburg and Belgrade, to say nothing of the cost and delay for upstream carriage in oar-driven boats: one month for a grain boat from Budapest to Vienna. Some progress was made later in the 1780s when the Turks again yielded over the use of the river downstream of Belgrade and Hungarian grain ships reached the Black Sea in 1787, but upstream navigation was a great problem, despite the use of convict labour on the tow-paths, until the introduction of steamships in the nineteenth century. Austrian commercial initiatives were based more on the maritime routes from Fiume and Trieste. Trieste was the more important of the two but Fiume's sugar refinery (arising out of Maria Theresa's ban of 1755 on the import of refined sugar) became the largest industrial enterprise in the Yugoslav lands during the eighteenth century. It survived well into the nineteenth century when it was undermined by the growth of sugar beet competition.

Contrasting urban fortunes: Bucharest and Dubrovnik

The buoyant Balkan trade stimulated growth in a number of provincial centres and especially Bucharest, which was probably the largest city in the Balkans after Istanbul. Goods entered Ottoman territory through the Carpathian passes and much of the trade was transacted with Leipzig (which accounts for the renaming of the city's main commercial highway as Lipsca street). Contact was made with Ottoman lands to the south with routes leading across the Danube at Giurgiu/Ruse and Calafat/Vidin to Bulgaria and Macedonia respectively. The British traveller Robert Stockdale found an ethnically-mixed population of some 16,000. No Turks were able to bring their families or exercise their religion: it was the religion of the Greeks that was enthusiastically projected. But the many shops, consisting of sheds which 'extend so far in many streets that they are nearly entirely covered', were run by Armenians, Germans, Greeks and Jews although these people nevertheless sat 'crosslegged on their counters' and the atmosphere was thoroughly oriental.[28] Stockdale would also have noticed that Bulgarians and Serbs had arrived as cloth and livestock merchants from Gabrovo and Vojvodina respectively. Bulgarian gardeners were much in evidence too, working in the grounds of villas built by Wallachian landlords moving into the city to escape the insecurity of the countryside, where the more prominent families were now obliged to reside in fortified tower houses.

All this created difficulty for Dubrovnik which had previously enjoyed a virtual monopoly on trade with the Balkans. Ottoman territorial contraction and the necessity to bow to other commercial interests lay at the root of the problem. Expanding western fleets eroded the lucrative business of collecting wool, hides and skins from all parts of the Balkans. Even trade with a much restricted hinterland was adversely affected because heavy taxes were levied on goods passing into the city from Bosnia, to help meet the financial strain of intermittent war with the Habsburg Empire. And part of Dubrovnik's territory was actually invaded during the Austro-Turkish War of 1736-9. There were some trading opportunities in the Black Sea theatre and further scope through the general growth in cereal exports from the Adriatic coast and various short-term possibilities arising out of Dubrovnik's neutral status in wars between France, Great Britain and Spain. All this prompted a growth of shipbuilding in the late eighteenth century. But Dubrovnik had to cope with stiff competition from other Adriatic ports like Bar, Budva, Hercegnovi and Ulcinj which Turks tended to encourage. Dubrovnik waged 'a continual diplomatic struggle between 1699 and 1740 to get the new harbours closed but increasing Turkish apathy in the affairs of Dubrovnik led to little success'.[29] The commercial decline was reflected in society as the timar system (under which the peasant enjoyed some security of tenure) was replaced by the ciftliks to which the peasants were effectively enserfed. Independence was finally snuffed out during the Napoleonic Wars when French and Russian forces competed with each other in an effort to occupy the city. The French succeeded (1808-14) but at the end of the war it was the Habsburgs who inherited Dubrovnik and presided over its further inevitable decline.

The political role of the 'Greek' traders

Overall the 'Greek' success was truly remarkable, politically as well as economically. The Greeks demonstrated an aptitude for commerce but they also combined their economic life with political and religious activities to create a comprehensive materialist philosophy in which business, politics and religion were one. The Orthodox ethic may have helped, as numerous fast days called for frugality and the accumulation of resources for future investment, while money lavished on the maintenance of buildings enabled the creation of wealth to appear virtuous in the eyes of the church. They aimed to become not just merchants but 'a political bourgeoisie in possession of the functions of banking, governing the Danubian Principalities, administering the civil and fiscal affairs of the Greek Orthodox Church and counselling the authorities at the imperial, provincial and even municipal level'.[30] Governorship of the Principalities dated back to 1716 when Phanariot Greeks (wealthy merchants from the Phanar quarter of Istanbul) were allowed to take the office of hospodar in Moldavia and Wallachia from native princes and thus gain control over many lucrative appointments and privileges. Their aggressive disposition in church affairs came out in pressure exerted on the sultan to eliminate the independent Serbian Orthodox Church. The patriarchate was first destroyed in 1459 but restoration had taken place in 1557; yet after the flight of the patriarch to Hungary with many of his followers in 1690 (followed by the flight of another Serb patriarch in 1737) the Greeks gained first the right to appoint some of the patriarchs and then succeeded in 1766-7 in getting the offices of Serbian patriarch and archbishop of Ohrid abolished, thereby increasing the power of the patriarch in Istanbul. On the whole the Balkan peoples who tried to emulate the Greeks did not succeed in acquiring the same simple outlook: their materialism seemed more ephemeral. Nevertheless the Balkan Orthodox traders created in their time a formidable hierarchy of activities which allowed the shrewd businessman to graduate from muleteer to forwarding agent, merchant, money lender and even banker. It also provided scope for graduating from small villages and towns, where the trading community added a distinct quarter (carsija in Macedonia or varos in Croatia) to agricultural settlements differentiated otherwise only on religious grounds upwards to the major trading centres, like those handling trade between the empires (Belgrade, Ruse, Vidin for example) and even to the great capitals of Istanbul and Vienna.

Yet the system was gradually exposed to new pressures. The Ottoman Empire could not maintain its embargo against foreign traders. In 1783 Russia won the undisputed right to send merchant ships through the Dardanelles and also to deal with Ottoman buyers and sellers: for the previous two centuries only the traders of Dubrovnik had been so privileged. The same rights were extended to the Habsburg Empire a year later (and to Great Britain, France and Prussia in 1799, 1802, and 1806 respectively). Initially this provided some new opportunities for Orthodox merchants. Greeks provided Russia with a merchant marine while other Greeks, along with Albanians and Serbs went to the Ukraine as settlers and traders, beginning with the Greek revolt in the Morea and the Russo-Turkish War of 1768-74. The Austrians were hard on the heels of the Russians. Once Ottoman insistence that Austrian goods shipped down the Danube be transferred to Turkish ships before entering the Black Sea was dropped the Austrian flag was the first among the non-Ottoman flags on the Black Sea by the late 1780s and remained so until the mid-nineteenth century. But when Austrian trade started to expand, Greek knowledge of the languages and of the terrain, both in the newly colonised lands and the primitive Balkan interior, suggested some cooperation in establishing a basic infrastructure of agents and warehouses. There was a considerable Greek and Vlach involvement therefore in the Orientalische Friesische Handlungs-Compagnie set up in 1777. But eventually foreign nationals were able to operate alone and promote their country's manufactures. The resurgence in Jewish activity was helped by this trend since Jews acquired the right to become Austrian subjects in 1796. Nor was the Greeks' position aided by the growth of overseas trade in Europe which brought, for example, American cotton to Germany. The anti-Greek tone of risings in Serbia and Wallachia gave notice that Greek commercial hegemony would not be tolerated in the nineteenth century as it had in the eighteenth, while the Greeks' own War of Independence convinced the Turks of the need to deprive them of their privileged status. But for the eighteenth century the Balkan merchants played a crucial role. Their itinerant trading life, sometimes growing out of brigandage and shepherding, provided an economic backbone for the Ottoman Empire and also supplied a catalyst for the exchange of ideas both inside and outside the empire and for the related political developments.

CONCLUSION

The growth of industry in the north was significant although the level of output and the scale of social change was restrained by West European standards. The East European aristocracy made a real contribution to government through the provision of army officers and efficient administrators, and it has been said that the Prussian Junkers were transformed through the late seventeenth and eighteenth century into a class of hereditary state servants. But the urban-based middle class was relatively small and this may have restricted interest in adopting the technology of the industrial revolution. A counter argument would however stress the differences in opportunity arising through the domestic resource bases of the European countries, the levels of home market demand and scope for external trade with its important overseas dimension for the West European colonial states. Despite good prospects in part of Eastern Europe the eighteenth century witnessed a deepening of the imbalance between Eastern and Western

Europe which had first emerged during the Medieval period. Progressive reforms such as those carried out in Prussia in 1734-8 under the Zunftordnungen (to regulate the guilds) did not have the desired effect and banking institutions like the Königliche Giro und Lehnbank founded in Berlin in 1765 suffered from limited investment capital, poor management and government manipulation. Yet a distinction must surely be drawn between the northern and southern parts of Eastern Europe with regard to industrial growth and modernisation generally. Failure in the Balkans may be linked with conservative attitudes in society which made any technical innovation difficult but if social change reflects an industrial stimulus then it may be necessary to look at the limited mineral endowment (fuels and ferrous ores) and also the relatively poor infrastructure of the European periphery. Landowners cannot be condemned for spending money on consumption rather than local industries for which there was no real potential. When factory-based manufacturing did begin in the more backward parts of Eastern Europe, in the context of a slowly-expanding middle-class demand for consumer goods or processing of export staples which could reach the west through an improved transport system, it was often through a large injection of foreign capital and management as well as foreign plant and machinery. The greater the lag the greater the probability that a local capitalist would have insufficient resources (of finance and technical/managerial expertise) to act alone.

NOTES

1. S. Pollard 1981, 199.
2. Ibid. 73.
3. W. Dlugoborski 1975, 'Peasant economy in the coal and smelting regions of Middle-East Europe before and during the early period of industrialisation' Studia Historiae Oeconomicae 10, 125-32; W. Klima 1979, 'Agrarian class structure and economic development in pre-industrial Bohemia' Past and Present 85, 49-67.
4. H. Freudenberger 1967, 'State intervention as an obstacle to economic growth in the Habsburg monarchy' Journal of Economic History 27, 493-509.
5. A. Klima 1974, 49.
6. Ibid. 51.
7. Ibid. 52.

8. Ibid. 54.
9. H. Freudenberger 1963, 7.
10. H. Freudenberger 1977, 4.
11. Ibid. 31.
12. Ibid. 142.
13. H. Freudenberger 1960, 'The woollen goods industry in the Habsburg monarchy in the eighteenth century' Journal of Economic History 20, 383-406.
14. W.O. Henderson 1958, 'The state and the industrial revolution in Prussia 1740-1870' (Liverpool: Liverpool University Press). Also H. Kekse 1980, 'International migration: Germany in the eighteenth century' Central European History 13, 322-47.
15. W.P. Jervis 1861, 'The Mansfeld copper mines' Journal of the Society of Arts 9, 592-632; C.J. Schmitz 1974, 'German non-ferrous metal production in the early nineteenth century' Journal of European Economic History 3, 129-47.
16. F. Redlich 1944, 'The leaders of the German steam engine industry during the first hundred years' Journal of Economic History 4, 121-44.
17. H. Kisch 1959, 'The textile industries in Silesia and the Rhineland: a comparative study in industrialisation' Journal of Economic History 19, 541-64.
18. S. Pollard 1981, 102. See also C.T. Smith 1967, 575-9.
19. F. Redlich 1953.
20. For contextual information see G. Livet 1983, 'Roads and transport in pre-industrial Europe' (Brighton: Harvester Press).
21. F. Redlich 1953, 92-4.
22. Ibid. 141.
23. Ibid. 149.
24. N.J.G Pounds 1969, 267.
25. J.R. Lampe and M.R. Jackson 1982, 78-9.
26. T. Stoianovich 1960.
27. Ibid. 276-7.
28. E.D. Tappe and T.J. Hope 1980, 598-9.
29. F.W. Carter 1972, 410. See also F.W. Carter 1968, 'The decline of the Dubrovnik city-state' Balkan Studies 9, 127-38.
30. T. Stoianovich 1960, 271.

Conclusion

Eastern Europe in 1815 showed a marked polarisation between the Habsburg and Prussian Empires where modernisation was under way, albeit slowly by West European standards, and the Ottoman Empire where radical reform was resisted. The continuation study on '<u>Eastern Europe 1815-1945</u>: <u>an historical geography</u>' reveals a further widening of the gap during the nineteenth century until the new nations of the Balkans implemented state programmes to remedy the situation, culminating in the present communist strategies. So it may not be too much to argue that the problems of economic backwardness and virulent nationalism which have dominated East European politics in modern times can be traced back to constraints on reform in the Ottoman Empire which first annexed Balkan territory in the fourteenth century. The Medieval period saw much of Eastern Europe consigned to an alien pattern of development after a long period of continuous association with the rest of the continent.

Until the Medieval period the whole of Europe could be considered a zone of prosperity, thanks to the ample capacity to innovate (between the sixth and eleventh centuries) in agriculture through new types of plough, horse harness, field system and crop rotation. The positive influence of peoples previously dismissed as barbarians was now evident. The Medieval centuries introduced deep divisions in Europe: culturally through the spread of Islam and economically through the colonial interests of the West European powers. Ironically these two developments are related. The ambivalent attitude to Byzantium meant that what was gained by the crusades, thanks to the element of surprise and the temporary weakness and disorganisation of the Arab world, was lost through the Ottoman conquests in the Balkans. Yet this devastating setback stimulated overseas discoveries, in order to outflank the Turkish blockade in the east, and the possession of exotic products then gave the colonial powers great advantages in trade with the rest of the continent: Eastern Europe became part of Western Europe's periphery.

All this may suggest a colonialist thesis with Eastern Europe, especially the Balkans, consigned to economic oblivion as part of Western Europe's economic system. Yet there was no inevitability that the west would rise to the challenge of Ottoman supremacy in the east. It is easy to look back with the benefit of hindsight and claim that success was inevitable, for contemporary perceptions of Europe's opportunities may well have been plagued by pessimism. Clearly there was readiness to grasp nettles and a disposition to innovate. Perhaps plague in Europe in the fourteenth century provided a motive for the introduction of labour-saving devices and, before that, perhaps the fresh outlook of the German people overcame a lack of receptivity to foreign ideas which had, arguably, characterised the later years of the Roman Empire with its condescending attitudes to outsiders as barbarians. The great fascination with mechanical aspects of technology (seen in the development of clocks) evident after the twelfth century meant that the west had the basic equipment to undertake voyages of discovery. And there were other elements in the situation. From the thirteenth century the Venetians demonstrated advanced business techniques and Byzantine merchants were forced to give way to their new and aggressive competitors. In the fourteenth and fifteenth centuries such manufactures as glass, soap and textiles which had previously gone to the west from the Middle East were flowing in the opposite direction.

The roots of Eastern Europe's modern problems cannot be related simply to economic issues. The permanent marchland character of the region is outstanding. The major political and cultural achievements of the ancient period took place on the shores and islands of Aegean which provided the site for the first great European civilisation. The Greeks settled on the coast of the Black Sea and the Adriatic but the colonists remained on the periphery of the peninsula: they did not attempt any conquest of the interior despite the scope for movement along the Danube and for contact between the Maritsa and Morava-Vardar valleys through the Dragoman Pass. The theme of Greek culture in the Balkans may be followed through the Dark Ages with Byzantium as heir to the Roman imperial idea: the most powerful empire in the western world at its height with its great wealth from trade and the land, its sound bureaucracy and military organisation and its civilisation which provided patterns for culture and government in the Balkans. Yet the peoples who came into contact with the Byzantines could not identify sufficiently with the prevailing imperial idea to adopt any but a thoroughly ambivalent stance so that the empire was threatened by Avars and Slavs as well as Arabs and Persians, to say nothing of the Christian Knights who turned on Constantinople when their objective was supposed to be the recapture of lands taken by the Muslims in the Middle East. Despite the restoration of the empire in 1261, with some Balkan territory, any student must be impressed by the anomaly of this assault on a Christian stronghold compared with later western support for the Ottoman Empire which, as history has demonstrated, was not capable by virtue of its Muslim ideology of maintaining its position in the Balkans indefinitely.

Thus the southern part of Eastern Europe has historically witnessed tensions between the national and imperial idea. These have not been eased by external interventions although at root they arise from a combination of incomplete colonisation, economic backwardness (in relation to the imperial core) and a perceived territorial basis for an independent national existence evident in the activities of Bulgarians and Serbs in Medieval times. Meanwhile, in northern part of Eastern Europe has no history of state development until the Dark Ages but over the last thousand years the growth of German power and influence has triggered off a roughly similar scenario, marked by strong ideological impulses through the Catholic Church and more sustained efforts in colonisation and economic development than were evident in the south. However, notwithstanding the Teuton-Slav dichotomy and the ethnic distinction of the Magyars, the territorial basis for national independence has been less than compelling while, once again, the issues have been decisively influenced by external pressures, from both Russia and the west.

The eighteenth century saw an impressive growth in the capacities of the German peoples to induce economic and cultural advances throughout Eastern Europe, so that it might be an interesting matter for conjecture how far they might have succeeded in integrating both northern and southern parts of Eastern Europe into a single coherent entity - Mitteleuropa. Arguably the heavy legacy of history would always have rendered the task an impossible one, even without the world wars of the twentieth century which have proved to be self-defeating in terms of support for some kind of German commonwealth. But the mutual interest of Russia and the west in frustrating an intervening build-up of power has also proved decisive. Today Eastern Europe has found an apparent unity based on Russia's Marxist-Communist ideology, yet in view of the stresses within the main international organisations of the bloc, and the fact that Albania and Yugoslavia stand apart from them, it seems that the historic struggle between nationalism and imperialism continues; while economic difficulties are expressed by the acute dependence of the region on external energy sources. Eastern Europe continues to be an economic periphery with stable political organisation constrained by national antagonisms and great power interests.

Bibliography

The following list includes some of the principal works available in the English language. It is supplemented by further references in the notes at the end of each chapter which it is hoped are reasonably comprehensive. But it has not been possible for reasons of space and research time to introduce material in other languages, and in particular the languages of the various East European nations. However most of the items listed below contain substantial bibliographies which include foreign language publications. A concise survey of East European geographical journals is provided on pages 375-9 of R.H. Osborne's book on East Central Europe (London: Chatto & Windus, 1967). Readers may well find it useful to consult a historical atlas in order to supplement the basic cartography included in this book. Suitable English language works include: H. Kinder and W. Hilgemann 1978, Penguin atlas of world history (Harmondsworth, Middlesex: Penguin Books, 2 vols.); R.I. Hoor 1981, The Hamlyn historical atlas (London: Hamlyn); W.R. Shepherd 1970, Shepherd's historical atlas (London: Philip). The reference below to D.E. Pitcher (1972) is excellent for the Ottoman Empire. Two German atlases may also be mentioned: the work of T. Kraus et al. 1959, Atlas östliches Mitteleuropa (Bielefeld: Neinajen & Klasing) is excellent for the GDR, Poland and northern Czechoslovakia, while the remaining parts of Eastern Europe feature in the Atlas der Donauländer by J. Breu (Vienna: Osterreichisches Ost- und Sudosteruopa Institut, 1970). Various atlases have been published in Eastern Europe, including national atlases for Bulgaria (Atlas NRB, Sofia 1973), Czechoslovakia (Atlas CSR, Prague 1966) and Romania (Atlas RSR, Bucharest 1979). Another Czechoslovak atlas Atlas ceskoslovenskych dejin (Prague 1965) contains a wealth of historical material.

Finally it is worth noting that volumes on Albania (J.D. Dwyer), Hungary (T. Kabdebo), Poland (R.C. Lewanski) and Romania (A. Deletant and D. Deletant) have appeared in the World Bibliographical Series.

Anderson, M.S. 1961, Europe in the eighteenth century 1713-1783 (London: Longman).

Barley, M.W. (ed.) 1977, European towns: their archaeology and early history (London: Council for British Archaeology).

Barraclough, G. (ed.) 1970, Eastern and Western Europe in the Middle Ages (London: Thames & Hudson).

——— 1976, The crucible of Europe: the ninth and tenth centuries in European history (London: Thames & Hudson).

Benecke, G. 1978, Germany in the Thirty Years War, (London: Arnold).

Black, C.E. 1971, 'Eastern Europe in historical perspective': C.E. Black (ed.) Challenge in Eastern Europe (Port Washington, N.Y.: Kennikat Press) 3-27.

Byrnes, R.F. (ed.) 1976, Communal families in the Balkans: the zadruga (South Bend, Ind.: Notre Dame Press).

Cadzow, J.F. et al. (eds) 1983, Transylvania: the roots of ethnic conflict (Kent, Ohio: Kent State University Press).

Cahnman, W.J. 1949, 'Frontiers between East and West in Europe', Geographical Review 49, 605-24.

Carter, F.W. 1972, Dubrovnik: a classic city state (London: Academic Press).

——— 1983, 'Cracow's early development', Slavonic and East European Review 61, 197-225.

Clarke, H.B. and Simms, A. (eds) 1985, 'Comparative history of urban origins in non-Roman Europe British Archaeological Reports International Series 255.

Dann, O. and Dinwiddy, J. (eds) 1987, Nationalism in Europe in the age of the French Revolution (London: Hambledon Press).

Davies, N. 1984, Heart of Europe: a short history of Poland (Oxford: Clarendon Press).

Deletant, A. and Deletant, D. 1985, Romania (Santa Barbara, California: Clio).

de Vries, J. 1984, European urbanization 1500-1800 (London:Methuen).

Dwyer, J.D. 1986, Albania (Santa Barbara, California: Clio).

Fedorowicz, J.J. et al. 1982, A republic of nobles: studies in

Polish history to 1864 (Cambridge: Cambridge University Press).
Fischer-Galati, S. (ed.) 1970, Men state and society in East European history (London: Pall Mall).
—— (ed.) 1982, Romania between East and West: historical essays in memory of C.C. Giurescu (Boulder, Colorado: Social Science Monographs).
Fleckenstein, J. 1978, Early Medieval Germany (Amsterdam: North-Holland Publishing Company).
Freudenberger, H. 1963, The Waldstein woollen mill: noble entrepreneurship in eighteenth century Bohemia (Boston, Mass: Baker Library, Harvard Graduate School of Business Administration).
—— 1977, The industrialization of a Central European city: Brno and the fine woollen industry in the eighteenth century (Edington, Wilts: Pasold Research Fund).
Gimbutas, M. 1971, The Slavs (London: Thames & Hudson).
Giurescu, D.C. 1981, Illustrated history of the Romanian people (Bucharest: Ed. Sport-Turism).
Gutkind, E.A. (ed.) 1964, Urban development in Central Europe (New York: Free Press).
—— (ed.) 1972, Urban development in Eastern Europe: Bulgaria Romania and the USSR (New York: Free Press).
—— (ed.) 1972, Urban development in Eastern Europe: Poland Czechoslovakia and Hungary (New York: Free Press).
Halecki, O. 1978, A history of Poland (London: Routledge & Kegan Paul).
Hoddinott, R.F. 1981, The Thracians (London: Thames & Hudson).
Hodges, R. 1982, Dark Age economies: the origins of towns and trade AD600-1000 (London: Duckworth).
Jelavich, B. 1983, A history of the Balkans (Cambridge: Cambridge University Press).
Jones, A.H.M. 1971, The cities of the eastern Roman provinces (Oxford: Clarendon Press).
Kabdbo, T. 1980, Hungary (Santa Barbara, California: Clio).
Klima, A. 1974, 'The role of rural domestic industry in Bohemia in the eighteenth century', Economic History Review 27, 48-56.
—— 1975, 'The beginning of the machine building industry in the Czech lands', Journal of European Economic History 4, 49-78.

Koch, H.W. 1978, A history of Prussia (London: Longman).
Lampe, J.R. and Jackson, M.R. 1982, Balkan economic history 1550-1950 (Bloomington, Ind.: Indiana University Press).
Lengyel, A. and Radan, G.T.B. (eds) 1980, The archaeology of Roman Pannonia (Budapest: Hungarian Academy of Sciences).
Lewanski, R.C. 1984, Poland (Santa Barbara, California: Clio).
Lewis, A.R. 1958, The northern seas: shipping and commerce in northern Europe AD 300-1100 (Princeton, N.J.: Princeton University Press).
Macdermott, M. 1962, A history of Bulgaria 1393-1885 (London: George Allen & Unwin).
McNeill, W.H. 1974, Venice: the hinge of Europe 1081-1797 (Chicago: University of Chicago Press).
Maczak, A. et al. 1985, East-Central Europe in transition: from the fourteenth to the seventeenth century (Cambridge: Cambridge University Press).
Millar, F. 1981, The Roman Empire and its neighbours (London: Duckworth).
Okey, R. 1982, Eastern Europe 1740-1980: feudalism to communism (London: Hutchinson University Library).
Osborne, R.H. 1967, East Central Europe (London: Chatto & Windus).
Parry, V.J. et al. 1976, A history of the Ottoman Empire to 1730 (Cambridge: Cambridge University Press).
Pollard, S. 1981, Peaceful conquest: the industrialisation of Europe 1760-1970 (Oxford: Oxford University Press).
Pollo, S. and Puto, A. 1981, History of Albania (London: Routledge & Kegan Paul).
Postan, M. and Habakkuk, H.J. (eds) 1962, The Cambridge economic history of Europe: trade and industry in the Middle Ages (Cambridge: Cambridge University Press).
Pounds, N.J.G. 1969, Eastern Europe (London: Longman).
—— 1973, Historical geography of Europe 450 BC-1330 AD (Cambridge: Cambridge University Press).
—— 1974, An economic history of Medieval Europe (London: Longman).
—— 1979, Historical geography of Europe 1500-1840 (Cambridge: Cambridge University Press).
Redlich, F. 1953, 'A German eighteenth century ironworks during its first hundred years: notes contributing to the unwritten history of European aristocratic business leadership', Business History Society Bulletin 27, 69-96;

141-57; 231-59.

Roberts, B.K. and Glasscock, R.E. (eds) 1983, 'Villages fields and frontiers: studies in European rural settlement in the Medieval and Early Modern periods', British Archaeological Reports International Series 185.

Rothenburg, G.E. et al. 1982, East-Central European society and war in the pre-revolutionary eighteenth century (Boulder, Colorado: Social Science Monographs).

Rothschild, J. 1974, East Central Europe between the two world wars (Seattle: University of Washington Press).

Schutz, H. 1983, The prehistory of German Europe (New Haven, Conn.: Yale University Press).

Seton-Watson, R.W. 1963, History of the Roumanians (Hamden, Conn.: Archon Books).

Smith, C.T. 1967, Historical geography of Western Europe (London: Longman).

Spector, S.D. 1971, A history of the Balkan peoples (New York: Twayne Publishers)

Spira, T. 1977, German-Hungarian relations and the Swabian problem (Boulder, Colorado: Social Science Monographs).

Stavrianos, L.S. 1958, The Balkans since 1453 (New York: Holt Rinehart & Winston).

Stoianovich, T. 1960, 'The conquering Balkan Orthodox merchant', Journal of Economic History 20, 234-313.

Sugar, P.F. 1977, Southeastern Europe under Ottoman rule 1354-1804 (Seattle: University of Washington Press).

Temperley, H.W.V. 1947, History of Serbia (London: Bell).

Todorov, N. 1983, The Balkan city 1400-1900: its socio-economic and demographic development (Seattle: University of Washington Press).

Treasure, G. 1985, The making of modern Europe 1648-1780 (London: Methuen).

Vlasto, A.P. 1970, The entry of the Slavs into Christendom: an introduction to the Medieval history of the Slavs (Cambridge: Cambridge University Press).

Vucinich, W.S. 1954, Serbia between East and West (Stanford, California: Stanford University Press).

Wanklyn, H.G. 1941, The eastern marchlands of Europe (London: G. Philip).

Warriner, D. (ed.) 1965, Contrasts in emerging societies (London: Athlone Press).

Whitting, P. (ed.) 1981, Byzantium: an introduction (Oxford: Blackwell).

Index

Cities are listed according to their present names: thus for Constantinople see Istanbul

abandonment see desertion
access/accessibility 10, 24, 103, 179, 214, 249, 253, 278, 284
Acropolis see Church
Ada Kaleh 249
Adamclisi 42, 69, 71
administration 5, 54, 62-4, 67, 70, 74-9, 84, 91, 94, 112, 126, 140, 147-8, 166, 177-80, 183-5, 235, 250, 257-9, 264, 273, 277-9, 285, 295-9, 304
Adriatic 10, 19, 26, 31-2, 36, 40, 52, 77, 90-1, 108, 126-7, 192-9, 205, 291, 294-6, 303
agriculture 5-11, 20-3, 31-6, 53, 57, 65-7, 70, 74-6, 80, 86-8, 92, 101-3, 111-13, 119, 133-5, 147, 154, 157-72, 180-1, 188-9, 191, 196, 210-19, 238-9, 244, 252-3, 257-64, 270-2, 278, 284-6, 298, 302
Alba Iulia 42
Albania 4, 10, 77, 125, 136-7, 143, 146-9, 193-7, 248, 255, 292-4, 298, 305
alcohol see distilling
Altenburg 181, 203
Amber/Amber Route 9, 23, 31-2, 55, 58, 77, 81-5, 132
Angevin Dynasty 114
Annaberg 181
Antler 88
Apuseni 51 see also Carpathians
arable farming 5, 76, 127, 144, 154, 160-9, 181, 215-17, 223
Arges 41
aristocracy 33-5, 40, 54, 66, 78, 82-4, 92-4, 101, 104-9, 115, 118, 123, 130, 140-4, 159-61, 176-7, 183-8, 194, 197, 210-23, 226, 235-7, 241-3, 251, 257-64, 273-8, 284, 289, 293, 299
armed forces/army see military
Arpad Dynasty 114, 119, 134, 190, 244, 255, 258
art 38, 78
artisan see craftsman
assimilation 86, 158, 193
Atlantic 10
Attila 60
Aurelianus 81
Aurelius, M. 56
Aurignacian culture 20
Austria 32-3, 106, 113, 144, 172, 175, 241, 244-6, 250, 273-5, 284, 289, 295, 298-9
Austria-Hungary see Habsburg Empire
autonomy 140, 183, 186, 194, 250-2
Avars 60-1, 69, 83-7, 93, 120-1, 127, 190-3, 304
axes 23

Babadag 37
backwardness 9-10, 241, 264, 300-2
Baia 133-4
Baile Herculane 33
Bakony 60
Balaton 55, 61-4, 87-9
Balkans 1-5, 9-11, 19, 23-30, 37-43, 48-9, 77-81, 84-6, 107, 122-49, 154, 163-70, 178, 191-9, 219-23, 243-55, 292-6, 299-304
Baltic 10, 23-4, 31-3, 55, 85, 93-5, 111-12, 132-4, 174, 180, 192, 204-19, 239, 244, 302
Banat 24, 66, 121-2, 139, 246, 258

Index

banditry 222-4, 249, 253, 256, 291-4, 299
banking 279-81, 292, 297-300
Banska Bystrica 173-6, 181-2
Bar 91, 108, 127-8, 192-5, 297
Baragan 5
Baranya 137
barbarian 1, 54-60, 64, 68, 74-6, 79, 90, 105-7, 111, 302-3
barley 20-2, 28
barrier see frontier
barter 94
Basarabi culture 38
Bastarnes 40
Bathory, S. 185
Battle Axe culture 30-1
Bautzen 87
Bavaria 83, 88, 105, 116, 120, 171, 182, 219, 247, 295
Beakers 23, 30-1
Bega Canal 259
Belgorod Dnestrovsky 132-4, 204, 220, 224
Belgrade 11, 51, 123, 139, 163, 194, 197, 246, 250, 293-5, 298
Belo-Brda Culture 88
Berlin 95, 103, 188-9, 281-3, 288, 300
Berounka 35
Bessarabia 42, 57, 68-9, 133, 246
Birlad 224
bishop/bishopric see Church hierarchy
Biskupin 36-7
Bistrita 41, 134
Bitola 139, 197, 293
Black Death 163, 211
Black Sea 9-10, 19, 25, 36-41, 69, 134, 146, 180, 192, 195, 204-5, 219-23, 245-6, 291, 295-8, 303
blast furnace see furnace
Bohemia 9, 22, 31-2, 35, 54, 81, 90, 93, 106-7, 121, 125, 147-8, 154, 160-1, 171-7, 180-2, 186, 217-19, 237, 244, 266, 272-7, 280-1, 284, 289
Boian culture 28
Boleslav I-III 93, 116
Bolesław I-IV 117-18, 205
bone 32, 88
Bosna 129
Bosnia 32, 52, 109, 121-2, 125, 129-30, 143, 148, 181, 194-7, 222, 247, 250, 294-6
Botosani 39
boulder clay 22-3, 162
Braila 57, 135, 141
Brandenburg 103, 178, 189, 209-10, 239-41, 264, 281
Bran Pass 41
Brasov 28, 122, 135, 220, 223
Brass 283
Bratislava 88, 119, 218, 295
Breclav 88
breeding see livestock
Bremen 157
brewing 215-17
bribery see corruption
brigandage see banditry
Brno 32, 277-81
Bronze Age 9, 28, 30-8
Bucharest 71, 134, 192, 238, 251-3, 295
Bucovina 140, 246
Budapest 35, 55-64, 119, 143-4, 190-1, 205, 219-20
buffer state/zone 135, 243, 247
Bug 85, 93
Bükk 26
Bulgaria/Bulgarian 26, 40, 69-70, 77-9, 83-91, 122, 126-7, 131, 136-8, 142, 146, 164, 195, 219-22, 248, 253-5, 258, 292-6, 304
bureaucracy see administration
Burebista 42, 65-6
Burgas 38, 52, 123, 224
businessman see entrepreneur
Buzau 33, 256
Bydgoszcz 36, 244
Bytom 159, 175, 181
Byzantine Empire/Byzantines 1, 10-11, 51-3, 60, 69-70, 77-9, 83-94, 105-10, 121-30, 136-8, 143, 155, 164, 169, 189, 193,

196, 204-5, 220, 302-4

Calafat 220, 296
Calamine 282-3
Calarasi 41
camp see garrison
canal 118, 163, 259-61, 283, 286-8
Cantemir, D. 164-5
capital/capitalism 12, 158, 176-7, 186, 211-12, 222, 225, 239, 248, 271, 284, 300
capital cities 103, 119, 129, 134, 190-2, 223
carantari 83
caravan 191, 197, 220, 224
Carinthia 113
Carolingian Empire 1, 87-8, 94, 101, 105, 155
Carpathians 9, 23-4, 28, 31, 34, 38, 42, 56, 65-70, 81, 107, 121-2, 130-5, 164-9, 177, 180, 224, 249, 295
Carpians 57, 136
castle 84, 104, 112, 132-6, 178-80, 183, 189, 197, 295
cathedral 95, 187-8
Catholic Church 43, 89-91, 109-15, 118-20, 130, 135, 148-9, 225, 243, 257-8, 304
cattle 22-3, 26-8, 85-6, 219, 233, 239, 245, 294
caves 33
Celts 39-40, 51, 54-5, 66, 80-2
centralisation 273
ceramics 20-4, 27-30, 34-42, 61, 65-8, 86, 281-4
cereals 23, 26-7, 38, 57, 68, 76, 81, 104, 119, 138, 168, 185-7, 196, 204, 207-26, 244, 248, 252, 256, 260-2, 291, 294-6
Cernavoda/Cernavoda culture 33, 69
Ceska Lipa 275
chalk 296
charcoal 272, 277, 286
Charlemagne 82-3, 87, 111, 154, 205
cheese 194, 293
chemicals 286
Chernozem 28, 258
Chilia 139, 204, 220, 224
Chorzow 282
Christianity 48, 52, 79, 83, 86-90, 107-15, 118-23, 139-42, 146-8, 185, 190, 198, 205, 209, 246, 249, 255, 276, 304
Church 78-9, 87-91, 105, 124, 143, 147-9, 162, 176, 179, 183-8, 293, 297
Church hierarchy 110, 117, 124-7, 135, 143, 147, 155-7, 160, 190-2, 215, 298
Cimpulung 133, 192
cities 48, 51-2, 56, 64, 76-8, 90, 93-6, 107, 117, 130, 145-6, 171, 291-3, 298
civilisation see culture
climate 5-11, 20-2, 28-9, 37, 64, 133, 163, 219, 256-8, 272
cloth 171, 188, 191, 209, 223, 245, 253, 275-7, 280, 285, 290
Cluj 40, 62, 71, 223
coal 9, 282-3, 289-90
coast/coastline 5, 23, 85, 91, 94-5, 111-12, 126, 132, 193-9, 204, 209, 244-8, 291-3, 296, 303
coins 38, 68
coke 283, 290
colonialism see colonisation
colonisation 9, 51-2, 60-2, 74, 84-5, 92, 103, 106, 111-13, 134, 147, 157-63, 171-3, 179-81, 191, 205, 212, 222, 239, 253, 256-60, 263, 294, 299, 303-4
commerce 36, 84, 94, 107-8, 112-13, 122-3, 128, 145, 168-70, 177-220, 245, 250-7, 291-300
communications see transport
communism see socialism
competition 9, 180, 207-9, 217-19, 274, 279, 284-6, 289
conquest see invasion

Index

Constanta 38, 69
Constantine 57-9
constitution 101, 106
consumption 300
cooperative 70
copper 23, 28-34, 67, 173-6, 195, 223, 281-3
corruption 76, 238, 253
costs see prices
Cottbus 87, 112
cotton 222-3, 237, 276, 280, 285, 291, 299
crafts/craftsmen 23, 35-7, 41, 65-6, 74, 94-5, 142-3, 170-9, 183-7, 190-3, 196-8, 213, 216, 223, 236-8, 258, 272, 278, 286, 289-93
Cris/Cris culture 26-7, 132
Crisana 132
Croatia 32, 90-1, 121, 130, 143-4, 148, 193, 255-7, 298
crops 181, 249, 257-9, 262, 291, 302
Crown see monarchy
Crown land see Royal estate
Crusade 107-8, 110-11, 126, 138-9, 163, 204, 237, 302
Cucuteni culture 27-9
culture 1-5, 9-12, 19, 49, 53, 56, 65-70, 77-8, 87, 104, 107, 110, 123-4, 130, 142, 145, 147-8, 158, 160-1, 193, 237, 246, 250-1, 257, 265, 292, 302-4
Curtea de Arges 133, 192
custom 233
customs duties 195, 245, 292
Cyril 89-90, 124
Cyrillic 89, 124
Czech lands/Czechoslovakia 10, 85-7, 113-14, 154-5, 179, 205, 209, 223
Czestochowa 110

Dacia/Dacian 38-43, 49, 55-8, 65-70, 81, 107, 131-2, 136
Dalmatia 55-7, 60, 90-1, 108, 130, 169-70, 192-9, 204, 246, 249, 278
Danube 9-11, 19, 22-8, 31-8, 43, 49-51, 55-62, 65-71, 76-7, 81, 84-6, 105, 113, 119-20, 123-7, 130-2, 135-41, 144, 190-1, 197, 205, 219-20, 223-4, 246-9, 253-5, 278, 303
Dark Ages 12, 37, 70, 74-98, 130-1, 193, 304
Debrecen 119
Decebalus 65-6
decline see depression
deer 20, 24
defence 28, 33, 39-42, 57-70, 80, 92, 103-4, 107-8, 132, 139-40, 164-6, 170, 178-9, 185, 188-94, 199, 223, 282
deforestation 144, 163-7, 174, 252, 257, 284
demesne see estate
demography see population
depression 64, 183-6, 213-17, 248-9
desertion 144, 163, 214-16, 253
destitution see famine
development see economy
diffusion 9, 19, 37, 76, 111, 158, 172
Dimbovita 41
Dinaric Alps 9-10, 20, 137, 174, 220
Diocletian 56-9, 74, 77-8, 178, 190
diplomacy 78-9, 106, 114, 239-41, 265
disease see plague
distilling 259, 262
diversification 284
Dnieper 204, 219, 247
Dniester 22, 41, 91, 132-4
Dobrogea 5, 27, 37, 43, 57, 68-9, 81, 133, 141, 248
Domitian 58
Dorohoi 224
Dragoman Pass 304
drainage see rivers
draught animals see horses
Drava 55, 61-2, 83, 121

Dresden 285-9
Drin 127
Drobeta-Turnu Severin 57, 67-9, 249
drought 256
Dubrovnik 78, 90-1, 108-9, 127-30, 140, 174, 178, 191-9, 204, 223, 255
Dunaujvaros 61
Durrës 52, 90-1, 108, 127-8, 137-9
Dusan, S. 129, 138
dwelling see house
dyeing see textiles
dyestuffs 39

earthquake 256
East Prussia 240, 265
economic development/economy 3-5, 9, 12, 19, 48, 57-8, 66, 78-84, 92-6, 101-3, 107, 110-11, 143-9, 154-239, 245-8, 252, 257, 263-5, 271-305
Ecumene 10, 103, 117, 121, 129, 136, 247
Edirne 53, 77, 81, 123, 139, 146, 197, 224, 291-4
education 177, 250, 258-9, 273, 286
efficiency 272
Elbe 9, 31, 36, 53, 86, 105, 109-11, 115, 157-9, 163, 207, 210, 239, 285-6, 290
Elblag 112, 185, 214, 245
elite 78, 138, 194, 210-19, 271, 291
elk 20
emancipation 260-3, 284
empire 3, 13, 84, 101, 105-6, 110-11, 127, 137-9, 147
employment 260-3, 284
energy see fuel
engineering 280-2, 285-90, 300
enlightenment 233-9, 260, 263-5, 273, 285, 289
entrepreneur 182-3, 236-7, 248, 272-3, 290
epidemic see plague
Erfurt 83, 95, 180
erosion 28, 144, 257
estate 64, 74, 78, 92, 104-6, 142-4, 148, 162, 213-18, 222-4, 237, 248, 252-3, 259-63
Esztergom 58, 110, 119-21, 190, 205
ethnicity 3, 70, 77, 80-1, 101, 121, 136, 149, 159-63, 184, 198, 240, 250, 255-8, 292, 296, 304
exports 57, 64-7, 77, 176, 195, 204-29, 245, 258-62, 291, 296-300

factory 262, 272-90, 300
Fagaras 132-5
fair 175, 198, 204, 276, 291
famine 168, 193-4, 209, 236, 256
farm 160-2, 180, 214-17, 223
farming see agriculture
Feoderati 58-60, 69, 74, 81-4
fertility see soil
feudalism 12-13, 49, 54, 65, 74, 88, 103-5, 117-18, 123, 130, 133-4, 138-40, 143, 148, 154, 158, 169, 172-3, 177, 183, 186, 191, 210-19, 235-44, 253, 259-63, 271-7, 284, 295
field system 78, 92, 217, 253, 302
figs 169-70
finance see capital and money
fishing 20-4, 27, 37, 53, 65, 70, 179, 184, 207-9, 218-20
flax 22, 172, 187, 209, 214, 218, 274, 280
fleet see shipping
flood/floodplain 28, 37, 163, 187, 219, 256
fodder 26, 252
food 20, 38, 94, 145-6, 158, 162, 171, 181, 187, 225, 247, 252, 256-62, 277
foreigners 176, 184-5, 191, 205, 235-8, 250, 273, 276-9, 284-5, 298-300
foreign policy 135

Index

foreign trade see trade
forest/forestry see wood/woodland
fort see garrison
fortification 35-7, 41, 52, 57-61, 64-6, 69, 81, 84, 88, 92-5, 143, 193
foundry 65, 182
fowling 20
Frankfurt/Oder 179, 208
Franks/Frankish culture 1, 79, 82-3, 87-91, 101, 105, 109-10, 115, 120, 124
Frederick the Great 235-6, 240, 282
free trade 273
Freiberg 173, 176, 181, 283
frontier 1-3, 11, 68-9, 74-8, 81, 87-8, 103, 109, 123, 127, 132-9, 143, 162-3, 193, 245-7, 257-8, 283, 292-3
fruit 27, 167, 218
fuel 9, 182, 210, 284, 289, 300
Fuggers 174-6, 182
fur 209, 224, 294
furnace 171-7, 213, 237, 280-2, 285-90

Gabrovo 296
Galati 68, 224
Galicia 121, 244, 273
gardening 23, 184, 296
garrison 56-9, 62-77, 88, 92-4, 107, 124, 138, 144, 189-90, 197, 249, 257
Gdansk 113, 157, 163, 170, 179-80, 204, 208, 213-16, 223, 240, 244-5, 262
Genoa/Genoese 107-8, 138-46, 220
Gepids 56-7, 69
German Democratic Republic 10, 188-9, 210
Germans/Germany 1-5, 9, 35-6, 53-6, 67, 74-6, 80-3, 86, 93-5, 101-6, 111-18, 122, 130-6, 141, 149, 157-63, 172-5, 178-91, 205-8, 211, 223, 235, 239-40, 253, 257-61, 264, 284
Geto-Dacians see Dacians
Geza 120
Giant Mountains 284
Giurgiu 141, 220, 253, 296
glass 35, 65, 88, 177, 244, 275, 284, 302
Glina culture 33
Gliwice 282-3
Gniezno 110, 117-18, 175, 180, 205, 215-16, 244
goats 20, 26-7, 53, 86, 163
gold 23, 33, 38, 52, 61, 67, 159
Goths 56-60, 68-9, 76-7, 81, 85
government 188, 194, 198, 211, 215, 226, 236-8, 248, 251-2, 271-3, 277-9, 283-4, 295, 299-300
Gradistea Muncelului 42, 66
grain see cereals
grazing see pasture
Great Moravia 87-90, 93, 109, 178
Great Poland 92, 118, 159, 175, 244, 252
Greece/Greeks 11, 19, 22, 32-42, 48, 51, 65-71, 86, 124-7, 137, 141-2, 146-7, 180, 187, 191, 196, 221-3, 250-2, 255, 292-9, 303-4
Grody 94
guilds 170-2, 184, 198, 219, 278, 284, 300
Gumelnita culture 27-8
Györ 58, 62, 189-90

Habsburg Empire/Monarchy 3, 11, 71, 106, 115, 122, 139, 144, 233, 239-40, 245-7, 250, 253, 257-60, 264, 272-4, 277, 282-3, 292-7, 302
Hadrian 51-3, 64, 77
Halberstadt 95, 239
Halle 32, 175
Hallstatt culture 34-6, 39
Hamangia culture 27
handicrafts see crafts
Hanseatic League 48, 85, 205-10

hard coal see coal
Harz Mountains 157, 163, 175-7, 237
Hateg 67
Hatvan 59
Havel 210
heartland 4, 48, 67
heath 22, 160, 238, 256
Hellenisation 39-42, 86, 124-6, 251, 292
Hercegnovi 191
Hercegovina 193-7, 250, 294
Hercynian Chains/Lands 20, 80-1, 163, 180
herding 53, 292, 299
hides see skins
highlands see mountains
hill forts 42
hinterland 204, 220, 296
Hirsova 41, 69
Histria 38, 41, 69-71
Hodonin 87
Holy Alliance 5
Holy Cross Mountains 173, 237
Holy Roman Empire 82, 103-6, 116-18, 189, 225, 233, 239-40
home industry 274-291
home market see market
homestead see house
honey 38, 125, 165, 168, 220, 294
horse 31, 25, 61, 65, 86, 184, 272, 281
hostilities see war
Hotin 68, 134
house 24, 279, 36-7, 40, 86, 92, 131, 143, 157, 160, 171-4, 187-9, 198, 249, 253, 259, 274-5, 279, 293, 296, 302
Hoyerswerda 286
Hunedoara 67
Hungarian/Hungary 3-5, 10, 84-7, 91-4, 110, 114-15, 119-22, 139-43, 146-9, 154, 160, 171-4, 182, 189-91, 195-6, 205, 209, 218-20, 244-6, 250-9, 264, 273, 293-5, 298, 304
Huns 56, 59-61, 80, 85
hunting 20-4, 27-8, 33, 65, 70, 88
Hunyadi, J. 139
Hussites 114, 117, 148, 217
hut see house

Iasi 27, 41, 134, 192, 224, 251
ideology 5, 74, 83, 94, 101, 104-6, 118, 149, 161, 265, 304
Illyria 40, 51, 55, 82, 136
Imperial Estate see Royal Estate
imperialism see empire
imports 34, 64, 95, 196, 204-29, 236, 286
Industrial Revolution 9, 145, 299
industry 20, 28-9, 33, 56, 62-5, 76, 88, 94, 103, 107, 113, 135, 145-6, 154-77, 182-8, 191, 209, 211-13, 221-3, 236-7, 241, 244, 260-4, 271-302
infield see field system
inflation 107, 248
infrastructure 300
inn 52
innovation 9, 19, 29-30, 74, 158, 172, 238, 244, 289-90, 300-3
Inowrocław 244
intellectuals 251, 260, 263-5
invasion 77-93, 134, 137-43, 155, 159, 174, 178, 205, 216, 246-7, 256-7, 277, 296
investment see capital
iron 159, 171-7, 196, 213, 237, 280-2, 285-90
Iron Age 23, 32-47, 66-7, 82, 86-8, 131
Iron Gate Pass 67
iron gates 1-3, 11, 20, 138, 219-20, 246
iron ore 9, 163, 285-90
Isaccea 69
Iskar 126
Islam 85, 93, 107-8, 123, 130, 137-48, 193, 237-9, 247-50, 253-5, 271, 292, 302-4
Isonzo 11
Istanbul 3, 43, 51-2, 62-4, 76-85, 90-1, 107-8, 123-6, 138, 146-8, 194-5, 219-24, 247, 291-3, 296-8, 304

Istria 91
Italy 40, 64-5, 81, 105-8, 135, 149, 155, 171, 176, 191-6, 204-5, 220, 223, 247, 292

Jachymov 176, 181-2
Jagiellon Dynasty 115, 241
Jajce 129, 195
Janissaries 146
Jena 240
jewellry 88
Jews 142, 146-7, 178-80, 184-8, 191, 205, 223, 255, 259, 292-3, 296, 299
Jihlava 173, 181-2, 277-80
Joseph II 261, 273
Junkers 261
Justinian 60, 77, 84-5, 178

Kaliningrad 112, 217, 245
Kalisz 37, 186-7
Karanovo culture 27
Karl Marx Stadt 285, 290
Karlovac 294
Karst 191
Kazan Pass 124
Kazanlik 27, 38-40
Kazimierz I-IV 115, 186-7, 213
Kecskemét 144
Keszthely 57, 61-2
Kiev 85, 94, 125, 205, 219
king/kingship see monarchy
Klodnice Canal 283
Kolin 278
Kołobrzeg 94, 117, 180, 185, 204, 209
Körös see Cris
Kosice 225
Kosovo 127, 138, 143, 250
Kotor 108, 127-8, 191-2, 195-6
Krakow 23, 93, 114, 117-18, 147, 175-6, 179-88, 205, 210, 214, 219, 223-4
Kremnica 173, 176
Kuciuk Kainardji, Treaty of 245
Kujawy 23, 37, 163, 175
Kurgan culture 31
Kutna Hora 173-6, 182
Kyustendil 53, 107

Labe 88
labour/labourer/labour force 32-3, 53, 65, 86, 104, 154, 173, 183, 193-5, 210-23, 239, 248-9, 252, 261-4, 271-9, 293-5, 303
lace 237, 285
land/land use 8, 108, 141-4, 154, 157-70, 188, 196, 248-9, 252, 261, 272, 304
land development/reclamation 158, 163, 264 see also colonisation
landowner 104, 126, 157-61, 172, 177, 183-5, 188, 211-17, 248, 252, 255, 261-2, 271-2, 284, 296, 300
language 13, 81, 89-91, 105, 116, 122-4, 128, 148-9, 160-1, 179, 184, 191-4, 259, 292
La Tène culture 35, 38-40, 55, 65
Latin 91, 107, 116, 126-8, 191-4, 259
Lauchammer 285-90
law 101, 104, 111, 159, 173, 179-86, 191, 226, 247, 260-1, 264
lead 159, 175-6, 195, 223, 282-3
learning see scholarship
leather 244
Leipzig 171, 175, 219, 224, 284-5, 291, 299
Lengyel culture 27
Lepenski Vir 24
liberation 250
Liberec 280
lignite see coal
Limes 52-65, 68
linen 171-2, 237, 274-5, 283-5
literature 103
Lithuania 112-15, 118, 162, 185, 188, 241-5
Little Poland 118, 187
livestock 64, 69, 86, 104, 166, 170, 187, 194-6, 205, 209, 212-16, 223, 244, 252, 294-6

Ljubljana 53, 58
loan 279
local authority see administration
Loess 9, 22-3, 26, 80, 126, 180
Lombards 60, 81, 191, 220
Lovech 126
lowlands see plains
Lübeck 4, 85, 179-80, 207
Lublin 92, 162, 185, 188, 219
Lunca see floodplain
Lusatia/Lusatian culture 36, 111, 171-2, 237, 285
Luxemburg Dynasty 114
luxury 38-9, 95, 145, 171, 209-13, 259
Lvov 132, 187, 192, 205, 220, 220, 223-4

Macedonia 10, 26, 34, 40, 51-3, 76-7, 84, 123-6, 138, 147-8, 178, 251, 292-8
machine/machine building see engineering
Magdeburg 22, 93-5, 110, 117-18, 179-80, 184, 188-9, 239, 281
Magyars see Hungarians
maize 222, 252, 291
Majdanpek 30
malaria 256
management/manager 276, 279, 289, 300
Mangalia 38, 69
manor 78, 211-19, 222, 226, 277-9
manpower see labour
Mansfeld 175, 281-3, 289
manufacturing see industry
Maramures 132-4
Marcomanni 53, 56, 59-61, 67
Maria Theresa 240, 260-1, 273-4, 278, 295
maritime power see sea power
Maritsa/Maritsa culture 28, 123, 126, 218, 238, 303
Mark 80, 103
market 9, 57, 87, 90-2, 104, 168-70, 177-99, 204-28, 237, 272-9, 284, 291-300
marsh 20, 54, 80, 92, 117-19, 144, 157, 160, 163, 178-80, 189, 252-3, 256-8, 286
Marx/Marxism see socialism
Matthias 114
meadow see pasture
mechanisation 274-6, 290
Mecklenburg 94, 160, 204, 209, 235
Medias 40
medicine 258
Medieval period 3, 9, 12, 54, 74-6, 79, 82, 95, 100-229, 300-4
Mediterranean 5, 9-10, 19, 22, 26, 31-2, 48, 93, 108, 201, 221, 248, 252
Meissen 111, 159, 188-9, 286
Menzlin 94
mercantilism 236, 277-83
mercenaries 65, 85, 138, 255, 292-3
merchants 40, 94-5, 178-99, 204-29, 237, 251-2, 257-9, 276, 289, 291-300
Merseburg 111
Mesolithic culture 22-4, 27
metallurgy 30, 35, 39, 66, 125, 172-7, 272, 282-4
Methodius 89-90, 124
Metkovic 52
Metohija 137
middle class 273, 299-300
Middle East 9-12, 19, 24-6, 29, 303-4
Mieszko 93, 117, 180, 186
migration 5-11, 19-23, 27, 31, 34-6, 40, 53-5, 68, 77-93, 101, 131-3, 137, 143-9, 157-60, 169-70, 177, 180-5, 193, 198-9, 212, 246, 253-8, 285, 293
Mihai (Michael) the Brave 141
military 48, 51, 55-70, 74-8, 81-7, 91, 94, 101, 104-5, 110-12, 120-5, 130, 137-44, 164, 177-81, 197-9, 225, 233-6, 239-40, 243, 246-50, 255-9, 273, 292,

Index

299
military frontier 257, 294
mill/milling 168-71, 184, 216, 253, 259, 274-80, 285, 294-5
millet 27-8
Millet 142
minerals 9, 35, 67, 93, 107, 157, 172-7, 191, 195-7, 205, 223, 253, 272, 284, 300
mining 51, 113, 172-7, 180-3, 192, 281-2, 288-9
mission/missionaries 109-13, 120
Mitteleuropa 305
modernisation 11-12, 145, 162, 170, 226, 233-6, 292, 300
modern period 3, 9, 12, 302-5
Moesia 55, 67, 76
Mohacs 57, 174, 257
Moldava 134
Moldavia 5, 24-6, 29, 39-41, 57, 68-9, 130-6, 139-41, 164-9, 192, 209, 222-3, 239, 251, 255-6, 297, 302
monarchy 26, 53-4, 65-6, 80, 88-91, 101, 105, 112-25, 130-2, 136, 148, 173-6, 179, 182, 188, 190-1, 195, 213-17, 236, 241, 274
monastery 109-10, 116, 124-6, 129, 140, 147, 162, 178, 188-92, 208-9, 217, 224, 256, 275-6
money 244, 262, 291, 296-7, 300
Mongols 76, 113, 138
monopoly 146, 170, 175, 197-8, 264, 294-6
Monteoru culture 33
moorland 57, 80, 157-8
Morava 81, 87-90
Morava-Vardar 9, 27, 34, 124, 127, 137, 219, 303
Moravia 5, 9, 32, 36, 61, 81, 84, 87-93, 112, 115-16, 120, 124, 146, 272-3, 277-80
Moroboduus 53-4
morphology 253 see also urban morphology
Moslems see Islam
mountain 5-11, 126-7, 135-6, 142, 163-71, 178, 181, 194, 199, 214, 222, 253, 274, 284-5
Mousterian culture 27
movement see transport
Muntenia 43, 69
Mures 132, 257
music 103
Muslims see Islam
Mycenae see Greece

Nagyrév culture 33
Napoleonic Wars 104, 233, 240, 285, 297
nationalism 35, 141, 147-8, 160, 246-7, 250-1, 259, 264, 274, 302-4
natural resources 9, 103, 139-41, 161, 180, 194, 235, 247
navigation 9, 205, 210, 295 see also shipping and water transport
navy 61, 108, 138, 233, 246, 253
Neolithic 20-34, 51, 175
Neretva 194-6
Neubrandenburg 189
neutrality 194, 246, 296
Nicephorus 78, 125
Nin 90-1
Nis 123, 137-9, 163, 194, 197, 246
Nitra 87-90
nobility see aristocracy
Nomad 70, 85, 119, 134, 169
North European Plain 1, 9, 22, 30-1, 36, 54, 80, 112, 157-60, 239, 253
Noua culture 34
Novipazar 127
Novi Sad 253, 258
Nürnberg 147, 171, 176, 224, 275

oats 21
Obuda see Budapest
occupation see invasion
Oder 32, 53, 80-1, 85-7, 94, 111, 157, 162-3, 204, 210, 237-40, 283

Ohrid 123-8, 131, 139, 298
oil 39
Oituz Pass 41, 81
olives 170, 220, 294
Olomouc 88, 116, 147, 205
Olt 56, 69
Oltenia 24, 57, 246
open field see field system
Opola 92
Opole 180, 237
Oppida 35-41, 62, 67
Orastie 42, 66-7, 71
orchards 181
Ore Mountains 159, 171, 177, 181, 237, 283-8
Orsova 220
Orthodox Church 1-3, 79, 89-91, 109-15, 121-3, 127, 130-1, 135, 142, 145, 148, 243, 257-8, 292-4, 297-8
Osijek 62, 257
Otakar 113
Otto 85, 105, 111, 117, 134, 271, 277, 302-4
Ottoman Empire 1-3, 10-11, 108-9, 135-6, 149, 155, 164, 174, 197-9, 220-6, 233, 237-41, 245-52, 255, 258, 264, 291-300
outworkers see home industry
overlordship see suzerainty
oxen 22

paganism 88, 123
Palaeolithic 20, 36
Panagjuriste 38
Pannonia 1, 9, 20-30, 35, 42, 52, 55-67, 81-5, 89-90, 119-23, 130-2, 136, 139, 178, 181, 190, 194, 219, 223, 246, 256-60, 294-5
papacy 89-91, 118, 128, 138, 148
paper 284
Pardubice 278-9
partition 175, 237-45, 262-3
pastoral farming 5, 28-9, 37, 57, 65-7, 143, 258, 293
pasture 9-11, 65, 119, 127, 161, 165-9, 184, 194, 214, 253, 256
patriarchate see Church hierarchy
Pazardshik 197
peasant 22, 74-8, 107, 112, 117, 130, 139-43, 157-72, 178, 187, 210-23, 247-52, 255-63, 272-9, 284, 291-2, 297
Péc 128-9, 148, 192, 195
Pécs 57, 62, 84, 114, 143-4, 190
Peene 94
Periam-Pecica culture 33
Petchenegs 119
Phanariots 141, 251-2, 297
physical environment 5-11, 103, 127, 163, 257
Piast Dynasty 93, 114, 160, 186, 205
Piatra Neamt 42, 134
pigs 20-3, 27-8, 86, 294
pilgrimage 110, 190, 199
piracy 108, 169, 294
plague 67, 107-8, 154, 170, 198-9, 212, 217, 238, 255-6, 303
plains 199, 256, 284, 293-4
planning 179, 184, 253, 273
Plauen 171, 285
Pliska 124-5
Płock 92, 184
plough 32, 155, 158, 161-3
Plovdiv 34, 52, 81, 107, 125-6, 139, 293
Poland 10, 22, 35-7, 80, 85-7, 92-5, 103, 110-18, 132-5, 139-41, 147, 154-63, 171, 175-7, 180-8, 205-19, 223-6, 235-7, 240-5, 252, 261-3, 291
political organisation see state development
pollution 181
Pomerania 95, 115, 155, 159-62, 178, 182, 205, 209, 239-40, 244, 264
Popesti 41
population 20, 26, 57, 65-7, 74-80, 85, 107, 111-13, 123, 138-9, 145, 154-5, 162-4, 166-71, 182, 185, 188, 194, 198, 205,

212, 216-17, 221, 236, 239, 252-63, 271, 274, 284
port 52, 90, 93-5, 107-8, 111, 146, 180, 185, 190, 199, 204-29, 239, 253, 291, 294-6
Porte see Ottoman Empire
power see fuel
Pozarevac 246
Poznan 110-12, 117-18, 175, 179-80, 184-5, 205, 214-16, 241, 244
Prague 35, 88, 93, 110, 114-17, 178, 183, 187, 205, 237, 274-6, 281
precious metals see treasure
prehistory 5, 9, 19-47, 92, 122, 130
Premyslids 113-14
Preslav 124-5, 219
Presov 86
Pribina 83-4, 89
prices 145, 174, 177, 211-18, 223, 237, 248, 262, 271, 283
principalities see Moldavia and Wallachia
Pripet 85, 93
Pristina 127-9
privilege 181-3, 186, 193, 213, 218-19, 258, 264, 284, 293, 297-9
Prizren 129, 194-5
profit/profitability 10, 277-9
protection 273-4, 291
Protestant 149, 172, 257-8
proletariat 172, 198, 273
proto-industrialisation 272
Prussia 103, 112-17, 149, 161, 172, 209-12, 233-45, 260-3, 272-3, 281-4, 288, 299-302
Prut 39, 81, 133, 246
Przemysl 205
Pszczyna 283
Pula 53, 192
pumping 174, 282
Puszta 119

Quarantine 292

Raba 60
railway 118, 261, 290
Rastislav 87-8
raw materials 64, 141, 145, 198, 262, 272-3, 280, 284, 290-3
rebellion 117, 139, 250, 298
reclamation see land reclamation
reform 218, 236, 245, 256, 260, 263-4, 271-3, 300-2
Reformation 49, 116, 144, 149, 188, 208, 278
refuge see castle
refugee 284 see also migration
Regensburg 93, 109, 115, 205, 220
reindeer 20
relief 5-13, 103, 122, 126, 133
religion 1, 29, 39, 66-7, 77-9, 82-4, 88-91, 106-15, 141-2, 198, 296-8
Renaissance 135, 145, 187, 259
rent 214, 217-18, 244, 252, 261-3, 271, 291
resettlement see colonisation
resins 39
revolt see rebellion
revolution 11-13, 250, 273
Rhodope 49, 293
Rijeka 108, 294-5
rising see rebellion
rivers 9, 28, 86-8, 176-8, 189, 205, 210-12, 219, 239, 294
roads 51, 61-4, 94, 118, 258, 286-8
robbery see banditry
Romania 10, 70, 77, 121-2, 130-6, 144, 164-9, 192, 221, 247, 250-8, 292-4
Rome/Roman Empire 1, 19, 36, 39-43, 48-83, 101, 105-7, 118, 124-6, 131-2, 139, 177-8, 188-90, 302-4
Rosiorii de Vede 33
Rostock 188, 204
rotation 222
routes see transport
Royal Estate 216, 264, 278-9
royalty see monarchy

Rügen 111
ruling class see elite
Rundling 92, 161-2
rural industry 20, 28-9, 33, 56, 62-5, 76, 88, 94, 103, 107, 113, 135, 143-6, 154-77, 271-80
rural settlement 5-13, 21-9, 35-7, 57, 62-4, 68, 76, 81, 85-6, 92, 111-13, 135, 141-4, 157-72, 179-80, 184, 191, 199, 252-63
Ruse 41, 124, 197, 223, 253, 295-8
Russia/Russian Empire 3-5, 11, 80, 95, 133, 177, 185, 205, 233-6, 240-6, 250-2, 255, 283, 291-3, 297-8, 304-5
Ruthenia 175
rye 21

Saale 31-2, 81, 210, 281
Salcuta culture 28
salt 9, 33-4, 119, 135, 163, 194-6, 220, 223, 262, 281, 294
Salzburg 84, 87-90, 109-10
San 224
Sandomierz 216, 252
Sarajevo 129, 194, 197
Sarmatians 55-9, 67-9, 85
Sarvar 58, 64
Satu Mare 27, 40, 264
Sava 11, 32, 55, 62, 83, 246, 257, 294
Saxony 9, 82, 105, 115, 154-7, 171, 174-6, 182, 186, 191-2, 210, 235, 240-1, 257, 282-90
Scandinavia 1, 9, 84-5, 93-5, 111, 155, 161, 205-7, 214, 239-43, 271
scholarship 78
school 274-5, 283, 293
Schwerin 20
science see technology
Scythians 35-41, 85
sea power 4, 29
sea trade see shipping; trade
Second World War 1
security see defence
self-sufficiency 12, 168, 172
Serbia/Serbs 52, 77-9, 91, 125-9, 138, 142-4, 148, 191-7, 221, 246, 249-59, 292-9, 304
serf/serfdom 65, 74, 104, 143, 161, 185, 210-36, 252, 271-5, 293, 294
settlement 5-13, 21-9, 35-7, 57, 62-4, 68, 76, 81, 85-6, 92, 111-13, 135, 141-4, 157-70,179, 195, 207-9, 222, 252-63, 283
Seuthopolis 40, 52
Seven Years War 240, 243
Severus, S. 56, 69
shatterbelt 1, 5, 12
sheep 20-2, 26-7, 86, 163, 166
shifting cultivation 23, 36, 92, 167, 253
shipbuilding 164, 193, 196, 209, 214, 297
shipping 61, 85, 107-9, 125, 169, 174, 194-6, 204-29, 245, 252, 294-8
Shkodër 108
Shumen 224
Sibenik 108
Sighisoara 192
Silesia 9, 61, 116-17, 146, 159, 172, 175, 184, 208, 216, 223, 236-7, 240, 245-7, 260, 272-8
Silistra 124-5, 224
silk 223, 237
silver 23, 38, 52, 66, 95, 159, 173-5, 195, 248, 282-3
Siret 39-41, 69
Sisak 56-8, 62, 294
skill 271-90, 293
skins 194, 197, 293, 296
Skopje 127-9, 137-49, 197, 255
Slaves 35, 38, 64-70, 78, 93, 103-5, 108-9, 113-19, 154, 161, 194
Slavs 1, 9, 36-7, 43, 70, 77, 83-96, 115-30, 138, 158-70, 178-82, 188-9, 192-4, 205-7, 247-51, 255, 292-4, 304

Slovakia 33, 85-6, 115, 172-7, 181-2, 209, 258-9
Slovenia 83, 113, 120, 191
smelting 164, 172-7, 181-2, 272, 283-90
soap 244
social geography/social structure 10, 30, 54, 74-9, 92, 105-7, 118, 122-3, 138, 148, 160-70, 183, 192-4, 197, 205, 209-11, 226, 233, 245, 262-5, 271-2, 277, 299-300
socialism 12-13, 302, 305
Sofia 53, 81, 107, 194-7
soft coal see coal
soil 5-11, 22-3, 26, 164, 252, 258, 274, 284
Sopron 55, 60, 64
Sorbs 87
Soroca 68
specialisation 12, 23, 290
spices 107, 146, 205, 220, 223
spirits 214
Split 52, 78, 90-1, 108-9, 174, 178
Spree 103, 189, 283
Sremska Mitrovica 11, 51, 57-64, 77, 83, 86, 89, 194-5
Sremski Karlovci 246
Stara Planina 34, 293
Stara Zagora 28-30, 34, 107
Starcevo Culture 27
state development/state system 10, 49, 74, 87, 91, 94, 101, 154, 179, 205, 226, 233-70, 302-4
steam/steam engine 281-2, 285-9, 295
Stefan (Stephen) the Great 139
Steppe 9, 26, 29-31, 35-7, 51, 70, 121, 132-5, 139, 165, 220, 258
stockraising see pastoral farming
Stradonice 35-6
Stralsund 180, 208
stronghold see castle
Struma 126
Subotica 256
subsidence 181
subsidies 283-4
subsistence see self-sufficiency
suburbs 179-80, 183-91
Suceava 86, 134, 192, 220, 224, 247
Sudetan Mountains 32, 177
sugar 245, 294-6
suzerainty 89, 111, 115, 127-8, 138-41, 192, 197, 247, 252
Svatopluk 84, 87-90, 115
Svishtov 197
Swabians 105, 177, 257-9
Szczecin 179, 204, 208, 239, 245
Szeged 27, 144
Szekely 122
Székésfehervar 119-21, 191
Szombathely 55, 61-2

Tabor 114, 117
tariffs see customs and tolls
Tarnowskie Gory 282-3
Tartars 121, 134, 165, 190, 220
Tatra Mountains 223
taxation 74-8, 104, 117, 142-6, 160, 166, 169, 176-7, 181, 197, 219, 223, 236, 247, 258, 261-4, 273, 284, 296
technology 9, 19, 22, 30-4, 37, 40, 65-7, 76, 79-80, 104, 111, 135, 140, 155, 158-61, 172, 212, 233, 238, 263-5, 273, 278, 282, 286, 289, 299-302
Tecuci 41
Tei culture 33
Teplice 289
Teutonic Knights 112-34, 158, 180, 205-8, 211-13
textiles 65, 107, 125, 146, 171-2, 182, 195, 209, 216, 220, 223, 244, 272-86, 291-3, 303
Thessaloniki 81, 86, 123-4, 139, 291
Thirty Years War 106, 172, 177, 210, 216-18, 224, 233-5, 239, 284-5
Thracians 19, 33, 37-43, 49-52, 55, 65-7, 70, 130-1
Thuringia 32, 35, 82, 105, 176

Tighina 134, 204
timber see wood
Timisoara 220
tin 23, 31-4, 174-5, 181, 283
Tirgoviste 33, 134, 192, 220
Tirnave 70
Tisza 26, 42, 55, 87, 119, 144, 257, 294
Tiszazug 25
Titograd 51
Titov Veles 77, 124, 293
tobacco 222, 258
tolls 186, 213, 245, 288
Torun 112-13, 163, 185, 210, 213, 240, 244, 252
trade 3-4, 10, 23, 29-34, 39-42, 54, 69, 81, 84-5, 93-6, 103, 107-8, 110-11, 117, 125-7, 132-5, 146, 155, 171, 175-99, 204-29, 283-9, 244-5, 251, 274-5, 281, 291-304
Trajan 51-8, 66-8
transhumance 28, 127, 165-7
transport 9, 30-3, 39, 48, 67, 107, 181, 210, 214, 239, 259-60, 272, 283, 291-4, 300
Transylvania 29, 34, 41, 55, 66-71, 81, 121-2, 130-6, 140-1, 166, 195, 207, 219-20, 223, 246, 251-7, 291
travel see transport
Travnik 129
Trianon, Treaty of 122
tribes 19-70, 82, 87, 92-5, 101, 105, 178-80
tribute 40-2, 108, 125, 140-1
Trieste 4, 294-5
Tulcea 125
Turks 10-1, 107-8, 119, 121-2, 126, 130, 135-47, 164-5, 196-7, 193, 205, 213, 241, 245-52, 255-7, 292, 297-9
Turnovo 126, 131
Turnu Magurele 141
Tutrakan 68
Tvrtko 130

Ukraine 86, 139, 209, 219-20, 223, 298
unemployment 248, 278
Uniate Church 243, 251
university 114
uplands see mountains
urban morphology 184, 197-8, 298
urban settlement 37-42, 53, 64, 69-70, 80, 93-6, 107, 117, 141, 145-7, 155, 162, 170-99, 204-29, 255, 299
urban system 185-99, 259
Urnfield culture 19, 32, 35
Urstromtaler 22

Vaclar (Wenceslas) 115-16
Vadastra culture 27
Vah 87
Valentinian 59-60
Vandals 56, 81
Vardar see Morava-Vardar
Varna 30, 38, 53, 138
vegetables 184, 215, 252
Venice 3, 90-1, 105-9, 138, 146, 164, 169-70, 174, 193-7, 204, 220, 223, 246, 302
Veselinovo culture 27
vessels see shipping
Veszprem 84, 190
Vidin 126, 138, 246-8, 253, 296-8
Vienna 58, 61-4, 81, 114, 128, 139, 146, 205, 220, 233, 239-41, 257-9, 273, 276-9, 295, 298
Vikings see Scandinavia
Villa 57, 64-5, 105
village 23, 26, 65, 80, 86, 92, 107, 135, 158-70, 222, 244, 252, 258-9, 274-6, 293, 298
Vilna 118
Vinca culture 27
vines/vineyard 23, 167, 170, 181, 196, 218-20, 257
Visegrad 59
Vistula 30-2, 36, 53, 80-1, 85-7, 92-3, 103, 112, 118, 163, 176, 179, 204, 210, 213, 216, 224, 240

Vlachs 292-5, 299
Vlöre 108, 137
Vltava 103, 115
Vogtland 171, 285
Vojvodina 20, 253, 259, 296
Volga 93
Vrancea 165-6

wages 214, 248-9, 263
Wallachia 121, 130-6, 139-41, 164-9, 192, 195, 220-2, 252, 255-6, 296-9
walls 39, 59, 64-71, 181, 184, 192
war 34-5, 55-61, 78-9, 82, 108-10, 137-41, 147, 154, 161, 180, 194, 197-8, 216-19, 221, 236, 247, 253-6, 259, 265, 296-7
Warsaw 118, 185, 188, 216, 243-5
Warta 32, 115, 118
water 26, 42, 144, 176, 181, 189, 257-8, 278-9, 294
water power 159, 174, 184, 212, 253, 284-6, 289, 295
water transport 9, 61, 216, 262, 283, 286-8, 294-5
wax 194, 197
weapons 33, 38, 56, 61, 66, 95, 104, 138, 213, 281, 286-8
weaving see textiles
Weitenberg culture 233-4
West/Western Europe 1-5, 9-12, 19, 83, 93-6, 101, 105, 108-10, 116, 135, 145, 157, 174, 177-9, 185, 194, 207-13, 217, 235, 238-9, 247-8, 251, 291, 296-304
Westphalia, Peace of 106
wheat 20-2
Wieliczka 159, 175, 181
wild boar 20
windmill 163
wine 38-9, 57, 65, 125, 167, 170, 209, 218-19, 223, 245
Wismar 180
wood/woodland 9-11, 20-4, 27-9, 32, 36, 57, 65, 80, 88, 92-3, 113, 117, 157-66, 172-3, 176, 180-2, 185, 193-6, 205-10, 213, 220-1, 237, 245, 272, 277, 285, 294
wool/woollens 146, 172, 187, 194-7, 237, 244-5, 275-80, 284-6, 291-3, 296
workers see labour
workshop 67-8, 88, 184, 187, 198, 244
World War 3-4
worstead see wool
Wrocław 118, 157, 179-80, 183-4, 205, 210, 245, 282-3, 290

Yambol 34
yield 216, 226, 252
Yugoslavia 4, 10, 85, 292, 295, 305

Zabrze 282
Zadar 91, 108, 121, 204, 220
Zadruga 164, 222
Zagreb 121
Zeitz 121
Zemun 258, 295
Zenica 129
Zielona Gora 162
Zimnicea 41
zinc 283
Zips 244
Zittau 171, 285
Zwickau 283